Go-To-Market Strategy

Go-To-Market Strategy

Advanced Techniques And Tools For Selling More Products, To More Customers, More Profitably

Lawrence G. Friedman

OXFORD AMSTERDAM BOSTON LONDON NEW YORK PARIS
SAN DIEGO SAN FRANCISCO SINGAPORE SYDNEY TOKYO

Butterworth-Heinemann
An imprint of Elsevier Science
Linacre House, Jordan Hill, Oxford OX2 8DP
225 Wildwood Avenue, Woburn, MA 01801-2041

First published 2002

British Library Cataloguing in Publication Data
Friedman, Lawrence (Lawrence G.)
    Go-to-market strategy: advanced techniques and tools for
    selling more products, to more customers, more profitably
    1. Marketing
    I. Title
    658.8

Library of Congress Cataloging in Publication Data
A catalog record for this book is available from the Library of Congress

ISBN 0 7506 7460 1

For information on all Butterworth–Heinemann publications visit our
website at www.bh.com

Typeset by Keyword Typesetting Services, Wallington, Surrey, UK
Printed and bound in the United States of America

Contents

Foreword by Neil Rackham

Few business books are well written. Ask me about it. For some sin committed in a former life, I'm condemned to read hundreds of the wretched things every year. And even fewer of the books that I wade through have real substance. So when I first read the manuscript of Larry Friedman's classic, *The Channel Advantage*, I was delighted. Here was exciting content written in an engaging way. In my back cover endorsement I wrote:

Its ideas will shape how companies use sales channels for years to come.

That was in 1999, at the dawn of modern channel history. And now, with all the benefits and the embarrassments of hindsight, I realize I was only partly right. The book certainly did shape how companies used sales channels. It was extraordinarily influential. It provided exactly the clear and concise guide that let organizations large and small slash millions from their costs while increasing their market coverage and sales volume. And it was almost alone among business books in that year for sounding a prophetic note of caution about the New Economy and the dot.com revolution. But when I wrote 'for years to come', I badly underestimated the speed with which the new field of go-to-market strategy was evolving.

In 1999, just as *The Channel Advantage* was hitting the bookstores, the prevailing wisdom of the strategists could be summarized in three simple tenets:

1. *Choose fewest channels for maximum economic coverage.* Channels are expensive to set up, so the argument went. They conflict with each other and they can confuse customers. So why have more channels than you must? In 1999 there was much talk of 'channel rationalization', 'channel pruning' and 'avoiding channel proliferation'. The experts advised you to reduce your

channels. The consultants' smart question of the month was 'what's the minimum number of channels to give you maximum economic coverage?'

2. *Set clear rules to minimize channel conflict.* Channels fight. As one Director of Channels put it, 'on a good day it's minor skirmishes, the rest of the time it's war'. So the 1999 wisdom for managing channel conflict was to set clear boundaries between channels to keep them as separate as possible. Channels were separated by product, by geography, by customer size, by industry or by the well-established first bite principle of 'Hands off! It's mine! I saw it before you did!'

3. *Allocate customers to the appropriate channel.* Left to themselves, customers have an inconvenient tendency to choose exactly the channels where you least want them. Much attention was being given in the year that *The Channel Advantage* was published to systems for allocating customers to the 'right' channels.

These three principles sounded sensible enough. They were logical and they made good economic sense. However, they suffered from one minor disadvantage – they didn't work. The reasons will become all too clear as you read this book. First and foremost, customers refused to be allocated to channels of the supplier's choosing. And they demanded channel choice. An increasing number of studies showed that those companies that restricted the channel choices available to their customers ended up with both fewer customers and a lower spend per customer. While it made logical sense from a supplier's point of view to minimize conflict and inter-channel fighting by keeping channels separate and watertight, it made no sense to the customer. Reducing channel conflict by building channel silos made it difficult for customers to choose and move between their preferred channels.

So, partly as a result of Larry Friedman's work, a new wisdom has emerged. Offer customers the product and service choices they want. Let them decide about how and when they want to do business with you. Make it easy for them to move between channels. Integrate channels rather than separate them. These are simple enough things to say; the trick is how to do these things without losing your shirt. Giving customers choices is an expensive business. How do you know which choices they want? Or which channels they will use? Offering too many choices is anarchy and the road to economic ruin. Offering too limited a range of choices will lose you customers in droves and get you to bankruptcy just as quickly. Marketing is caught in a paradox. Corporations can't afford to provide all that customers want, but they can't afford not to either.

Here's where *Go-To-Market Strategy* comes in. It will allow you to design and engineer your go-to-market strategies so that you can provide more of what your customers want for less than you are paying now. That's quite a trick. In nineteenth-century Scotland there was an elegant definition of an engineer as 'a man who can do for sixpence what any fool could do for a shilling'. (For those unfamiliar with the arcane currency of Britain, a shilling is two sixpences.) That's the role of good go-to-market strategy – and it's the mission of this book. Given a big enough budget, it doesn't take much talent to put together an impressive array of sales and service channels. Why not have a large direct sales force, plus a partner network, and telesales, and catalog sales – not to mention a few VARs and an impressive e-commerce capability? Oh, and while you're at it, why not spend a few extra millions on a CRM system to link them all together? But can you do it for sixpence? With the help of Larry Friedman you can, and he shows us how with that impressive clarity of thought I've come to expect from his writing since we co-authored *Getting Partnering Right*, in the truly prehistoric year 1996.

You'll find this book packed with ideas, case studies, things to do and mistakes to avoid. It's hard to pick out just one insight. But I have my own candidate, and it's fresh in my mind. A few weeks ago I was working with a large European multinational. In the room was the Head of E-Business, the Head of Sales, miscellaneous luminaries from Marketing, and the person whose unenviable responsibility was to oversee channels and agencies. We were putting together an important element of their go-to-market strategy and, for a couple of hours, we had been discussing what customers really wanted. We were quite pleased with ourselves and thought we'd come up with some elegant insights and strategies. Then I remembered Larry Friedman's first commandment: *Go-to-market strategy must start with the customer*. Here we were in a closed-door strategy meeting, each of us speaking convincingly on the customer's behalf. I recalled Larry's warning:

… **the only people who have a clue what customers will actually buy and how they will buy it – the customers themselves – are not in the meeting. They weren't invited.**

We experts were all confident that we were right. Each of us thought we understood what customers wanted. Some of us even had data. Yet in the few weeks since the meeting, preliminary research has collected the missing voice of the customer and I have to confess that we misjudged it. Fortunately, if belatedly through this research, we did give the customer a seat at the table. But had we been carried along by our own confidence we would by now be in deep trouble.

It's a simple point, yet we ignore it all the time. Go-to-market strategy is about customers – and customers are ever changing. Most of the data on which organizations base their go-to-market decisions are questionable and dated. This book will provide you with elegant strategies, tested models and sound ideas, but only your customers can tell you which of those ideas they will embrace. And, as Larry Friedman makes abundantly clear, everything you do has to be designed from the customer and the market, not from your preferred strategy.

Acknowledgements

Many people and companies have influenced the content in this book. It would be scary if that weren't the case, because otherwise I would have made all this stuff up. I'm happy to report that I didn't. This book is a continuation of the work of a large group of companies, academics, individual consultants and other experts who've gradually brought shape to the overall discipline of 'go-to-market strategy'.

I must first acknowledge the people working at the various companies mentioned throughout this book, such as Charles Schwab, Dell Computer, Marriott, FedEx, and Procter & Gamble. These companies have been fountains of creative energy in pushing the field of go-to-market strategy forward. My own clients – companies such as IBM, Oracle, General Electric and Hewlett-Packard – have equally been out in front of the pack, developing new go-to-market approaches and radically reshaping the way people think about selling.

I have also been influenced over time by significant thought-leaders in the field. First among them is Neil Rackham, who graciously provided this book with its foreword. Neil's book *SPIN Selling* basically created the field of sales effectiveness, from which many derivative works have since been spawned. His other books, such as *Rethinking The Sales Force*, *Major Account Sales Strategy* and one that I had the opportunity to co-author with him in 1996, *Getting Partnering Right*, have also been influential. He continues to exert thought-leadership and contribute actively to the field, with original contributions that shape and influence the strategies of a vast majority of the world's leading companies. We have been colleagues and friends for a long time, and we will be for many more years.

Other thought-leaders who've done path-breaking work include leading academics and top-notch consultants such as Michael Porter, Philip Kotler, ex-McKinsey principal John DeVincentis, Kenneth Rolnicki, and Rowland Moriarty. The latter, an advisor to many leading companies, contributed to the public debate and understanding of the field in his forward-thinking 1989 article in *Harvard Business Review* entitled 'Managing hybrid marketing systems'. It has stood the test of time as a major contribution to the field. My earlier writings and thinking were also influenced positively by the co-authors of my previous books, Richard Ruff and Tim Furey.

I'm particularly pleased to acknowledge the contributions of the staff of my firm, The Sales Strategy Institute, in Herndon, Virginia. Numerous employees played some role in the development of this book, while also working very, very hard to help build our company and attend to clients' needs at the same time. I must especially thank Suryo Soekarno and Michael Tan, two outstanding senior business analysts who researched and developed a number of the case studies and helped out with some of the key ideas. Suryo and Mike have been a real pleasure to work with over the past few years. Business analysts Sheena Chawla and Michael Moyer also made valuable contributions by helping out with some of the key case studies. My assistant, Edna Carrozza, did a great job of taking care of my schedule and keeping everything on track during the six months that I was writing this book, and also lent a helping hand with some of the research.

The biggest acknowledgement, and the one I am proudest to record here, must go to my wife Kim, and not just for being the proverbial supportive wife while I wrote this book, though she certainly was. Kim is in her own right one of the leading business researchers in the United States, acknowledged by many clients and staff at SSI to have a singularly encyclopedic knowledge of business and go-to-market strategy best practices – she was nicknamed The Human Search Engine by a top SSI client, and appropriately so. Kim served as editor and proofreader of the last book, *The Channel Advantage*, but this time around she did that and so much more. Kim led the five-month-long effort to identify relevant case studies and, through careful and painstaking research, develop them into hard-hitting examples that would illustrate and articulate key points. We got married a year ago, and our partnership is very strong.

Larry Friedman
Reston, Virginia

Author contact information

Lawrence G. Friedman
Chief Executive Officer
The Sales Strategy Institute, Inc.
1474 North Point Village Center, Suite 400
Reston, Virginia 20194
United States

Main office number: 703-326-0500
Mr. Friedman's assistant: Edna Carrozza, 703-547-1525
Fax: 703-547-1545

lfriedman@ssiadvantage.com

www.ssiadvantage.com

1

Go-to-market strategy:

A brief tour of the issues and opportunities

I t has often been said that 90 percent of everything that has been invented since the start of civilization has been invented in the last fifty years. I don't know who came up with that statistic, or if it's true (how would we know?), but it sounds good, and it's very compelling!

Much the same can be said of go-to-market strategy. People have been selling things – *going to market* with products and services – since the dawn of civilization, but not much, if anything, has changed in how they do it, until very recently. Make a product. Find a customer. Meet face to face to discuss the product with the customer. Negotiate. Close the deal. Check in with the customer to ensure he, she or it is happy. And then find another customer and start all over. Does this all sound familiar? Sure it does. People have been going to market in precisely this way, from the first suppliers of cave-painting tools, to hawkers of medieval battleaxes, to purveyors of steam engines and locomotives, to the blue suits in the 1970s pitching mainframe computers. The basic face-to-face sale – the process of going to market, in person, to meet customers and make deals – has a long, proud history. It's a model for doing business that predates the recent harping about 'business models' by at least ten thousand years.

And it's also dying out. No, it's not quite dead yet; people are still out there selling. But as the sole, or even primary, means of going to market, well, let's just say you might want to place some bets on a few other horses. Most executives today believe that going to market through a single, company-owned face-to-face channel is an expensive, growth-limiting and competitively catastrophic approach, and they're right. We live in a world of rapidly increasing go-to-market choices, many of which were created by recent technological advances. These choices have enabled today's successful business carnivore – the aggressive integrated multi-channel organization, the scary one who's actually figured out how to make sales reps, partners, the phone, and the Web all work together – to devour the friendly plant-eaters dressing up in suits and calling on their customers one at a time to talk about golf and the kids. I'm sure you can think of more than a few companies who've looked like *lunch* as they lumbered into the market place with fat, happy sales forces knocking on doors indiscriminately, while nimble, creative, aggressive competitors began approaching their best customers through a half-dozen new sales channels, each and every one of which was perfectly tuned to those customers' needs and buying behaviors. It can get ugly.

Unless you're the carnivore.

This book will help you become a go-to-market carnivore, transitioning to a fully competitive and winning go-to-market strategy, based on a solid game plan to be implemented over the next 18 months. There is no sense in talking about incremental change here. If your goal is to grow revenues 3 percent or improve profitability 'a little' then you may as well throw this book away. You don't need to rethink and redesign how you go to market to achieve those kinds of results. Just raise your prices a percent or two and fire a few under-performers. No, for the next few hours we are going after larger game: double-digit revenue growth and the slashing, at a minimum, of 10 to 15 percent of selling costs – absolutely realistic results that have been achieved consistently by companies that have become serious about go-to-market innovation. With all due respect to vegetarians, we are going to design a new go-to-market model that will help you devour the plant-eaters competing in your space and take charge of your markets. And we will do it without falling back on the bland, repetitive jargon of business books, in which every new thought is a 'revolution' or a 'paradigm shift', and in which you are just minutes away from going out of business unless you adopt the writer's five- or eight-step process immediately, without question. Forget all that. We are going to be practical, and we are going to put together an actionable game plan for going to market faster, cheaper, better, more effectively, and more efficiently than the competition.

Let's look at the new go-to-market choices and alternatives, and let's start with the star of the show. The big go-to-market innovation of recent years is, of course, the Internet. The 'noisy' part of the Internet story is the rise and fall of the dot.com companies: first threatening their bricks-and-mortar competitors, then anointing themselves the 'New Economy', then leading to a feeding frenzy by retail investors desperate to be part of the electronic gold rush, and finally dismissed as a juvenile experiment in excess and arrogance – all in a period of about four years! All those visions of Internet World Domination that made complete sense way, way back in, oh, February of 2000 seem positively ludicrous now. People running home to little Web devices on their kitchen counters, pulling down dinner recipes from the Internet and ordering milk online from the local supermarket.

Businessmen dashing through airports, checking their Ebay bids on their wireless-Web-enabled cell phones to ensure they win their share of other people's attic junk before anyone else can outbid them. Wars ending, and an era of world peace resulting from people using email to break down national borders by ... well, it was never quite clear how email was going to lead to world peace, but it sounded great at the time.

Truthfully, a few of us suspected all along that no one really wanted to sit at their computers all day buying lawn mowers and parrots and whatever else the inventors of the mythical New Economy thought they could sell us over the Web, but today it's downright trendy to be an Internet skeptic.

The quieter part of the story, though, and the much more important one, is the gradual, less flashy, but ultimately more meaningful adoption of the Internet by stable, successful companies. Even after you discount the hype and the shameless self-promotion of the Internet evangelists, you are still left with a technology that has changed, and continues to change, how people and organizations do business. Let's look at a few numbers. Office Depot booked $982 million in online sales last year, and now expects online transactions to account for $1 of every $7 in sales this year.[1] Ford Motor Company and twelve hundred steel producers and stampers will do over $1 billion in steel procurement this year on the E-Steel exchange.[2] Intercontinental Exchange, a trading site for electric power, gas and oil, has handled $100 billion in trades in the ten months since it opened.[3] Then there's General Electric's GE Global eXchange Services (GXS), a business-to-business e-commerce network that handles over one billion transactions and over *one trillion dollars* ($1,000,000,000,000) per year in goods and services between over 100,000 trading partners – companies such as Coca Cola, Daimler-Chrysler and FedEx.[4]

In short, the Internet is real. True, some of the early Internet pioneers have been killed off, but that's what has always happened to pioneers. My advice: be cautious about becoming a pioneer; most of them get

---

[1] Charles Haddad, Office Depot's e-diva. *Business Week*, August 6, 2001, e-biz section p. EB22.
[2] Richard Karpinski, E-Steel rising. *Internet Week*, July 20, 2001
[3] Bob Tedeschi, Some business-to-business marketplaces showing staying power. *New York Times*, July 16, 2001.
[4] Wiring your company – online business exchanges. Washington Post.com, June 20, 20001.

killed by the natives, starve to death, or succumb to unfamiliar diseases. No, the *smart* move is usually to follow the pioneers after they've cleared the forests, built some roads, and made friends with the natives. That's exactly what big, successful companies are now doing with the Web, and it's working. Skepticism is healthy and appropriate with new technologies, but facts are facts. The Web is becoming part of the fabric of Big Corporate go-to-market strategy.

Let me be clear, though, this is not a book about the Web. There are enough of those and, frankly, the Web is not all that interesting in-and-of itself. No, this book is about the larger and more strategic issue of how to take products and services to market more powerfully in order to increase sales, market share, profits, and customer loyalty. The Internet is certainly a *part* of the go-to-market story for many leading companies, but it is just a part, and for other companies it is not part of the story at all. The Web is just a *choice*, and the whole point of modern go-to-market strategy is that you have lots of different choices and alternatives today, depending on what you are selling, who you want to sell it to, and what you are trying to accomplish as a business.

Today you are not limited to a field sales force, and you're not limited to the Internet either. You could market, sell and support your products and services through any combination of field sales reps, strategic allies, business partners, master or local distributors, integrators, value-added resellers, manufacturers' agents, brokers, franchises, telemarketers, telesales agents, television, Web sites, email, extranets, e-marketplaces, auctions, fax machines, direct mail, newspapers and, depending on your markets, some ten or fifteen other channels as well. You could build and use any of these channels on their own, or you could build an integrated mix of them to serve customers faster, better and cheaper in concert. *That's* what I'm talking about when I say 'choices and alternatives'. There are all sorts of new opportunities out there to reach, do business with, and develop long-term relationships with customers. As a result, it's imperative to think creatively and carefully about how you go to market – about the choices you're going to make in a sea of choices.

> There are all sorts of new opportunities out there to reach, do business with, and develop long-term relationships with customers. As a result, it's imperative to think creatively and carefully about how you go to market.

Some organizations have been quite brilliant in taking advantage of new channel opportunities and building powerful, winning go-to-market strategies. Companies such as Dell Computer, FedEx, Southwest Airlines, Charles Schwab & Company, Marriott, and Land's End all come to mind. These organizations have built strong, successful positions in the market place, reduced selling costs, increased market share, and added thousands and in some cases millions of new customers, by going to market smarter, better, faster, cheaper, and more effectively than their competitors. They've all reorganized their businesses around the crucial concept that, today, it's no longer just about *what* you sell, it's also about *how* you sell it. They all have pretty good products that are perhaps marginally better than their competitors, but their success lies primarily in their creative use of new technologies and channels to reach more customers, in more markets, more efficiently, to do more business, more often. We'll look at some of these companies in depth in later chapters. We need to understand what they're doing and what we can learn from them.

> Today, it's no longer just about *what* you sell; it's also about *how* you sell it.

Before we start talking about 'best practices', however, it's important to recognize that for every successful go-to-market innovator there are dozens of companies that aren't cutting it in an age of expanding and confusing go-to-market opportunities and risks. The telltale signs are familiar: slow sales growth or increasing sales costs, or both; inefficient distributor networks in which just a tiny fraction of partners do any real selling; poor results from Web initiatives; conflict between channels; 'dormant' go-to-market IT solutions, such as ineffective and incorrectly used CRM packages; and an ever-expanding inventory of products and channels that generate few, if any, tangible business results.

The many companies who fit this description aren't, for the most part, 'go-to-market laggards' who are lazy and uncreative. Rather, they are companies that are earnestly trying to figure out what to do in a fast-changing world and yet who are unsure of how best to move forward. They're trying to deal with new go-to-market challenges by throwing huge amounts of money, time and energy at various gimmicks and fads. Fad-chasing, encouraged and driven by aggressive consultants pitching 'quick fixes' to complex strategic issues, has for many organizations been disappointing – and very, very expensive. Let's take a look at one of these companies.

NOMO CHEMICALS: GO-TO-MARKET FASHION VICTIM

Deep in the recesses of downtown Atlanta are industrial parks and smokestack-laden buildings that are about as far removed from the clean, slick offices of California's Silicon Valley as they could possibly be. There are no BMWs in the parking lots, no Starbucks on the street corners. A forty-minute taxi ride north from Atlanta's Hartsfield International Airport, and, *voila!*, you are transported into the 'Old Economy', a place many don't see everyday, derided endlessly in the business press, and yet where they make things people and companies actually *use*. Trucks carry pallets of machine tools, PVC pipes, and electrical fuses back and forth from buildings emitting scary-looking multi-colored plumes of smoke.

It is so easy to smile bemusedly and think about how these companies don't 'get it'. Why on earth are they polluting the atmosphere and not making cool Palm Pilot add-on software modules? But it is here, right smack in the middle of the Old Economy, that executives and managers are trying the hardest to come to terms with the enormous changes wrought by the explosion of new go-to-market choices.

The CEO of one of these companies, Nomo Chemicals, a $210 million manufacturer of specialty industrial lubricants,[5] grabbed a stack of thin, smudgy acetate slides. With a little adjusting and twisting, the ancient contraption of light-bulbs-and-mirrors on which the slides sat managed to put up a fuzzy little image on the wall. Squinting slightly, I made out the title image. It said:

> **Motivating The Sales Force: Morale,**
> **Retention & Re-Training After**
> **E-Commerce**

---

[5] Wherever possible, real names of companies and people are used throughout this book. In some cases (this being one) the executives of the companies in question demanded use of a pseudonym and/or minor changes to case information in return for permission to describe their go-to-market experiences.

I couldn't help but appreciate the irony. Two years earlier, the executive team had decided, on the basis of recommendations from some obscenely-compensated marketing consultants, that its four-hundred-person sales force was a dinosaur, a veritable tribute to quaint post-war thinking, an almost unbearably backward way to sell in an e-enabled world. The entire management team had gone into a panic and had a spending frenzy to get up to date. They spent $16 million – you read that right; there is no missing decimal point, SIXTEEN MILLION dollars – building Web sites, e-portals, call centers, and an integrated CRM system that tied it all together and could track a sales transaction from the very first contact with a customer through to the deposit of the last and final check for receipt of goods. The whole new 'sales model' went live on June 1, 1999.

By August 2000, sales, predicted to increase immediately by 35 percent, were down 18 percent. Margins, expected to go up 22 to 25 percent, had decreased by 14 percent, mostly to pay for all the new go-to-market infrastructure.

Almost a third of the sales force quit in fourteen months, including most of Nomo's best field reps. Of a shortlist of the twenty sales reps that 'we cannot afford to lose, no matter what, because they produce a huge percentage of the business', seventeen had quit. That's 85 percent attrition. The few of those seventeen who had bothered to explain why they were quitting made it clear that they no longer understood what the company was trying to accomplish, and didn't feel like hanging out trying to compete against their own Web site after devoting years, and in some cases decades, toward building personal relationships with their customers.

The company's one major distributor, representing over a fifth of total annual sales, had sent a threatening, angry letter, voicing 'concern' over the competition that the company's new Web presence had created. It read, in part:

Please respond within 10 days at the latest to our demand that you immediately cease transactional activity on your Internet site with respect to all products we are carrying. Failure to conform will lead us to drop all of Nomo Chemical's products and product lines, which totaled $43,505,200.61 in sales in 1999. If you will not comply, please advise us on where to return all unsold inventory.

As with Black & Decker, ordered by Home Depot in an infamous letter to knock it off with the e-commerce stuff or get lost (along with 300 other Home Depot suppliers), this is not quite what Nomo Chemicals had in mind when it was sold on a cheerful future of customers sitting at their computers engaged in 'frictionless' transactions over the Web, communicating effortlessly with their suppliers, customers, and partners. No, this was a nightmare – and a lonely nightmare at that. By this time, all the consultants were long gone. They'd moved onto their next projects, selling visions of effortless growth in sales and profits through technology, while Nomo's senior managers quietly weighed how long the money in the bank could support their negative cash flow.

My firm, The Sales Strategy Institute, was called in to figure out what had happened and to make recommendations for getting back on track. Over the course of a couple weeks, we looked around at all the technology and systems, the users' guides and internal procedure manuals, the consulting studies and the business plans. And nowhere – not in a single memo, not on one solitary overhead slide – was there any direct input from a Nomo Chemicals customer. The entire system had been created in a series of closed-door meetings, with lots of coffee and donuts and absolutely no input from the only people you'd think would count in a go-to-market redesign: the people who buy things.

So we asked the obvious question: 'Did you ask any of your customers how *they* want to do business, before you built all these systems?'

We were met with blank, confused stares, as if we had just asked what cashew nut shells look like.[6] Sixteen million dollars and two years' worth of work, and at no point in the process had anyone asked customers how they want to do business. Nor had anybody run the concept by key distributors or top sales managers and reps, or, for that matter, talked to anyone except each other and the consultants.

We promptly proceeded to call a hundred or so customers. We asked point-blank how they wanted to do business with our client and

---

[6] Yes, cashew nuts have shells. But inside the shells is a caustic black oil that has to be removed (i.e. not something you'd want to eat), so the consumer rarely gets to see the shell.

what they thought of the new Web-based strategy. The answer was simple: the single, only thing they thought was any different about our client – its *entire* competitive advantage – was the expertise of its sales force and the ability of its sales teams to design solutions to solve their unique technical problems. Take away those sales teams, and all customers saw was a relatively expensive supplier of lubricants. As sales reps quit in disgust over the uncertain future of their careers, and as brochures went out telling customers to go to the Web – and suggesting between-the-lines that they'd soon no longer be served by their trusted reps – these customers did what customers always do when they don't get what they want: they stopped buying. And they stopped placing orders in *every* channel; not just the Web, but through field reps and distributors too. Sales went down, but definitely not costs. Costs went way, way up, to pay for the computers, software packages, networks, integrators, VARs, consultants, tech support staff, and all the other accoutrements of go-to-market fad chasing.

All those investments might have made sense, by the way, and indeed would have made sense, if Nomo Chemicals had focused first on its go-to-market *strategy*, before investing in the techno-goodies. Nomo should have asked and addressed basic go-to-market strategy questions, such as:

■ Who are our target customers, and how do they want to do business with us?
■ What are our 'degrees of freedom' in channel expansion? What are the *boundaries* in terms of what our customers, distributors, and sales reps will accept from us?
■ Do we really want to *replace* the field sales force and our distributors with a Web channel, or do we want to use the Web to support and improve the effectiveness of our field reps and partners? What's the goal here?

Given that we were walking into an immediate panic over declining sales revenue, we decided to keep it simple and stay focused on two main questions: what do customers want from Nomo, and what would it take for Nomo to get back on track with them? What we discovered in talking to customers was that they were not anti-Web. Far from it! They were very enthusiastic about the Web for order tracking, product information, and routine re-purchases of simple commodity products. What they didn't want was to have the Web replace their sales reps in the crucial specification and design phases, and in the negotiation of prices and terms. So, in short, they were channel-flexible but they *did* have boundaries that had to be respected in the go-to-market redesign process. That's the kind of thing you find out if you talk to customers, listen carefully, and think strategically about what they're saying.

In the end, we recommended breaking apart the end-to-end sales process into discrete tasks, such as lead generation, specification development, pricing, and deal-closing, and *working with customers* to co-design a total customer experience – an end-to-end process addressing each and every 'touch point' between Nomo and its customers – that would truly give them what they want, at every step in the Nomo relationship.

Nomo acted on those recommendations, and built a powerful new sales model that provides field rep hand-holding where customers specifically require it within the sales process; efficient, Web-enabled support when, where and how customers are interested in getting it; and telecoverage (systematic phone calling into key accounts) to increase 'touch' and continuity with end-customers over time. It is working. Sales are headed back up, and costs are coming down as new, low-cost channels begin to deliver results. That's exactly what you'd expect when you focus on the customer experience and align your sales model with true customer needs and behaviors. Now Nomo can begin addressing its other go-to-market issues: distributor angst, sales force retention, etc. These tend to be solvable problems once you've built a sales model that's fundamentally aligned with customers' needs.

Is Nomo's experience unusual or surprising? Not really. Over the last few years lots of companies have chased go-to-market fads, believing, incorrectly, that gimmicks and technology could substitute for the disciplined work that's needed to build a customer-focused, high-growth go-to-market *strategy*. But there is just no substitute for having a strategy. It simply takes more than money, software and consultants to go to market effectively.

GETTING STARTED WITH GO-TO-MARKET STRATEGY: A DEFINITION, AND A FUNDAMENTAL PRINCIPLE OF GO-TO-MARKET SUCCESS

Hopefully, it's clear at this point that what we are *not* talking about in this book is jumping on the latest technology bandwagons or chasing the latest marketing fads. What we are talking about here is putting together a rock-solid, successful go-to-market strategy that will enable you to achieve high top- and bottom-line growth, real gains in market share and competitive advantage, and superior customer retention and loyalty. So how do you achieve all that? Let's start by putting some stakes in the ground and defining precisely what a 'go-to-market strategy' is.

What is a go-to-market strategy?

A game plan for reaching and serving the *right* customers in the *right* markets, through the *right* channels, with the *right* products and the *right* value proposition.

The purpose of a go-to-market strategy is to create a powerful, winning *total customer experience* that will:

- Attract, win, and retain the most desirable customers,
- While driving high sales and market share growth,
- At the lowest possible cost.

Now that we have a definition in place, let's talk about what it means, and let's begin with the fundamental purpose of a go-to-market strategy: a winning *total customer experience*. Throughout this book, we will continually revisit and bring shape to the idea that a go-to-market strategy must aim toward a superior total customer experience, and indeed that creating a winning total customer experience is the core purpose of investing time, energy and money in a go-to-market strategy.

So what *is* the total customer experience? As Gene McCluskey, a director at Cognos with fifteen years of channel and partner management experience, defines it:

> It is a continuing relationship with the customer, consisting of numerous interactions or 'touch points' that begin with brand awareness and continue through the first contact, pre-sales activities, the first purchase, installation, customer support, service, ongoing purchases, and long-term care. At each and every touch point, the customer has an experience with your organization. How good, bad, fantastic, or terrible those experiences are over time defines your company in the eyes of the customer, and shapes the long-term account growth opportunity. Every experience with your company has to be positive, consistent, high quality, and memorable, whether the customer is buying something, seeking information, meeting face to face, looking at your Web site, calling on the phone, et cetera. When you can deliver that, that's the Total Customer Experience. It's the whole point of having a go-to-market strategy.[7]

Gene's insight could be simplified as follows: you are not going to hit home runs in the market place unless everything you do – and everything you are – creates value and a powerful experience for your customers, whenever and however they interact with you.[8]

That may seem like common sense, but frankly it's not how many companies approach their go-to-market strategies. Most go-to-market initiatives are *internally focused* exercises driven by the vendor's own desire to make a lot more money a lot more quickly. But, as we saw at Nomo Chemicals, internally focused go-to-market strategies don't work. I am not going to beat around the bush here. You may – just *may* – be able to squeeze out a few dollars of margin by hammering away at channel costs or forcing customers into a lower-cost channel, but the results will be meager, and you won't sustain the gains for very long. Eventually your customers will become alienated and will move along to a competitor with whom it's more convenient, more satisfying, or just plain easier to do business.

If you want real sales growth, significant gains in market share, more loyal customers, and big profits, your point of departure *must* be that going to market is all about finding, attracting and ultimately keeping

---

[7] Interview with the author, Reston, Virginia, December 22, 2001.

[8] For an excellent discussion of value creation as the core purpose of sales, see Neil Rackham and John DeVincentis, *Rethinking the Sales Force: Redefining Selling to Create and Capture Customer Value.* McGraw-Hill, 1999.

the best customers out there. So how do you find and keep them? Today's customers expect and demand a coordinated, seamless buying experience and a set of touch points that meet their needs and map to their own buying behaviors. They don't want to hear about lost orders; or waste time educating sales reps who aren't up to speed on their phone purchases; or be told they have to use the Web when what they really want is to talk to a live person, or vice versa. They want something much better, and increasingly they are confident (and correct) that they can get it elsewhere. They want a *total customer experience* – a positive, consistent, high-quality and memorable experience that fits with their own needs and purchasing methods. They'll buy from whomever offers that experience – in many cases even if it's considerably more expensive to do so.

If that sounds improbable – customers paying a serious premium, not for a better gadget or widget, but for a better buy–sell relationship and a superior total customer experience – let's take a look at one company that's made billions, outlasted and outgunned most of its competitors, and held onto its huge client base in a bitterly competitive market … while selling the exact same products as its competitors for twice as much money.

When the SEC deregulated brokerage fees in 1975,[9] Charles Schwab & Company became one of the first discount brokerage firms. Schwab's brokerage concept, radical for the time, was aimed at investors who didn't feel they needed, and didn't want to pay for, the high-touch face-to-face relationships and heavily laden research services of traditional 'full service' brokers such as Merrill Lynch and Smith Barney. Prices were kept down by offering innovative and customer-focused, yet lower-cost, channels such as 24-hour telephone access. Of course, Schwab's customers did not get, nor did they want, the face-to-face attention (and sales pressure) associated with the full-service firms.

The discount brokerage market became increasingly competitive in the 1980s, but really took off in the early 1990s when new Internet upstarts began to offer online trading services. E*Trade in 1992 (originally as E*Trade Securities offered through AOL and CompuServe, and later, in 1996, as etrade.com), Ameritrade in 1996 and many

---

[9] SEC = US Securities and Exchange Commission.

others began invading Schwab's core space by aggressively courting the coveted 'do it yourself' discount brokerage customer. Competition for the many new bull market-tempted discount brokerage customers rose to a frenzy as the 1990s came to a close, culminating in no-holds-barred brand-building excesses such as the estimated $4.5 million that E-trade spent for two thirty-second spots during the January 30, 2000 Superbowl.[10]

Schwab's online competitors continue to this day to hammer down stock trading prices, in some cases charging less than a twentieth of what it used to cost to buy a few hundred shares of stock. Very active traders can do transactions online now for as little as $4.95.[11] In the face of this competitive onslaught and intense downward pricing pressure, Schwab, often perceived as yet-another Web-based brokerage, maintained – and continues to maintain – a high stock trading price-point, currently at $29.95.[12] That's about twice the average price for an equivalent stock trade at the various other discount brokers, and three times more than the lowest-cost alternative. With prices two to three times higher than its competitors, yet offering exactly the same products and basically similar services, Schwab is going out of business, right?

Wrong.

While Schwab's dominance in online market share has declined a tad from 27 percent in the first quarter of 1999 to around 23 percent in the first quarter of 2001, it remains the market leader, trailed by *all* of the other major players: E*Trade, Waterhouse, Fidelity and Datek. Schwab's 5 percent share of the entire seventeen trillion investable dollars in the United States grew 21 percent in 2000, leading all other financial services firms.[13] Schwab's stock price, depressed lately along with everyone else's, has provided a total shareholder return of 61.5 percent over the last ten years, putting Schwab in the number nine position on *The Wall Street Journal*'s list of the fifty best performing stock over the last ten years.[14] If you had invested $10,000 in Schwab

---

[10] Louis Trager, Some dot coms hedge Super Bowl bets. *Interactive Week*, January 24, 2000.
[11] www.etrade.com, reviewed on August 9, 2001. Based on rates for very active traders, listed stocks only.
[12] As of August 9, 2001.
[13] Investor Conference Presentation, Schwab Investor Relations, May 10, 2001.
[14] *The Wall Street Journal* Special Report, Shareholder Scoreboard, February 26, 2001.

stock in January 1990, you would have been able to cash in your stock and ring in the new year in style in December of 2000 – $1,070,000 worth of style, for a total gain of 10,600 percent.

Interestingly, while maintaining its high prices, Schwab has some of the highest customer retention rates in the business – people who voluntarily and knowingly pay a significant premium to buy the same goods and similar services as are offered elsewhere. All those 'sticky' Schwab customers must be staying for a reason.

Why are they staying?

The answer is that Schwab has designed, and brilliantly executed, a powerful total customer experience founded on the principles of customer choice; multiple, flexible channels; and 24 × 7 access to Schwab through convenient access points. Its retail branches are just minutes from most city or suburban dwellers in the United States. Its 24 × 7 international call centers handle trades, inquiries and problems when customers don't feel like going to a branch office, and, as is well known, Schwab has a solid Web site from which most, if not all, routine financial transactions and research can be performed. All of these channels are linked by one of the world's leading customer information systems, which enables immediate access and sharing of customer data across, between, to and from all channels. No matter which channel you use, the system will have accurate, up-to-the-minute information on your account. Throw on top of this Schwab's partnerships with hundreds of mutual fund companies to provide, in its OneSource funds, access to over a thousand funds in one centralized location, many of which are available at no fee to the customer.[15]

In sum, Schwab's channels and partnerships provide a sort of 'surround sound' customer experience, an approach we'll examine much more closely later on in the book. It has given Schwab a very powerful value proposition, which I would articulate as follows: 'You can do business with us whenever you want, however you want, wherever you want, in whatever ways you want. Want to visit us in person? Fine. Want to use the Web? Great. Prefer to use the phone? That's great too. Want to look over mutual funds on the Web site and then

---

[15] Or no overt mark-up, anyway. Of course, Schwab is getting paid for this service – from its partners, which eventually gets reflected in their own customer fees.

stop in to discuss them with an expert and then order them over the phone – hey, even better! You like our mutual funds? Excellent. Don't like ours – want to buy someone else's? That's fine too, and you can buy them through whichever Schwab channel you happen to prefer.'[16] Customer choice is a very, very powerful go-to-market concept, one that produces tangible and measurable gains in sales growth, customer retention and, ultimately, profits.

Schwab's go-to-market model, by the way, should not be mistaken simply for a channel story. Keep in mind that channels are just pipes to your customers. Schwab has spent years doing high-quality customer analysis and segmentation, enabling the company to provide custom-ized services that are 'tuned' to the needs of unique segments in order to establish more targeted, durable relationships with them. As Charles Schwab (the co-CEO, not the company) put it, 'The way you develop your customer base is by having important and in-depth relation-ships.'[17] Frequent traders, high net-worth investors, and other segments get specialized services such as proprietary research, trust and estate planning, and dedicated phone-based trading teams, while casual, low net-worth investors can still use all of Schwab's channels and most of its services any time they want, to do business in whatever ways they prefer.

Now *that* is a total customer experience, one rooted in flexibility, responsiveness to customers' unique needs, and partnerships to enable broad product and service offerings. This is a powerful value propos-ition – much more powerful than 'trade on the Web and save a few bucks'. It explains why the E*Trades and Ameritrades have never been able to topple the giant. My money's on Schwab, and companies like Schwab. Long after we've all gotten tired of Web outfits that come and go, or companies that try to force us to do business this way or that way, there's really something to be said for a memorable, consistent, positive, high-quality customer experience based on our own choices and preferences for doing business.

Of course, Schwab's orientation toward customer choice, 24 × 7 channel availability, and flexibility might not be precisely the answer for your organization. I'm not arguing it is. There are other models for

---

[16] Although in the next chapter, we'll see that there are some limitations on this model.

[17] myprimetime.com, Great entrepreneurs. Interview with Charles Schwab.

creating a total customer experience, and we'll look at them in this book. But I *am* arguing that as you think about how you go to market today and how you might do so in the future, the total customer experience is the appropriate, and indeed the only, valid point of departure. If the only drivers of your go-to-market activities and initiatives are internally-driven goals invented in closed-door meetings, such as 'let's cut sales costs' or 'we have to grow 30 percent this year', you are already on the wrong side of history, and you will fail. There are exactly zero companies succeeding today by defining the customer relationship on their own terms. You must always start with the customer – what the customer needs, expects, and demands; how the customer wants to do business and relate to you – and create a positive, memorable, consistent, and high-quality experience. Go-to-market strategy cannot deliver any serious results unless it significantly upgrades and enhances the experiences that customers have with your organization.

> Go-to-market strategy cannot deliver any serious results unless it significantly upgrades and enhances the experiences that customers have with your organization.

THE INGREDIENTS OF A WINNING GO-TO-MARKET STRATEGY

It should be apparent at this point that the phrase *go-to-market strategy* incorporates more than sales channels. We saw, for example, with Nomo Chemicals that while the company certainly had channel issues, the larger problem involved a flawed, poor understanding of its customers. With Schwab, we see a more sophisticated organization in which a deep understanding of, and responsiveness to, its customers is a core element of the strategy, alongside its superior channel mix. These two companies' experiences suggest an obvious although often ignored truth: going to market is a broad challenge in which choosing and building sales channels is just one piece of a larger puzzle. In fact, channels aren't always the most important piece of the puzzle, and though you may be surprised to hear the lead author of *The Channel Advantage* say this, sometimes they don't matter at all![18] If you try to

---

[18] Lawrence G. Friedman and Timothy R. Furey, *The Channel Advantage: Going to Market with Multiple Sales Channels to Reach More Customers, Sell More Products, Make More Profit*. Butterworth-Heinemann, 1999.

charge $1 million for a paper clip, it doesn't matter how clever or creative you are with your channels; you won't sell any.[19] If you try to sell UNIX servers to monasteries, it isn't going to work whether you do it over the Web or the phone, or whether you record your sales on a CRM system or an abacus. Appropriate pricing, and selection of an appropriate target market, and for that matter a host of other factors, can be as or more important than your choice of sales channels.

> Going to market is a broad challenge in which choosing and building sales channels is just one piece of a larger puzzle.

In short, let's acknowledge channels here for what they are: *part* of a go-to-market strategy, but just a part. Today's successful go-to-market strategist must look at the 'big picture', and not just at channels. This means thinking carefully and creatively about what it will take to reach the right markets and attract and serve the right customers, through the right channels, with the right products and the right value propositions. It's when all of these ingredients come together, in one coherent and coordinated system, that you get the magic: accelerating revenue growth with decreasing selling costs and happier, more loyal customers. You can't get that magic if any of the ingredients are out of sync with each other – if, for example, your channels are efficient and effective but don't reach the right customers; or if your products are superb but can't be sold by your channels or are unattractive in your target markets. It all has to fit together – markets, customers, channels, products, and value propositions. Let's take a brief look at each of the ingredients; we'll return to each of them – and to the issue of making them fit together powerfully – in much more detail later in the book.

Markets

Selection of the right markets is a crucial ingredient in *any* winning go-to-market strategy. The reason is simple. If you choose the right markets, you can make a lot of go-to-market mistakes. But if you choose the wrong markets, it's basically hopeless.

---

[19] Unless they're really incredible paper clips!

To take a simple example, if you discover that pharmaceutical firms desperately need your products and will eagerly line up to buy them, it won't matter much which channels you use to reach those customers, as long as you have some reasonable, efficient means to do business with them. But if companies in the pharmaceutical industry have no need for your products, reaching into that market with an expensive, fully-integrated database-driven Teleweb channel, backed up by a computer system which links telesales reps and national account managers, isn't going to help at all. Nor will improving the product, or coming up with a new tag line, or anything else. Put simply, you have to focus on the right markets for a go-to-market strategy to matter at all.

Lots of companies end up targeting and participating in the wrong markets, despite the endless purchase of market reports. Generic studies just don't cut it in a world of tough competitors who micro-segment their markets to pinpoint the specific markets and segments in which their value propositions will be strongest and best received. To compete in this environment, it is essential to ask yourself the question: am I really focused on the right markets, and do I even have the right information to know? It takes effort and energy to uncover, define, and validate the markets that offer the absolute-best selling opportunities, and then to carefully prioritize those markets for penetration. Rigorous, careful market selection and prioritization, however, reduces risks and ensures that *all* of your go-to-market strategies and tactics are aimed at the right sales opportunities in the right markets and segments. We will come back to this crucial topic in Chapter 3, where we'll look at a well-tested and successful process for uncovering, defining, validating, and prioritizing your target markets.

> It is essential to ask the question: am I really focused on the right markets, and do I even have the right information to know?

Customers

Even companies that have a pretty good understanding of their markets often have a superficial, anecdotal understanding of their customers. And that's a big problem. The reason is that markets don't buy things; *customers* do. You can do market research and analysis until the cows come home, and still end up with no idea how to sell effectively to the customers in those target markets. In fact, getting your arms around the fundamental needs and the buying behaviors of your target customers – with enough precision to make high-reward but also high-risk go-to-market decisions – is the very cornerstone of a winning strategy.

So what does it take to understand and align with your target customers' needs and buying behaviors? First and foremost, you must raise and develop answers to some very crucial questions. Questions like: Who are the customers in your target markets, and what do they need? What drives them to make a purchase? What kinds of experiences are they seeking from their vendors? What has real value to them in the sales process – value that they're willing to pay for? Which channels do they use to do business today, and which channels are they planning to migrate to over the next year or two? What specific actions or activities on your part would cause them to increase *significantly* their volume of purchasing activity with your organization?

It goes without saying that if you had answers to all of these questions, and acted on them, you would generate dramatic improvements in sales results. We are after nothing less than those dramatic improvements in this book. In Chapter 4, we'll drill down in detail on the techniques and tools of customer alignment – the specific things you can do, right now, to develop a deep understanding of the core needs, decision drivers, and buying behaviors of the most important customers in your target markets.

Channels and partners

Channels are a significant ingredient of a go-to-market strategy, for the simple reason that nothing happens until a channel connects you with a customer. They are the lifeblood of any business enterprise. If your channels disappeared overnight, you'd be unable to reach, sell to, or support any of your customers. You'd go out of business immediately, or as soon as the cash in the bank ran out. It's scary stuff – as Ebay or Amazon.com discover every time their servers go down for a couple of hours. Even slight improvements to, or problems with, channels or partners can have a huge impact on your sales and profits. Companies, such as Dell Computer, that have chosen the right channels for the right reasons have dominated their competitors; others who've made the wrong choices have suffered greatly or even folded their tents. Choosing the right channels, and aligning them correctly against opportunities in the market place, is very serious business.

In Chapter 5 we will dig into this topic in great detail. We'll discuss each of the major types of channels in use by companies today, and examine when, how, where and why they're appropriate. We will then examine a rigorous process for identifying and choosing the right sales channels and developing a market coverage plan to use those channels in order to connect the right customers with the right products. By the end of the chapter, you will know exactly what you have to do to choose channels and assign them to opportunities in order to drive top- and bottom-line performance.

The product and the value proposition

Some products aren't very good. Remember edible deodorant, garlic cake, and aerosol toothpaste? Back in the 1960s, there was the $7,000 Honeywell kitchen computer with a built-in cutting board, followed in the early 1970s by the $800 HP calculator wristwatch requiring that you carry around a separate stylus. More recently, we saw Pepsi A.M., a less-carbonated, higher-caffeine beverage aimed at the presumably fast-growth breakfast soda market, which turned out not to exist. Now *that's* bad. Bad products cannot be sold successfully, through any channel.

One basic question, then, is whether you have a good product. You have to sell a desirable product that meets a real need 'out there' in the market place – that people want and are willing to pay for. In this book we're going to assume that you have such a product, although we'll look briefly at ways you can make *certain* you have something sellable. You must ensure that your products and services are really in tune with your target customers' needs before spending a lot of time or energy on a strategy for taking them to market.

Our main concern with products in this book will be on how well products and their value propositions (the 'message') fit with the rest of your go-to-market strategy. New plans for markets, customers and channels can significantly impact on your products and value propositions. All sorts of products, from personal computers to life insurance and legal services to home mortgages, have had to be substantially redesigned and repositioned to 'fit' with new alternative channels or work in new vertical or geographic markets. When you create or change a go-to-market strategy, you must carefully re-evaluate your offerings and value propositions and make certain that they fit with your markets, customers and channels. In Chapter 6, we'll take a look at some practical tools to do that.

Putting it all together: the integrated multi-channel model

Make no mistake about it; 'integrated multi-channel strategy' is a hot topic these days, from the boardroom to the marketing department to the sales office. People are intrigued and excited about the possibility of achieving big financial gains through multi-channel selling, but are also confused about how, exactly, to go about doing it. The complexity and variety of new types of sales channels has not made the task any easier.

The fact is, if channel integration existed at all twenty years ago, it consisted of using direct mail to produce leads for the sales force, or a similarly simple formula. Now it has evolved into something much more complicated, due to the rise of telephone, Web, and business partner channels, all of which must be used in the right ways at the right times and coordinated in the sales process to deliver a seamless, coherent customer experience. Multi-channel integration today requires a careful analysis of which channels will be used, what they should each be doing, how they will coordinate and communicate with each other, and how technology will be used to make them all work effectively as one system in the market place.

Integrated multi-channel models come in many forms. To take just one example, Hewlett-Packard, a technology giant seeking to provide a more flexible customer experience and to do battle with tough competitors in a commoditized market, has put together a highly customer-focused model aimed at flexibility and convenience. The company offers a full-featured Web site so customers and prospects can learn and do their own research on HP's products and services. Customers who decide to buy can place orders over the Web or, alternatively, call in orders over the phone. Large corporate accounts also get the attention and hand-holding of key account reps. Post-sale support and problem resolution is provided first over the phone, and then through local business partners if needed, with Web-based support tools as well. HP, in short, has integrated its many channels to create a seamless customer experience, in which different channels take on specialized roles within the sales process and work together to serve customers.

That's just one example, out of hundreds of possible multi-channel configurations. A coordinated, integrated mix of channels can come in many other flavors, depending on what you sell, who you want to sell it to, and what you're trying to accomplish as a business. There is no one 'correct' approach; an integrated multi-channel model aimed at maximum sales growth will look very different than a model aimed at high margins or market share. It takes some work and creativity to develop an integrated multi-channel model that's right for a particular business. We will take a very detailed and thorough look at the issues involved in building a strong, winning model in Chapter 7.

So there you have it: a brief look at the ingredients of a successful go-to-market strategy. Just to recap: in order to develop a high-performance go-to-market strategy, you must target the right markets, align with the behaviors and needs of customers in those markets, choose the right sales channels, put the right products and value propositions into those channels, and pull it all together into an integrated, multi-channel model. When you've done all that, you will end up with a selling machine that delivers high revenues, margins, and customer loyalty.

WHAT TO EXPECT FROM THIS BOOK

At the completion of this book, you will have a clear and thorough understanding of the best practices, the core success principles, and the practical tools and techniques for taking products and services to market, which you will be able to put to good use whether you're launching a new product, targeting new markets, building new channels and partnerships, or taking a whole new division to market!

Specifically, you will be able to create a complete go-to-market plan that defines the optimal mix of markets, customers, channels, products, and value propositions needed to:

- Create a powerful, winning total customer experience that attracts and retains the best, most desirable customers
- Increase sales and market share
- Reduce selling costs and increase profits
- Ultimately, create shareholder value.

These are (hopefully) the reasons you purchased this book. So without further ado, let's get started!

2

Go-to-market strategy:

The ten commandments of going to market

T he Ancient Greeks (Socrates, Plato, Aristotle, etc.) spent a lot of time thinking and writing and arguing. Remember, this was in the days before home theater systems, the Internet, telephones, MP3 players, and shopping malls. There just wasn't a lot to do, especially if you weren't interested in attacking the neighboring city-states. With all that time on their hands, the Greeks developed some pretty important ideas, and one of them was the notion of universal truth: truth that applies everywhere, at all times, no matter what. For example, the idea that the three angles of a triangle *always* add up to 180°, or that 2 + 2 *always* equals 4. The argument over whether there's such a thing as a universal truth is still being debated in the universities, but practical sales-types know that 2 + 2 really does equal 4.[20]

The biblical Ten Commandments are great examples of universal truths. The whole idea of commandments such as 'Thou shalt not kill' is that they are just *right*, regardless of how we feel about them. They come from a higher source: from mountain tops and, for fans of Cecil B. DeMille and Charlton Heston, from burning bushes that speak to us in very authoritative, low-pitched voices.[21]

In go-to-market strategy there is no burning bush to speak to us, nor are there any stone tablets coming down from the mountaintop to suggest profound corporate truths. You are unlikely to spend time in a fiery, unpleasant place if you choose a bad sales channel. So perhaps it's a stretch to proclaim any true Commandments of Going to Market.

Or is it? Go-to-market strategists will probably never produce anything with the elegant simplicity of Moses' Commandments, but on the other hand there are some things about going to market that are so universally applicable and so useful as to deserve a special place as our fundamental guideposts for go-to-market strategy. With the typical modesty of a business strategy consultant, I call these guideposts *The Ten Commandments of Going to Market*. They are shown in Figure 2.1.

---

[20] Unless the customer says it equals five. Actually, modern science has basically proven that everything is relative, and that there's no such thing as a universal truth. But that is way, way beyond the scope of this book.
[21] Charlton Heston played Moses in Cecil B. DeMille's remake of the epic *The Ten Commandments* (©1956 Paramount Pictures Corporation).

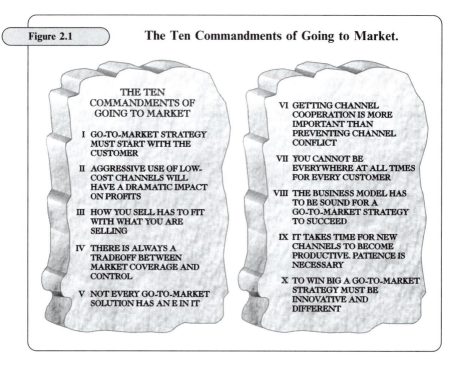

Figure 2.1   **The Ten Commandments of Going to Market.**

THE TEN COMMANDMENTS OF GOING TO MARKET

I   GO-TO-MARKET STRATEGY MUST START WITH THE CUSTOMER

II AGGRESSIVE USE OF LOW-COST CHANNELS WILL HAVE A DRAMATIC IMPACT ON PROFITS

III HOW YOU SELL HAS TO FIT WITH WHAT YOU ARE SELLING

IV THERE IS ALWAYS A TRADEOFF BETWEEN MARKET COVERAGE AND CONTROL

V   NOT EVERY GO-TO-MARKET SOLUTION HAS AN E IN IT

VI GETTING CHANNEL COOPERATION IS MORE IMPORTANT THAN PREVENTING CHANNEL CONFLICT

VII YOU CANNOT BE EVERYWHERE AT ALL TIMES FOR EVERY CUSTOMER

VIII THE BUSINESS MODEL HAS TO BE SOUND FOR A GO-TO-MARKET STRATEGY TO SUCCEED

IX IT TAKES TIME FOR NEW CHANNELS TO BECOME PRODUCTIVE. PATIENCE IS NECESSARY

X   TO WIN BIG A GO-TO-MARKET STRATEGY MUST BE INNOVATIVE AND DIFFERENT

Let's take a look at each of the commandments.

I

GO-TO-MARKET STRATEGY MUST START WITH THE CUSTOMER

The First Commandment of Going to Market states that you must start with the customer. The customer must be the focus of all of your go-to-market efforts, as well as the *primary source of information* used to make each and every go-to-market decision.

Some might argue that this commandment is obvious and trite – just common sense, like 'Thou Shalt Not Kill'. The difference is that while business people don't usually run around killing each other, there are very few organizations that understand their customers in enough depth to create powerful, winning go-to-market strategies. They think they do, but they don't.

Sure, lots of organizations conduct internal, closed-door strategy meetings, in which managers discuss the latest thinking *within the company* about customers' needs. There is never a shortage of people ready to speak on behalf of the customer. But where does their information come from? A few participants will discuss their 'gut feel' based on intuition about the market. A marketing director will bring in some market research reports, in which customers were asked superficial, multiple-choice questions such as whether their budget will increase or decrease next year. A product manager might take a few hours to explain the customer problem that was assumed to exist when the development team invented a new product or solution to solve it. A sales VP might volunteer what he or she heard while talking to some customers at a recent conference.

Of course, the only people who have a clue what customers will actually buy and how they will buy it – the customers themselves – are not in the meeting. They weren't invited.

Internally driven, behind-closed-door strategy development does not work; it never has. No one, no matter what their title or their sales and marketing expertise, no matter how much they think they understand the customer and the market place, is clever enough or clairvoyant enough to understand customers' needs or predict their behaviors in a vacuum. Generic market research reports won't help, and neither will the occasional, anecdotal conversation with a customer or two. There is only one way to start with the customer for real: systematic, rigorous, and careful analysis of what the customers in your various markets buy, why they buy it, how they buy it, and what will motivate them to buy more of it. Few companies have had the discipline to do that. That's why you end up with the ongoing stream of new products, marketing campaigns, and channels that are 'retired' almost immediately after their launch. Created in a vacuum, they never hit home with customers, and are quickly replaced with more guesswork-based initiatives.

That is how you end up with Starbucks selling furniture over the Web, based on the idea that what customers 'really' want is not just a good cup of coffee, but a Starbucks-style couch in their living rooms. It's how you get Merrill Lynch coming to the conclusion, a few years ago, that its customers wouldn't use the Web because they value the 'relationship' too much. It's how you get Coca Cola's *New Coke*, or marketing messages like 'the leading java-based e-commerce solution enabling enterprise portal functionality on cross-platform architectures' pitched to corporate customers who just want reliable Internet access for their employees. And it's how you get some of the really awful, total go-to-market failures of our age. Let's take a look at one, just to see how bad it can truly get when you don't start with the customer.

Iridium LLC, a satellite-based global wireless phone system, initiated voice and paging service in November, 1998. Its sixty-six satellites in low earth orbit (LEO) allowed wireless communication anywhere in the world. The basic idea was that busy globetrotters would be able to use the same phone whether they were ordering a pizza from home, sitting in a business meeting in New York, relaxing on a boat outside Sydney Harbour, vacationing in Kenya, or even stranded in a desert!

That's a compelling story ... if you happen to be sitting in an Iridium conference room guessing what customers want. But do people really need to talk on wireless phones while they're vacationing in Kenya? And how often do wireless phone users get stranded in deserts?

It turned out that Iridium had failed to test some pretty basic assumptions in the market place. Who would buy this service? How much would they be willing to pay? Where would they buy the phone or expect to find one? What, if anything, would they find compelling about it? Was it designed correctly for its target user? None of these questions had been answered conclusively.

I think you know what's coming.

By April of 1999, just six months after the launch, Iridium had burned through nearly a billion dollars and was almost out of cash. Only ten thousand of the fifty-two thousand anticipated subscribers had signed up. Its largest intended distributor, Sprint, had still not started offering Iridium voice service. Four months later, unable to keep its head above water and drowning in debt, Iridium landed in bankruptcy court. Seen as one of the most spectacular business failures in recent memory, the satellite network and phone system that had taken nine years and cost

$5 billion to develop was eventually sold for $25 million – or half a penny on the dollar.

What went wrong?

At a time when high-end mobile phones cost $400–800, an Iridium phone was priced at around $3,000. Shaped like a large house brick, and weighing over three times as much as a typical cellular phone, the Iridium phone didn't exactly slip into a shirt pocket or snap onto a belt. The Iridium service required an 'acquisition fee' of $70, and had a monthly access fee of $70. On top of that, usage fees were $3–6 per minute for international calls and $1.99 per minute for domestic airtime. In contrast, normal, everyday cell phones of the time fit easily into a suit pocket, had monthly fees of $20–50, and had usage fees of around 20–30 cents per minute.

Despite all this, the concept still might have worked. However, Iridium made one more mistake, and it was a big one. Instead of targeting discrete segments of users that might actually need the service, Iridium attempted to market its service generally to wireless customers who, of course, already had cell phones. And instead of forming partnerships with local cellular providers so it could offer cheaper rates for local use, Iridium went head-to-head against these companies as a direct competitor. As a result, users would have to choose between a convenient, small, reasonably priced cell phone and a big, bulky, expensive global phone charging exorbitant rates, even to call a neighbor from their living rooms.

Of course, on the off-chance that a user happened to be stranded in the middle of a desert or ocean, Iridium had a far better service than anything offered by local wireless providers. In the end, customers decided that was a risk they were willing to take.

The Iridium failure boils down to yet another concept designed, developed, and brought to market without the customer. What if Iridium had gone about it differently? What if it had called a few hundred wireless phone users, early in the design stage, to ask these kinds of questions:

■ Do you need a global cell phone?
■ How much more would you be willing to pay for global capability? How much would be 'too much'?

- Would you put up with a larger-sized and heavier phone to get global capability?
- What's the maximum size and weight you would accept?
- Would you require low-cost local service to be bundled in with the product?

Iridium could have saved itself nine years of work and $5 billion if it had taken the time to ask these simple questions and gain a real understanding of the customer.[22]

Iridium's arrogance in believing it could create a market opportunity through sheer cleverness, without involving the customer, is hardly unique. Many companies have done exactly the same thing, and continue to do so. It is a recipe for disaster. The fact is, all of the key go-to-market decisions you make depend on detailed, exact information gathered from target customers. Consider the following:

- *Products.* The only products you will be able to sell are the ones that customers want, need, and are willing to buy. So if you want to sell a product successfully and in high volume, it must map with great precision to the needs and expectations of your target customers – which, of course, you can only learn about by working directly with them and listening very carefully to what they have to say.
- *Channels.* The only purpose of channels is to reach and do business with your target customers. Whichever channels your target customers use, those are the channels you must provide. And whichever channels these customers believe they will use in the future, those are the channels you should start building. Again, this is information that is only available directly from your target customers.
- *The 'message', or value proposition.* In order to have a strong, successful message that compels purchasing activity, you must understand at a deep level what customers find compelling and

---

[22] Incidentally, the new (post-sale) Iridium Satellite has changed focus from the mass consumer market to clients who especially need global communications, in the maritime, heavy-construction, forestry, aviation, and emergency services industries. Iridium Satellite also no longer has the original aim of a million subscribers. Motorola, one of the bankrollers of the original Iridium, will supply the company with new equipment, and Boeing will operate and maintain the satellite operations. Before purchasing the old Iridium's assets, Iridium Satellite LLC finalized a deal with the Department of Defense for a two-year, $72 million contract to supply twenty thousand phones. Iridium has scaled down the phones, added data-transmission capability, and plans to offer text messaging services in the future. The new-and-improved Iridium Satellite may, in fact, have a decent future at this point – precisely because it started over with the customer in mind. Time will tell.

enticing about your product or service. There is only one place to get that information.

■ *Markets*. You should only be targeting markets in which customers have verified that they are highly interested in doing business with you. Otherwise, it's just luck of the draw – maybe you'll stumble onto the right markets, and maybe you won't. The only way to have certainty about your target markets is to work directly with customers in those markets to gauge their buying interest.

In short, the success of *every* go-to-market strategy decision you make depends on the depth of your understanding about customers' needs, expectations, and behaviors. Assumptions don't work, and neither does the occasional anecdotal information collected from a handful of customers. You must conduct detailed, thorough, and rich investigation into what makes your target customers tick. This is the core foundation of every successful go-to-market strategy.

II

AGGRESSIVE USE OF LOW-COST CHANNELS WILL HAVE A DRAMATIC IMPACT ON PROFITS

Over the past fifteen years, we have witnessed a cornucopia of new management theories, legitimate 'best practices', and some questionable fads too, all of which have basically had the same goal: finding the Holy Grail of Higher Profits. Everyone is trying to figure out how to improve bottom-line performance.

First we had process redesign, in which efficiency experts walked the halls with clipboards to cut out the waste (and people). Then we had re-engineering, which looked a lot like process redesign combined with expensive new computer systems. We've been through TQM, in which quality principles were applied to reduce errors and create more efficient (and profitable) processes. There have been numerous other theories and fads as well. Some of them have indeed led to cost savings, although many executives have been surprised and disappointed at the amount of work that it has taken to squeeze out small gains. Operational tinkering seems to be of limited usefulness. In any event, it is probably the wrong place to look for serious gains in profitability.

The *right* place to look is the sales function. Here is an area that represents a huge chunk of total expenses. The average company spends around 20–25 percent of revenues to sell its products and services. For a $10 billion company, that's roughly $2–2.5 billion per year to go to market. That's a lot of money – and a lot of potential cost-savings too.

Let me emphasize this point, because it's crucial. In many organizations, going to market is the single largest expense of any kind, with the possible exception of physically making the product. In a lot of companies, even making the product itself doesn't cost as much money as bringing it to market! Look at any company's income statement and go down to the row that says 'SG&A' which consists mostly of go-to-market expenses (sales and marketing costs).[23] You will see an absolutely huge number. Anything you can do to reduce your go-to-market costs will dramatically impact profit margins and actual profit dollars.

A $10 billion company, for example, that spends 20 percent ($2 billion) on sales and marketing expenses, and is able to reduce its sales costs by just 10 percent, will realize $200 million in new operating profits. That is a lot of money. And it's a very conservative number. Companies that get aggressive about sales costs can typically achieve reductions in the 20–25 percent range. In our example of a $10 billion company, that's a saving of $400–500 million in sales costs.

There is probably nothing else you can do to save so much money, and to impact profitability so directly and significantly, period.

So how do you squeeze 10 or 20 or even 25 percent out of your sales costs? The simple answer is: you sell some of your products through lower-cost channels. All the money you save by making sales through lower-cost channels drops straight to the bottom line.

---

[23] SG&A = Selling & General Administrative expenses.

To illustrate, let's take a look at a helpful chart (Figure 2.2) that shows the typical transaction for selling a $5,000–7,500 product, in each of five different sales channels.

Figure 2.2 shows that, for an average, everyday $5,000–7,500 industrial product, the cost to sell it through a field sales rep is about $1,000. That $1,000 covers the sales rep's salary, commissions, bonus, travel expenses, dinners with the clients, brochures, laptop computer, sales training, and so on. It's the 'fully loaded' cost of a typical sales rep transaction.

Let's say you move a sale out of the hands of a field sales rep and into the hands of a value-added partner – a company that will resell your product and provide its own value-added services and support. Instead of paying all the costs of the sales rep, now you pay a 'cut' to the partner, and you'll also need some managers to keep an eye on the partners. When you add that up, selling through value-added partners

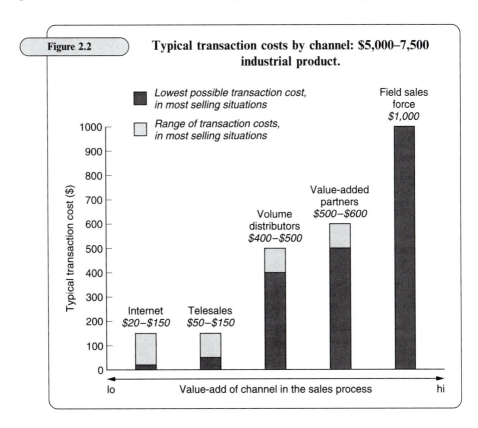

Figure 2.2   **Typical transaction costs by channel: $5,000–7,500 industrial product.**

typically costs about $600 per transaction. You've just saved $400. *Your cost to make the sale just went down 40 percent.*

Let's suppose your product could be resold by volume distributors – partners who add few services and little value to the product, but just sell it in quantity. Because they provide fewer services and generally have lower labor costs, they usually get a smaller cut than value-added partners. This kind of sale might cost you $450. In contrast to a sales rep, you just saved $550. *Your cost to make the sale just decreased by 55 percent.*

Let's get radical and suppose you could sell your product over the phone. It might sound improbable, but people are doing it; IBM sells over 15 percent of worldwide revenue over the phone, including complex, multi-million dollar computer systems. Phone reps cost a third or less than field sales reps, don't travel, and typically make eight to ten times as many calls per week. As a result, a $5,000–7,500 product can usually be sold over the phone at a transaction cost of around $120. In comparison to a field sales rep, that's a saving of $880. *Your cost of sale just got slashed by 88 percent.*

Perhaps you have a product that can be sold over the Web, at least to a few of your customers in some circumstances. Typical transaction cost: around $100, basically the cost to build and transact business on the Web site, divided by the number of sales transactions. *Now you've reduced the cost of sale by 90 percent.*

Of course, most companies that sell complex products and services can't, and wouldn't want to, sell to new customers over the Web and telephone. I'm not suggesting that you do. But let's say you moved just a quarter of your transactions to lower-cost channels – for instance, your routine add-on sales to existing accounts; or sales of simpler, commodity items to your smaller customers. Without going too deeply into the math, if you were to do that, your sales costs would go down by around 10–15 percent, depending on the channels you selected. For a company spending $2 billion per year on selling costs, that's $200 million to $300 million of pure new profit. That's a lot of coin.

The challenge, of course, is to figure out which alternative channels to use, and which sales transactions and customers to use them for. Some products and transactions require more complex, expensive channels – and yet, others don't. That's what you need to figure out when you put together a go-to-market strategy. We'll come back to this issue later in the book. For now, let's just establish the basic principle that *aggressive use of low-cost channels will have a dramatic impact on your profits.* Expect to save money – a lot of money – as soon as you start moving some of your sales transactions into alternative, lower-cost channels.

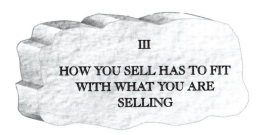

III

HOW YOU SELL HAS TO FIT WITH WHAT YOU ARE SELLING

The Third Commandment states that *how* you sell has to fit with *what* you are selling. Put another way, the sales channels you choose must fit with the products and services you sell – and vice versa.

Product–channel fit is a fundamental principle of successful go-to-market planning, and one that is easy to understand on an intuitive, commonsense level. Long-distance telephone service sold over the telephone: there's a strong product–channel fit. Books, CDs, and other simple, low-cost consumer items sold over the Internet: a pretty good product–channel fit. Recreational vehicles sold at automotive dealerships, with products on the lot and knowledgeable sales people to help customers take test-drives: excellent product–channel fit. So what's a bad product–channel fit? Services for the blind, sold on Web sites. $100,000-per-year field reps selling individually-wrapped chiclets. Open-heart surgery pitched over the phone to consumers during their dinner hour. Fur coats sold at People For The Ethical Treatment Of Animals (PETA) conventions. Land mines advertised in Peace Corps newsletters. Sometimes the fit between products and channels, or lack thereof, is very obvious.

But are all product–channel fit scenarios as straightforward as these examples? Not really. In truth, getting a strong, tight fit between what you sell and how you sell it is often a difficult challenge. Let's look at a company that struggled with this issue and failed, to see just what can go wrong and how serious a bad product–channel fit can be for the business.

Pets.com was one of the highest-profile late-1990s dot-coms; its site went live in February, 1999. The company's likable mascot, the Sock Puppet, was advertised endlessly on television, creating strong consumer awareness and making Pets.com an instant household name for anyone even remotely tuned into the Web phenomenon. Pets.com's business concept seemed sound. With a worldwide market for pet food and supplies estimated conservatively at $32.4–34 billion,[24] even a small portion of sales captured over the Web would provide Pets.com with a business opportunity measured in the hundreds of millions, if not billions, of dollars. And with 136 million cats and dogs in the United States alone, and 71.8 percent of US households owning cats or dogs or both, Pets.com was entering a stable market unlikely to go away or contract anytime soon.[25]

Pets.com's Web site offered a broad range of products, from 50-pound bags of dog food and 25-pound bags of cat litter to leather motorcycle jackets for ferrets. The value proposition to customers seemed pretty good. Why bother driving to a retail store to pick up food and supplies for your pets, when you can order them efficiently over the Internet?

Yet despite the seemingly reasonable marriage between the product – pet food and supplies – and the Internet channel, it turned out not to be a good fit at all. For one thing, many pet supplies, such as bags of food or cat litter, are bulky and heavy, leading to prohibitive shipping costs. Pets.com had to absorb most of these costs in order to be competitive in a low-margin, price-sensitive market. As a result, the company lost 19 cents on every incoming $1 of revenue – even before paying for overhead.[26] In fact, in its final quarter before going belly-up on November 6, 2000, Pets.com collected $277,000 less in sales than it had taken to purchase the products from suppliers. The economics just didn't work. That quarter, Pets.com lost $21.7 million on sales of just $9.4 million.[27]

---

[24] Estimate from The Sales Strategy Institute research in 2001, based on a number of industry sources and estimates.
[25] Number of cats and dogs, source: The Food Marketing Institute, *Supermarket Research*, 2(4), 2000. Percent of households owning cats or dogs or both, source: The Pet Food Institute, Pet Population Study finds More and More US Households own Pets, web reference: http://petfoodinstitute.org/reference_pet_data .cfm
[26] Matt Krantz, What detonated dot-bombs? *USA Today*, December 4, 2000.
[27] Troy Wolverton, Pets.com: latest high-profile dot-com disaster. *CNet News*, November 7, 2000.

If unsound economics was the only problem, you could write it all off to poor business planning by inexperienced dot.com executives. But the problems went further. The real issue was one of customer behavior. Customers, simply put, were satisfied with their existing channels – supermarkets and pet supply stores – and didn't line up to do business over the Web. Much has been written on the topic of Pets.com's inability to attract a critical mass of customers. As the owner of two cats, I think I can bring some clarity to the discussion. When you're a little behind in your cleaning responsibilities – when the cats are circling the litter box emitting snarls communicating 'No way!' – are you going to place an order over the Web for delivery in four days, or are you going to rush over to the grocery store to get some clean litter? It's pretty simple, really. In the end, the so-called inconvenient trips to retail stores turned out to be pretty convenient, after all. With pet supplies and food readily available in supermarkets, one short aisle away from the people-food that you have to buy anyway, there's little incentive to power up the PC, go to a Web site, type in an order, and wait days for delivery.

What's to be learned from Pets.com? Well, don't try to sell big bags of cat litter on the Web. More seriously, even when a product and a channel seem fairly well suited to each other, it's important to step back and evaluate how good the fit really is, because the fit might just be poor. There are three basic things to consider.

1. *Customers*. The channels you select must be the ones that customers actually use to buy the things you are selling. If they buy products like yours over the phone, then sell over the phone. If they buy products like yours over the Internet, then sell on the Internet. If they buy product like yours in supermarkets, then you will have to get your product onto the supermarket shelves. There are no ifs, ands, or buts about it. You must ensure that your product is available in the channels that customers use when they look for, and buy, that type of product.

2. *Economics*. The channels you choose must make economic sense, given what you are trying to sell. Pets.com couldn't do profitable business, because the channel itself added extra costs (shipping, logistics, etc.) that the company had to absorb in a price-sensitive market. The fact is, even if a product can be sold in a particular channel, that does not mean it can be sold *profitably* in that channel. That's why you don't see $100,000-per-year field sales

reps selling individually wrapped chiclets; a sales force is way too expensive for such a simple, low-cost product. You have to choose channels that are financially suitable, given the price-point, margin levels, and other financial dimensions of the product.

3. *Complexity*. Some products are simple and 'off the rack' and can be sold through simple, low-cost channels such as the Web or phone. But not every product fits this description. Offerings such as medical diagnostic equipment, custom software development, and engineering services are complex and require channels that can handle product configuration, customer training, ongoing face-to-face support, complex negotiations, and long-term customer coddling. More complex channels, which are able to provide these kinds of services, include field sales forces and high-end value-added resellers. You may have to use one of these channels if your product is highly complex, customized, or expensive. The channel must be well suited to the complexity of the product.

In the end, your degrees of freedom in designing a go-to-market strategy are constrained and shaped by product–channel fit issues. You must take a very careful look at your products and your potential channels, and determine which ones are optimally suited for each other.

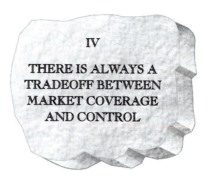

IV

THERE IS ALWAYS A
TRADEOFF BETWEEN
MARKET COVERAGE
AND CONTROL

On a United Airlines flight to Sydney a few years ago, I cautiously requested a cup of coffee after the meal. We've all gotten used to bad airline food and coffee over the years, and as a seasoned traveler, I was ready for another cup of the bitter, foul-tasting stuff. But United had just entered into a new partnership, bringing us something we jaded business travelers wouldn't have expected to see in a million years. Not 'okay coffee', not 'pretty good coffee', but ... Starbucks coffee!!!

The only problem was that it was awful. The flight attendants, racing back and forth with meals, getting the fidgety kids out of the aisles, and fixing the broken in-flight movie system, lacked the attention to detail and the fanatical quality control of the crews in the retail Starbucks shops. The coffee was overdone, and not just a little over-done. It was burnt, and almost undrinkable. In a retail store, they would have quickly tossed it in the garbage and made a new one. On an airplane, you get what you get. I drank it dutifully. It was not Starbucks' shining moment.

Starbucks has taken its upscale $3 cup of coffee and other offerings, sold initially through its company-owned retail shops, into a massive, global customer base, through dozens of new alliances, distributor channels, and partnerships such as that with United Airlines. The only catch is, to reach all the customers served by all of those new channels, Starbucks has had to put its products and its pristine reputa-tion for quality into the hands of a multitude of new players who are not employed by Starbucks, and who are therefore not as interested in whether a cup of coffee is 'perfect'. But that is the price of growth. If the goal is to ensure that every cup of coffee is perfect, then you stick to company-owned retail stores – and write off the potential growth and market expansion that new channels and partners can make possible.

Starbucks is just a simple illustration of one of the essential truths of going to market. *There is always a tradeoff between market coverage and control.* You cannot reach deeply into new markets and cover the broad range of potential customers, while fully controlling the sales transaction, the customer relationship, and the delivery of your pro-duct or service. Every time you expand your channels to reach and serve more potential customers, you reduce your ability to control events. This occurs with *any* new channel. Selling over the phone will reduce your control. Selling over the Web will reduce your con-trol. Selling through distributors and partners will greatly reduce – and perhaps eliminate – your control. In fact, selling through anything except a company-owned, company-paid, and company-trained sales force will reduce your control. Loss of control is a price many com-panies are willing to pay to achieve high growth, but the tradeoff is

initial results in eight weeks. A consultant hired by the team suggested that a CRM system would integrate all of the company's channels and create a powerful experience for customers. So the team spent most of its eight weeks evaluating CRM packages, at the conclusion of which they made a $4 million software investment. The team's final presentation suggested that its task had basically been completed.

There was just one problem. There was no strategy. The CRM system was slick, but CRM is just software – a tool – and not a strategy. *None* of the fundamental questions of going to market had been answered:

1. Which markets offer the best growth opportunities?
2. Which prospects should the company target in those markets?
3. Which channels could most efficiently and effectively reach those prospects?
4. Which products should be emphasized in new sales opportunities?
5. Did the company have the right message? Would *new* customers find it compelling?

Since none of these questions had been answered, the team couldn't identify a single new customer or a single new euro of revenue from all of its work.

So the team was sent back to the drawing board, again with an eight-week deadline, and this time with a charter to recruit business partners. Frenetic activity took place to meet the deadline – without bothering to validate that business partners were the right channel in the first place. Eight weeks later the team had a list of forty partners, which it presented to the board, knowing full well that most of the partners were on the list just because they'd shown up to the company's regional conferences. The board understood this, too. Everyone agreed there were, at most, five good partners on the list.

Worn out from racing from deadline to deadline, the team decided to stop wasting time on 'strategy' and get down to the task at hand: implementing the huge CRM system that had already been paid for … and which was sitting in a corner collecting dust. A 'Big 5' consultant was called in, and three million euros were spent over six months to customize and tune the software. No one used the system. Since the team hadn't identified or built any new channels, the only people around to use the software were the field sales force. Reps didn't feel like banging data into their computers all day, and since there weren't any other channels to communicate with, or new customers to strategize about, or new products to sell, they didn't bother.

Total cost: ten months; seven million euros.

Total benefit: None. Not a single new customer. Not a single new channel.

The frenetic pace at which companies attempt to 'nail down' their go-to-market strategies and roll out new channels is wrong. It *never* produces the right results. It just creates rework and continued frenetic activity, as teams jump around from one initiative to another. Nothing ever really gets built. The ongoing frenzy to hit the market place with half-baked ideas leaves people too exhausted and cynical to do anything useful and practical, such as identifying fifty or a hundred new prospects, or sitting down with prospective partners to see what it would take to drive deals together.

If you get nothing else out of this book, get this: It takes twelve to twenty-four months to build and roll out a new go-to-market strategy, and in most cases it's around eighteen months. If you put in that time, you can get great results. If you short-change the process, you'll end up with nothing. Here's why it takes eighteen months.

1. *Strategy development.* You can't successfully build and integrate channels until you understand, at a minimum, which markets and customers those channels have to reach and serve. What if you end up choosing business partners that don't sell to your target customers? What if you invest in a call center or e-commerce site and your best prospects won't do business over the phone or Web? It can all end up being an enormously expensive waste of time, and it often is. To avoid time-wasting, you must carefully analyze which markets offer the best opportunities for growth; what the customers and prospects in those markets need, how they buy, and how they will do business in the future; which channels will reach and be able to serve the most customers in those markets; and which partners can best help you achieve your goals. From this fact-gathering and analysis, you will be able to put together an overall go-to-market strategy that has a sound

basis in actual market realities – and that will therefore win. It takes three to four months to do all this, and never less.

2. *Channel planning and design.* Let's say you do your homework and determine that systems integrators are the right new channel. Do you just pick up the phone and call them? They'll have questions you won't be able to answer. What is the revenue sharing plan? What kinds of sales, marketing and technical support will you provide? Are you going to give them leads, or are they on their own? It isn't just a partner channel that will create a need for channel planning and design. If telesales is to be the new channel, where will the call center be located, who will you hire to staff the center, and which customers will it serve? If it's a Web site, what will the features be, and which products will it carry or not carry? And then you get to the really big questions: how will all of your channels integrate and work together seamlessly? Who will manage the overall go-to-market system? Typically, answering these questions through good channel planning and design takes about three months.

3. *Implementation.* Finally, you have to build the actual channels as well as the integrating mechanisms (CRM system, management team, etc.). For example, Web sites, call centers etc. must be designed and built. Business partners must be recruited, trained, and launched into the market place with an effective campaign. The sales force may require new training programs. Getting all of this up and running can take anywhere from six to eighteen months.

The bottom line: it takes twelve to twenty-four months to build a new go-to-market model and roll it out into the market place.

As a result, it's important to put a stop to the various frenetic go-to-market strategy activities taking place within the organization. A much better approach is to develop a thoughtful, solid plan that will deliver results in the market place on a realistic timeline. It probably took ten or twenty years to build your sales force, so it shouldn't come as a surprise that you cannot redesign and deploy an entire go-to-market model in a month or two. Forget it. Get everyone on board with the fact that it takes about eighteen months to roll out a winning new go-to-market model. Everyone – top executives, middle managers designing and building channel programs, sales reps, etc. – must be given target dates that have a basis in reality.

X

**TO WIN BIG A
GO-TO-MARKET
STRATEGY MUST BE
INNOVATIVE AND
DIFFERENT**

You cannot dominate your markets and become *the* company to do business with, just by doing the same things everyone else is doing. If your ambition is to achieve serious growth and be a real leader in your markets – if you want to win big – then your go-to-market strategy must be innovative and different. This is the Tenth and final and, for an ambitious, growing company, the most important Commandment of Going to Market.

Of course, it could be the case that you don't want to win big. For some organizations, modest, incremental sales growth, combined with reasonable profitability, is acceptable. You may even be happy right where you are, at current revenue and profit levels. There's no shame in that. Not everyone is trying to win big. If that's the case at your company, then the Tenth Commandment is not for you.

But most organizations are more ambitious than that. They have set their sights on aggressive revenue and profit targets. They want to be Number One or, at worst, Number Two or Three in their markets. They want the loyalty of the *best* customers. They want to be the supplier of choice. They want customers to know that they are much better to do business with than the competition.

To achieve these things, you cannot just plod along with a 'me too' go-to-market strategy, continuing with what you are doing or copying the strategies of others. The fact is, even the best go-to-market strategies out there today, the ones you might choose to imitate, will eventually become commonplace and stale. Dell's winning Internet and 'teleweb' approach, and Schwab's 'surround sound' channel model, are great innovations. But within a few years, putting up an outstanding Web site or providing customers with a multi-channel experience will become 'normal' – just a routine expectation of customers, not a source of advantage. Go-to-market innovation has a short shelf life; it always has. Once a great go-to-market idea 'hits the street', it immediately gets copied and begins losing its currency and differentiation. Let's take a look at two historical examples.

Sears & Roebuck, formed in 1886, was perhaps the first great go-to-market innovator. Initially a jewelry and watch store, in 1897 Sears introduced one of the first general mail order catalogs.[49] In its time, the mail order catalog was a radical go-to-market innovation. The fast-growing population of the US was basically unreachable in the 1890s; there was no Internet, of course, but there was also no fax, TV or radio, and the phone had just been invented. There were few ways to reach the dispersed customers spread out across the US; that's why most businesses at the time were local and small. The new, and ubiquitous, Sears catalog put the company's name out in front of millions of customers, and made it easy and convenient for them to purchase, right from their living rooms. It turned Sears into a $1 billion per year household-name brand by 1945. The catalog model was quickly replicated, due to its success. In 1915, for example, Burpee, the seed company that invented iceberg lettuce and the Brandywine tomato,[50] shipped over one million catalogs to reach the nation's dispersed farmers and planters. As more and more companies brought out their own catalogs, this channel gradually lost its cachet, and became just another way to reach and sell to customers. Today, it's expected that you will have a catalog (both in print and online) if you sell a broad range of products – but you get no special credit or advantage from doing so.

Amway is another great go-to-market innovation story. Launched in 1959, Amway, which sells typical household products such as soap and shampoo, created a very clever channel consisting of independent distributors who sell Amway's products in neighborhood door-to-door transactions, while also buying and using the products themselves. Today, with over three million distributors selling and consuming Amway products in more than eighty countries, the company has become a $5 billion per year behemoth with a cult-like following. The

---

[49] The first Sears catalog appeared in 1888, but featured only watches and jewelry.
[50] The Brandywine tomato is also called the Mikado tomato.

Amway model, unquestionably, is one of the most successful go-to-market strategies ever developed. Like the Sears catalog, it provided the means for the company to penetrate dispersed markets and reach millions of new customers. But like the Sears catalog, the Amway model has also been replicated by hordes of imitators, including companies such as HerbaLife and Mary Kay Cosmetics, as well as hundreds of companies pushing various 'multi-level marketing' schemes. What worked for Amway probably will never work again on any kind of massive international, or even national, scale.

The lesson in these historical examples is simple. Eventually, even a great new go-to-market model becomes commonplace and routine. This will happen to today's go-to-market channels and strategies, just as it happened with the mail-order catalog and the distributor model. The question is: When that happens, what's your plan? What are you going to do to stay on the cutting edge and maintain your leadership position?

The good news is that you will probably not have to come up with a whole new channel. The reason is that we will all be immersed for at least a decade in trying to figure out what to do with the Internet. This coming decade will be about companies finding new and creative things to do with the channels they already have, and not about companies discovering entirely new channels. The leaders of the next decade will figure out how to use channels that already exist, but much more aggressively and creatively. There are already a few companies going down this path, and they are experiencing great successes. Let's take a quick look at one of them.

Dreyer's Grand Ice Cream manufactures and distributes premium ice creams under its own brand name, Dreyer's and Edy's, as well as 'private label' brands such as Starbucks and Godiva's. With an 18 percent share of the US market, Dreyer's manufactures and distributes more packaged ice cream than any other company in the US, and had robust sales growth of 13 percent in 2000.[51]

While Dreyer's *Rocky Road Ice Cream* (a flavor which it invented) is delicious, the company's innovative distribution model is primarily

---

[51] Rob Wherry, Ice cream wars. *Forbes Magazine*, May 28, 2001.

responsible for its market dominance. Dreyer's has the only national direct store distribution (DSD) system in the frozen dessert category, servicing 59,000 retail stores in forty-eight states and reaching approximately 90 percent of Americans.[52] Its distribution system links Dreyer's five manufacturing plants through a network of regional warehouses and cross docks, which enable a fleet of both company-owned and independent frozen-delivery trucks to service all 59,000 retail outlets several times per week! Add to all this a state-of-the-art information system that handles order processing, order tracking and routing, and you end up with Dreyer's route salesmen and merchandisers consistently delivering the highest in-stock rates in the industry.[53]

So what do you do once you have the best-in-class distribution system that reaches a vast majority of the nation's customers? Dreyer's raised precisely this question, and came up with an innovative answer: sell competitors' products through it! It's certainly a counterintuitive approach; who competes by making competitors' products easier to buy? Yet it's worked fantastically well. In 1986, Dreyer's began distributing Ben & Jerry's Ice Cream, and is credited with making Ben & Jerry's into a national brand.[54] Dreyer's also distributes Nestlé's ice cream novelties; manufactures and distributes Healthy Choice Ice Cream; has a joint venture with Starbucks to manufacturer and distribute Starbucks Ice Cream; and has a joint venture with M&M Mars to market their premium packaged ice cream products. Dreyer's more recently entered into a venture with Godiva Chocolatier in 1999 to produce ice cream that incorporates Godiva ingredients. In the second quarter of 2001, sales of these companies' brands and distribution of their products through Dreyer's distribution system accounted for 37 percent of sales, a 56 percent increase from the previous year.[55]

Dreyer's has effectively 'rented out' its channel to competitors, in order to increase its own sales and profits. At the same time, the company is now using its distribution system to create new growth opportunities outside the traditional grocery channel, by targeting other retailers such as convenience stores, drug chains and supercenters.

---

[52] Fact sheet, www.Dreyersinc.com.
[53] *Ibid.*
[54] Since April 2000, Ben & Jerry's has been owned by Unilever.
[55] Press release, www.Dreyersinc.com. July 25, 2001

In sum, Dreyer's distribution model enables the company to reach more customers, as well as to charge its competitors to reach their own customers, thus benefiting Dreyer's *again*. The company has clearly profited by thinking innovatively and exploring 'out of the box' channel options for increasing its business.

Not everyone is going to become a Dreyer's, but it's a good example of an important new trend. Companies such as Dreyer's are looking beyond recent go-to-market developments, such as corporate Web sites, and thinking 'outside the box' about how to leverage their existing channels, partners, and distribution systems for greater competitive advantage and financial returns. Of course, for most organizations, coming up with a winning new model is not a two-hour design project. It will take time to figure out how to get the most out of your go-to-market channels, and the time to get started is *now*. Some of today's go-to-market channels and fads are already looking a little long in the tooth. The winners of tomorrow will be those companies who are able to be innovative and different – who bring energy and élan to the task of figuring out how to do more with the channels and go-to-market approaches that are already available.

SUMMARY

In this chapter, we looked at ten bedrock principles of going to market. These principles so consistently determine go-to-market success – or failure – that they're appropriately named the *Ten Commandments of Going to Market*. They are universal truths of going to market, useful not only in evaluating an existing go-to-market approach, but also as guidelines for moving forward with a new strategy.

Think of the Ten Commandments as philosophical direction setting for a go-to-market planning effort. Moving forward, we'll be focusing on more practical matters – the tools and techniques of successful go-to-market strategy development. Let's get started by looking at the identification, evaluation and selection of the right mix of target markets.

3

Go-to-market strategy:

Targeting the right markets

Would you invest in a company that planned to sell cigars and other tobacco products to health clubs and hospitals? Probably not.

But what if you were informed that the company intended to sell only the *very best* hand-rolled cigars, at wholesale prices? Would you find that more interesting? On top of that, what if the company said it planned to conduct a $200 million advertising campaign to explain the benefits of cigar smoking to the health-minded public? Finally, what if, in an effort to pique your interest, the investor relations manager told you that they'd hand out cigars for free at health clubs and hospital emergency rooms over the next month?

Would you be excited about this investment opportunity? Or would you find it ludicrous?[56]

Your company is probably not trying to do anything as outrageous as selling cigars to health clubs and hospitals. At least, I hope not! Nevertheless, you face a similar challenge. Just as our hapless cigar manufacturer must choose the right markets in which to sell its products, so must you. No one is exempt from this fundamental law of go-to-market success. No matter how good your products are, and no matter how cleverly you price, package, advertise and promote those products, in fact *even if you give them away for free*, you won't succeed unless you focus your efforts on selling them into the right markets.

Your choice of target markets is important in itself, but it's also a crucial factor that influences every other go-to-market strategy decision that you make. For example, consider your selection of sales channels. It's impossible to choose a *successful* mix of channels until you determine which markets those channels are supposed to reach. If your goal is to dominate the health-care market, you must choose channels that reach health-care buyers. If your goal is to be a player in financial services or consumer packaged goods (CPG), you must choose channels that reach

> It's impossible to choose a successful mix of channels until you determine which markets those channels are supposed to reach.

---

[56] Incredibly, this example is based on an actual personal experience. On my way into the Worldgate Athletic Club in Herndon, Virginia, I encountered a salesman in the elevator on his way up to pitch the idea of selling premium cigars in the club's health food café. He saw nothing unusual or ironic about this sales call.

financial services or CPG customers – and those will be very different than health-care channels. Channel selection is just one example of a go-to-market decision that depends on your choice of target markets. *All* of your choices regarding products, marketing and promotion initiatives, business partnerships, messaging, value proposition development, pricing, etc., require that you first clarify and choose the markets in which you intend to participate and win.

Choosing your target markets is a good start, but it's just that – a start. As suggested with the cigar vendor, you not only have to choose markets; you also have to choose *good* ones. At a very minimum, this means choosing markets in which there are customers who will purchase your products and services. But of course 'very minimum' isn't the goal here. Where you really want to be is in your *optimal* markets – markets in which customers are highly receptive to your message and your offerings, and where you can sell the highest-possible volume of products and services to the most possible customers at the lowest possible cost.

To be blunt, at the moment it's unlikely that you are focused on your optimal markets. If you're in the majority, you are probably wasting a lot of time, effort and money chasing sales in mediocre or even undesirable markets. The fact is, most organizations have a sub-optimal mix of markets because they don't have the tools required to assess and choose their markets with any precision. Lacking these tools, they select their markets based on generic third-party market research reports that rarely apply to their unique circumstances, on hype about 'hot' market opportunities that usually turn out not to be so hot (and that almost always evolve into next year's duds), and on guesswork that has no roots in verified market conditions and proven customer behavior.

In this chapter, we're going to make sure that it's *other* companies who have this problem – and not you. Here, you'll get the tools you need to identify, evaluate, choose and prioritize your markets, and ensure that your sales efforts are laser-focused on the right opportunities in the market place.

We'll begin by discussing the four basic pitfalls of market targeting, and how to ensure that you avoid them. Then we'll examine a rigorous, proven process for evaluating new markets that will help you focus on the best possible opportunities. We'll conclude by looking at a company that has done a lot of things right, and established itself as a true leader in market targeting. To get started, though, let's take a look at the market targeting experiences of Enconix, a company that unfortunately fell into a number of the usual traps of poor market selection.

'OOPS! PICKED THE WRONG MARKET' ... ENCONIX AND THE MANY PITFALLS OF MARKET SELECTION

Amid the stifling heat and superb golf of Scottsdale, Arizona, the executive team of software developer Enconix[57] took a three-day off-site in April of 2000. It was no celebration. At issue was the very future of the company, which looked much in doubt when the CEO, a personal friend of mine, called his team together to discuss their dire situation.

Enconix was a classic 1990s software success story. From a 1989 launch with three co-founders, $5,000 in cash, and 'corporate offices' in the CEO's living room, this provider of Enterprise Resource And Planning (ERP) software and services had grown to 246 employees and over $55 million in sales by 1998. Enconix's success was due mainly to the disciplined and savvy business development focus of its cofounders. Cognizant of the overwhelming dominance of well-established players such as SAP and Baan in the Fortune 500 'enterprise' space, Enconix had carefully carved out a niche of small-to-mid sized industrial manufacturers with $50–250 million in revenues, who were often overlooked by larger competitors.[58] By focusing exclusively on this market, Enconix had developed a thorough understanding of the needs and information technology requirements of mid-market industrial manufacturers. As these customers' interests meandered during the 1990s from ERP to SCM (supply chain management) to CRM (customer relationship management), Enconix developed new software and services to meet the expanding needs of its customer base, positioning the company for strong continued growth. Enconix

---

[57] A pseudonym.
[58] The $50–250 million space is often termed the 'lower middle market', distinguished from the 'higher middle market' consisting of companies with $250 million to $1 billion in sales.

entered 1998 with a realistic plan for 35 percent revenue growth and a long-term objective of $250 million in annual sales.

And then Enconix got greedy.

In 1998, entranced by the huge opportunity presented by Y2K, Enconix changed direction. That year, customers were lining up to pay IT consultants big bucks to analyze their exposure to Y2K issues. Who could afford to stand on the sidelines and miss this once-in-a-lifetime opportunity? Not Enconix! Scores of the company's software developers were converted into 'Y2K specialists' who prior to 1/1/00 would help customers ensure that they were 'Y2K compliant', and who after 1/1/00 would help customers deal with their catastrophic computer crashes, lost data, and (hopefully!) development of entirely new IT systems. Enconix put the word out to its entire customer base that they needed to look no further than Enconix for a vendor to help them deal with the coming Y2K information technology apocalypse.

At midnight on January 1, 2000, Enconix discovered, along with everyone else, that the whole Y2K thing was a big bust. The world's banking systems were still functioning. Nuclear weapons slept peacefully in their silos. Hospitals' emergency rooms still had power. Manufacturers kept churning out products on their assembly lines as if nothing had changed. Even the traffic lights were working! Life went on as it always had; there was barely a dollar's worth of IT consulting work to be done. For Enconix, it was back to square one.

At the Scottsdale off-site in April 2000, the executive team had to admit one thing: while the company had wasted two years chasing the Y2K dream, the ERP software business, where the company had its roots, had changed dramatically. Enterprise, resource and planning solutions were losing popularity as companies began questioning the high cost of these solutions and the bizarre, almost Byzantine complexity of implementing ERP packages across an organization. In addition, the stock market had just taken a nosedive, causing many customers to reduce their overall IT spending in anticipation of an economic slowdown.

Enconix's executive team believed there was a silver lining in all of this. A report published by a leading market research firm indicated that while IT spending was slowing down, there was a 'hot next wave' of buying activity coming up – something called 'Partner Relationship Management', or PRM. Partner relationship management solutions would connect companies with their distributors and partners over the Web, reducing distribution costs and tightening up relationships with partners. According to the report, PRM would be a $2.1 billion per year business by 2004, and no vendor had yet staked a credible claim on this opportunity. Enconix's executives quickly renamed their Y2K specialists as PRM consultants, redeveloped their main software product into a PRM product in three months of intense work, and refocused their marketing efforts on the three segments named in the market research report as super-hot for PRM solutions: consumer goods manufacturers, food distributors, and computer hardware vendors. The Enconix sales force, consisting of thirty-eight account executives, was expanded to fifty-four reps and split into three teams of eighteen each, targeting consumer goods, food distribution, and computer hardware. Out they went, flying around the country to call on customers in their new target markets.

Enconix proceeded to learn all about the importance of sound market targeting … the hard way.

Ignoring its core, traditional customers – small to medium-sized industrial manufacturers – Enconix redirected its sales efforts toward pitching a brand-new product into three markets in which it had no experience and no understanding of customers' needs. Those customers, already working with their own IT vendors, were reluctant to switch to Enconix, particularly since it lacked references in their markets and was unable to articulate clearly how its solution solved industry-specific problems. The market research report on PRM, from which all the key decisions had been made, turned out to have been based on a couple of dozen phone calls to companies that were already evaluating PRM solutions – an insignificant and biased sample, which led to wild market projections that had no relationship whatsoever to reality. The demand for PRM solutions was nowhere near as large as the report had claimed; as of the writing of this book, many customers still have no idea what the acronym 'PRM' even means. While Enconix chased delusions of grandeur about selling a hot new product into hot new markets, it increasingly ignored its traditional customer base – industrial manufacturers – and destroyed a decade's worth of relationship-building, causing over half of its accounts to switch to competitors.

I wish this story had a happy ending because, for one thing, I was a shareholder in Enconix. But alas, it doesn't. By March 2001, Enconix's sales had declined to an annualized rate of just $34 million, and by August 2001 they had declined to $28 million. Enconix had lost its image as a company dedicated to the needs of mid-market industrial manufacturers, and yet it couldn't put together a credible story – or product – for customers in other markets. The company went through a few more visioning exercises to try to get back to its roots as a disciplined, high-quality provider of IT services. A meeting was scheduled for September 11, 2001, to review its options and decide how to proceed. That very day, the World Trade Center and the Pentagon were attacked by terrorists, and most of Enconix's few remaining customers immediately froze their IT budgets. Lacking a broad enough customer base to withstand this latest challenge, and running out of cash, Enconix filed for bankruptcy protection on November 1.

Needless to say, a number of things went wrong at Enconix. Lurching from product to product in a vain attempt to find something 'hot' – in Enconix's case, hopping from ERP to CRM to Y2K to PRM solutions – certainly didn't help. Neither did abandoning its traditional customer base in favor of new, untested markets. Reliance on a fatally poor market research report added to the mess. Of course, choosing markets and products in an off-site meeting as far removed from customers as possible didn't exactly help the company stay in tune with market conditions. These are all, unfortunately, common problems. I've seen the same issues pop up at dozens of companies. To ensure that *your* company does not end up looking like Enconix some day, let's take a look at four of the most common pitfalls of market targeting – and how to ensure that you don't fall into them.

THE FOUR PITFALLS OF MARKET TARGETING ... AND HOW TO AVOID THEM

Market targeting trap # 1: Chasing untried and unproven 'blue sky' markets ... and neglecting solid, available business that's close to home

The seductiveness of 'blue sky' markets – hot new opportunities, in which you target new groups of customers with new types of products and services – is powerful indeed. As we saw with Enconix, in its self-reinvention as a PRM software company moving into three brand-new markets, the notion of escaping the challenges and limitations of the existing business by doing something entirely new and different is very compelling. But chasing blue sky markets is often a real problem. It has driven many fine companies into the dust, just like Enconix.

Certainly, it's more exciting to focus on new markets and new products than it is to slug it out against the competition with your boring old products in your slowing-growth markets. Many companies, egged on by consultants with visions of hot new market trends, feel not only justified in redirecting resources from familiar markets and products to unproven ones; they feel obligated to do so. Technology companies in particular, always searching for the Next Big Thing, find the notion of new groups of customers ready to pounce on a new product concept to be irresistible. But even non-tech companies get caught up in the act, believing they've tapped out in their existing customer list and need to do something different. Blue sky markets also satisfy the need of many executives to 'reinvent' something and make dramatic changes. By pursuing these markets, they can stop fussing with the daily ritual of calling on the same old customers, with the same old message and the same old products.

Unfortunately, the pursuit of entirely new market opportunities is usually the slowest, least effective, most expensive, and least certain way to increase revenues, for two reasons.

First, *new customers in new markets are much more difficult to identify, contact, and penetrate than existing ones.* These customers have different business needs, purchasing behaviors, and expectations than those you're accustomed to in your existing markets. Pursuit of these customers makes the sales cycle longer, less certain, and more open to competitive threat. It also increases selling costs dramatically, since it costs four to six times as much to acquire a new customer as it does to make new sales to an existing one. In addition, a by-product of the continual search for new markets and customers is a tendency to neglect and take for granted the existing customer base. Customer satisfaction and loyalty decrease in the existing customer base, exposing you to new competitive threats in your established accounts.

Most importantly, many companies haven't even begun fully to penetrate their core customer base and shouldn't be looking to new markets as a source of salvation. With share-of-customer typically running at 5–35 percent, even successful vendors haven't yet begun to tap into the revenue opportunities that are sitting in their laps. Better-planned, better-executed sales calls to cross-sell products and services more aggressively into the existing customer base would, for most companies, provide huge gains. This is the low-hanging fruit – money sitting on the table. It's a far more effective, quicker, and more predictable way to generate revenues than jumping from market to market in a frenetic search for new customers.

Second, *new products are much more difficult to sell than existing ones*. Every new product requires customer education and digestion-time. Customers must learn what the product is, why they need it, what problems it solves and how it solves them, how to use the product, and when, where and how to purchase it. They must evaluate it against competitors' offerings and decide if it truly meets their needs better than the alternatives. In addition, your sales force, partners, and other channels must learn and master the 'pitch', figure out which customers to sell it to and how to sell it, and stumble and fall while determining how best to close deals. All of this takes time, increasing the length and uncertainty of the sales process. In addition, historically, 90 percent of all new product introductions fail, making this a risky bet. The truth is, most companies already have good products, and need to learn how to sell them more effectively.

The bottom line is that companies tend to fall into one of two camps: those who continually chase new market concepts, pulling them away from their core business base, and those who take a disciplined, build-on-your-strengths approach (Figure 3.1).

1. *The 'blue sky' approach*. In this approach a company lurches, like Enconix, from an established business base into uncharted, unknown markets, selling new, untested offerings. Sometimes it works, and often it doesn't.
2. *The 'build on your strengths' approach*. In this approach, the first action is to grab the low-hanging fruit, through deeper penetration and cross-selling of existing products to existing customers. Once that's in place, new products are carefully introduced to existing customers, to leverage the customer base and extract

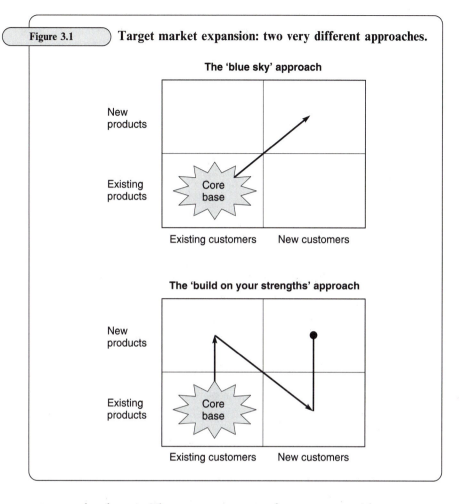

Figure 3.1 **Target market expansion: two very different approaches.**

The 'blue sky' approach

New products

Existing products

Core base

Existing customers   New customers

The 'build on your strengths' approach

New products

Existing products

Core base

Existing customers   New customers

greater value from it. Then, new segments of customers are identified and approached – with tried-and-true products that have been tested and proven in the core base. Finally, when it's really time to try something new, forays are made into new markets with new products, to tap into hot opportunities coming up on the horizon.

I am not suggesting that you ignore hot new markets, or plod along with your existing core base to the exclusion of new potential opportunities. There's a time and a place for growth through new market development. Recognize, though, that selling new products into new markets is expensive and risky, and takes time to pan out. Chasing blue sky markets is a trap into which many well-meaning companies fall, as they get impatient with their existing business base. To avoid this trap, it's well worth keeping in mind that most companies have more potential business than they could ever handle, in familiar territory where they understand the market and can easily compete and win.

Market targeting trap # 2: Putting too much weight on third-party market research reports, which often have inaccurate, agenda-driven estimates

Research reports from market research firms can play an important role in your market selection efforts. While these reports can be useful, however, you must be wary about their estimates of market sizes and their conclusions. You should *never* make the decision to participate in a market solely on the basis of a third-party research report.

There are certainly lots of research houses that do solid, accurate market analysis. However, in recent years a number of market research firms have taken to publishing highly inflated, sometimes hyperbolic, estimates of the revenue potential in new markets. These unrealistic estimates have become so commonplace that you will instantly recognize the look and feel of them. For example:

- 'Wireless Web to be a $65 billion market by 2008, says top analyst at ...'
- 'Sales of remote-access pet-food dispensers to increase from $2 in 2002 to $7 billion in 2007, says ...'
- 'ASP market to grow from $800 million to $22 billion by 2004, noted high-tech research firm ...'.

Inflated estimates such as these almost always turn out to be wrong. Markets claimed to be worth $10 billion in sales turn out to be worth $100 million. Markets claimed to be worth $2 billion turn out not to exist. How can this be?

A benign view is that some research firms have optimistic, overly enthusiastic analysts who love the markets they're studying, genuinely believe in these markets' huge opportunities, and learn very slowly from their past mistakes in overestimating market sizes. Perhaps due to the dot.com craze, when many of these analysts got started in the business, they are accustomed to 'thinking big' when they ponder the potential size of a new market opportunity.

A less benign view is that these companies' market analysts, who are often inexperienced and junior, sometimes use questionable methodologies, drawing conclusions about entire markets from surveys of twenty or thirty customers, for example, or from a review of already-published sources, which are themselves based on bad data. These methods stand in stark contrast to the in-depth, thoughtful analysis of customers, partners, suppliers and competitors that is needed to validate and assess a market opportunity accurately.

To gain a better understanding of how market research can negatively impact your market targeting decisions, let's take a look at an *entire industry* that was led astray by misleading and poorly executed market research.

In 1998–1999, technology companies and analysts stumbled onto a new idea, the 'Application Service Provider' (ASP). With slowing growth in software sales to large corporate customers, all eyes were focused on the small-to-medium business (SMB) market. Troubled over the difficulties of reaching these customers profitably, and aware of their limited IT budgets, technology vendors and analysts came up with the idea that software vendors could 'rent', or host, applications over the Web for a monthly fee. Customers would require none of the hardware, support staff, and in-house expertise that they'd need if they purchased the applications outright, and the lower rental fees (versus purchase costs) would encourage new customers to flock to this new model. Overall, the value proposition didn't sound too bad!

Driven by an intense need to get customers and investors to take this new concept seriously, the technology industry's leading vendors and analysts immediately published highly optimistic estimates of the potential size of this market. Though total dollar volume in application rentals in 1999 was relatively insignificant – $1 billion at best, and probably a lot less – most analysts predicted that the ASP market would be in the $10 billion range just a year later in 2000, and two leading research firms published widely-quoted estimates suggesting that the ASP market would exceed $20 billion by 2003. To put that in perspective, that is a claim of 2,000 percent revenue growth in three years, for an unproven, brand-new technology offering.

As a result of these research reports, accepted as 'true' by many in the industry, a feeding frenzy ensued. Large software vendors, such as Microsoft and Oracle, announced that they would become ASPs by hosting applications for their own customers; some claimed that within a short period of a year or two they would no longer sell software through any other channel. Telephone companies made multi-billion dollar investments in the infrastructure needed to host applications over the Web. Start-up ASPs, funded by giddy venture capitalists, spent billions of investors' dollars to launch application-hosting operations. By early 2000, the ASP model was the topic of entire technology conferences; it even spawned its own association, the ASP Industry Consortium.

At the same time, serious warning signs were on the horizon. The original research reports suggesting the existence of a $20 billion market had been based mostly on the opinions of industry analysts and insiders. How these insiders concluded that customers would want $20 billion worth of ASP services is anyone's guess. When customers were interviewed in 2000, they told a different story and voiced deep concerns. They questioned whether storing their data on ASPs' servers would provide adequate security for their mission-critical information. They questioned whether they wanted to 'outsource' their software and data in the first place. They questioned the ASP pricing model, which was (and remains) very fuzzy and complicated. While many admitted that the concept might someday be useful, they weren't exactly rushing to sign up for the services of ASPs.

Faced with unanticipated customer resistance, technology industry groups fought back with new research. A study in the summer of 2001 claimed that 64 percent of respondents meeting the survey criteria currently accessed applications that were paid for on a rental or as-needed basis (i.e. through ASPs). Encouraging, yes. But it was bad data. The report failed to explain that to meet the criteria for the survey, respondents either had to be currently using an ASP or had to be planning to use one in the next 12 months. This was agenda-driven market research, to say the least.

Despite the frenzied effort to keep the ASP story alive, eventually facts began to replace the original theories. Newer reports suggested that around 70 percent of customers had heard of the ASP approach, while just 8 percent were actually renting applications. The implication was clear when you compared those two numbers: customers were aware of, but were not interested in, the ASP model. Low customer usage and interest, of course, translated into disastrous results for everyone. Between July 2000 and July 2001, twenty ASPs closed up shop, and not a single publicly traded ASP reported a profit – not one.[59] More recently, it's been estimated that 60 percent of the remaining ASPs will go out of business in the next year.[60] As an example of the financial carnage that's ensued, one ASP, Interliant (symbol: INIT), has declined in price from a high of over $50 per share in early 2000 to 38 cents on December 20, 2001. And Interliant is a *successful* ASP, insofar as it hasn't yet gone out of business.

Needless to say, a lot of people got burned by the ASP hype. Several research firms are still claiming that this will be a $20 billion business in a couple of years. The model may eventually take hold and be successful – after all, it's basically a good idea – and perhaps it will achieve the $20 billion mark some day. For the moment, however, everyone's paid dearly for the inflated, pie-in-the-sky market projections invented by over-eager research analysts in the early days of this story.

Don't think the ASP hype story is unusual – it isn't. It exposes a basic flaw in the market research business that you must keep a careful eye on if you're using third-party research to evaluate new markets. Fueled perhaps by good intentions and enthusiasm for the markets they study, many research firms develop inflated, unrealistic market projections without due regard for the risks that these estimates pose to the companies who make decisions based on them.

At the very minimum, you should always get multiple, independent sources of information when you're evaluating a market. You should also take the time to learn how your research vendors arrive at their conclusions. Are they drilling down into the customer base to uncover real customer needs and drivers of purchasing decisions? Or are they relying on second-hand information and superficial customer surveys?

If you really want to do it right, you must assume at least some in-house responsibility for the validation of a market opportunity. This

---

[59] Source: Giga Information Group.
[60] Source: Gartner Group.

could be as simple as calling a range of prospects in a new market to ask whether they're interested in your product or service. You'll learn more by doing this than by reading a thousand pages of market research reports, and it'll provide a useful check-and-balance on third-party conclusions and recommendations about new target markets. There has never been a substitute for listening directly to customers. In the end, you can only eliminate the risks of over-reliance on third-party market research by doing some of the work yourself.

Market targeting trap # 3: Assuming that markets can be 'good' or 'bad', outside of the context of your unique offerings and your business goals

> Just because a market is growing quickly, is already big, or is getting a lot of attention doesn't mean it's a good opportunity for *you*.

You cannot assume a market is a 'good' one, or for that matter a 'bad' one, in a vacuum. Just because a market is growing quickly, is already big, or is getting a lot of attention doesn't mean it's a good opportunity for *you*. And just because a market is growing slowly, is relatively small, or is out of favor with analysts or other vendors doesn't mean it isn't the perfect selling opportunity for *your* company and offerings. Until you evaluate whether a new target market fits well with your offerings and your business goals, it's impossible to know whether it's right for your business.

Let's begin with your offerings. The size or growth rate of a market says a lot about whether *someone* out there will succeed in the market, but very little about whether *you* will succeed. It all depends on what you're trying to sell. For example, consider the high-technology industry, which, though it's had some ups and downs, has been on an upward-growth trajectory for many years. You could say that high-tech markets are (or at least until very recently were) 'good' ones for suppliers, since companies in these markets spend huge sums to fuel their growth. But what if you sell paper-based calendars and day-planners, overhead slide projectors, and calculators? Most companies in the high-tech industry are 'early adopters' of new technologies. Their employees use electronic handheld devices to maintain their calendars and schedules; electronic systems to make presentations; and PCs and handheld devices to do numeric calculations. As a result, the high-tech market would be a poor choice if you sold those kinds of products, regardless of whether the high-tech industry is growing at 3 percent or 1,000 percent per year.

On the other hand, there are markets that aren't growing quite so quickly, such as engineering and manufacturing, where you can sell tons of calculators, paper-based day planners and the like. If you sell these kinds of products, you might be far better off selling into these slower-growth markets, where you can find customers who use – and will want to buy – your products.

In short, the 'right' target market depends on what you're trying to sell.

You must also consider carefully whether a new potential market fits with your business goals. A super-hot, $100 billion market that's growing 70 percent per year may sound great in theory, but it may not fit with what you're trying to accomplish. If your sole corporate goal is maximum sales growth, then yes, a fast-growing market is probably a good fit. But sales growth is not the only type of goal that companies can have. If your primary corporate goal is profitabil-ity, it's possible that the fastest-growing markets, which sometimes have high costs of entry and require years of heavy investment, will not be the right choices. If your goal is to grow steadily while ensuring that shareholders get a predictable, low-risk return on investment, then it's even more unlikely that fast-growth markets will be your best choices.

Take China as an obvious example. With over a billion people entering the modern world economy, the Chinese market is a one-of-a-kind growth story that has proven irresistible to many com-panies. Numerous western firms have spent years and years attempt-ing to establish themselves in China and get a slice of this pie. Some companies such as IBM and McDonald's have succeeded, but it's not an inexpensive, short-term, or low-risk proposition. For every IBM or McDonald's there are hundreds of companies that wiped out in China and lost millions or even billions. If long-term growth and international expansion are your most important goals, and if you are willing to do whatever it takes and assume high risks, China might be just the right target market for you. However, if you are seeking high profits, or immediate growth in sales, or low-risk expansion, China is not the answer, despite its size and growth potential. There are other markets, closer to home and easier to penetrate, that will deliver more profitable, faster, lower-risk trans-actions. China's just a simple illustration of the fact that your mar-kets must fit with your business goals; there's no 'always right' answer.

The trap of picking markets that are 'good' in a general sense, but perhaps not good for *you*, can be avoided. You must ask whether customers in new potential markets need, and are increasing their spending on, not just products and services in general, but *your* types of products and services. You must ask whether the costs, risks, and time-horizon of market entry fit with your own business goals. You must, in short, recognize that there is no such thing as a 'good' or 'bad' market, and evaluate every market opportunity in light of your unique business situation.

Market targeting trap # 4: Ignoring crucial *internal* sources of information when evaluating new market opportunities

The marketing director of a Florida-based management and technol-ogy consulting firm informed me last year that the company had decided to target the community banking market. While they did have a number of community banks as customers, they hadn't pene-trated this market in a systematic, organized manner. 'Why commu-nity banking?' I asked. 'One of our consultants suggested that we reorganize the business to focus on vertical markets in financial ser-vices, and we agreed it was a good idea,' he told me. 'The consultant recommended several verticals, of which community banking was one. Since there are thousands of community bank branches in the region, we figured it was a large potential market worth at least $30 million in incremental revenue to us, so we decided to go for it.'

The reasoning sounded plausible, but soon proved to be flawed. A massive six-month sales effort by the company's sixty-five account executives (AEs) and forty business partners yielded a grand total of thirty new accounts and just over $2 million in sales – or $28 million short of expectations. The company decided to ask its account execu-tives why this market had been so difficult to penetrate. The AEs pulled no punches. Community banking, they explained, was the worst possible choice of market, and they had been stunned when it was defined as a key marketing initiative. Most community banks, they knew from personal experience, had no money to spend on consulting services. The few community banks that did have money already had consultants and weren't shopping for new ones. The entire industry was consolidating and contracting, leaving fewer and fewer prospects to pursue. Several AEs pointed out that they had tried to tell executives about these problems when the community banking initiative was first announced, but no one had listened.

Concerned, the marketing director interviewed the company's six alliance managers, who oversaw the efforts of the forty partners. They told a very similar story, based on the feedback they'd received from partners. Customers without budgets. An industry in turmoil. Tough, entrenched competitors. Like the AEs, partners had been vocal in their belief that community banking was a dismal choice for a marketing initiative.

Needless to say, it would have made a lot of sense to get the input of these people *before* embarking on the community banking initiative.

Within most organizations lies a real wealth of information about opportunities and risks in the market place. I'm not referring to complex numerical data buried deep in the bowels of corporate databases, the extraction of which would require high-end data-mining software. I'm referring to something much simpler: the insight about customers and markets that is already residing in your employees' heads. This insight can bring shape to a market targeting effort, but it rarely gets collected and is often ignored. Be sure not to fall into this trap. You cannot afford to overlook the insights – both positive and negative – held by key groups of market-facing employees. Specifically, look to three sources of market insight within the organization:

1. *The sales force.* Whose opinion is always considered valuable in a typical market selection effort? Key executives, of course. Then there are the various marketing analysts and managers whose job is to study, size and define new markets. Product groups are often consulted, and you might even see the inclusion of someone from finance. What you *rarely* see is a sales rep. Sales reps are usually the last people to be consulted on new market initiatives. They're

supposed to be out there selling, not strategizing. They are not often thought of as visionaries and marketeers who would have value to contribute in the market targeting process. But this view of sales reps is misguided. Think about it. Who is actually out there, in daily, one-on-one contact with end-customers, learning continually about their needs, issues, and purchasing trends? Who knows *for a fact* what works and what doesn't, based on direct, personal experience? Answer: the sales force. The sales force is the only part of an organization that interfaces directly and continually with customers. The amount of insight about customers and markets residing in any sales organization is huge. Here are some basic questions to raise with the sales force regarding new markets:

- Has anyone in the sales force already been selling or prospecting in the new market? If so, what have they learned? Do they think it's a good opportunity?
- Are there existing customers that look (and act) similar to the customers in the new target market (e.g. size, business needs, purchasing behavior, etc.)? What are these customers' needs, and how well are we able to address those needs? What is the most effective way to reach and attract these customers?
- What kinds of expectations should we have for the new market, based on our experiences with similar customers in other markets? Will we win one customer out of three? One out of fifty?

2. *People who deal with partners or distributors.* Another crucial group within the organization consists of the people who manage or interact with business partners (distributors, VARs, etc.).[61] Partner managers and channel executives, like sales reps, hear constantly about what's going on in the market place, but are sometimes an even better source of information. Since partners are rarely as concerned as your own employees with toeing the party line or telling people what they want to hear, the people who deal with them usually hear a less-edited and more honest version of what's going on 'out there'. As a result, they often have an accurate, intuitive grasp of market conditions and opportunities. These people should always be consulted when considering new markets.

---

[61] VAR = Value Added Reseller.

3. *People who know a lot about the competition.* Within any large organization are a number of people who study the competition. These people reside in market research departments and competitive intelligence groups, within the sales organization, in product marketing groups, and even in product development. These people should all be consulted. They can help you determine which markets and customers are being targeted by competitors, and where competitors are increasing or decreasing their market coverage investments (e.g. recruiting distributors for specific markets, etc.). This is an invaluable source of information for market selection. Of course, competitors may not know any more than you do about how and where to sell. However, when viewed collectively, the strategies and market initiatives of a group of competitors tend to say a lot about where the buying interest and activity is taking place.

Simply put, many companies do a poor job of extracting the market information they already have at their disposal. They don't think to tap into the extensive knowledge of market conditions and opportunities residing within their own organizations. Sitting down with the people who are out on the street meeting with customers and partners, and getting their views, is an excellent way to ensure that you avoid this trap.

MOVING BEYOND THE AVOIDANCE OF PITFALLS: A DISCIPLINED, ORGANIZED PROCESS FOR TARGETING NEW MARKETS

Earlier, we noted that the first major pitfall of market targeting involves the pursuit of new opportunities at the expense of your core base – your existing accounts and markets, where you may barely be scratching the surface of the total sales opportunity. It just might be the case that all you need to do, in order to achieve moderate, successful growth, is to focus on fully penetrating the customers in your familiar markets.

With that important caveat, let's acknowledge that, for a lot of companies, focusing solely on existing customers and markets is not a complete strategy. Particularly for growth-oriented organizations, the ability to identify, evaluate, choose, and penetrate the right new markets is a crucial component of long-term go-to-market success. In this section, we will examine a solid, battle-tested process for doing just that. We'll be practical about it, because your task in targeting good new markets boils down to some pretty simple things. You must uncover and identify new market opportunities, evaluate those markets to test whether they meet your specific requirements, and prioritize them to ensure that you go after the right ones first. The process we'll use to do all this is shown in Figure 3.2.

Figure 3.2   **Six-step process for targeting new markets.**

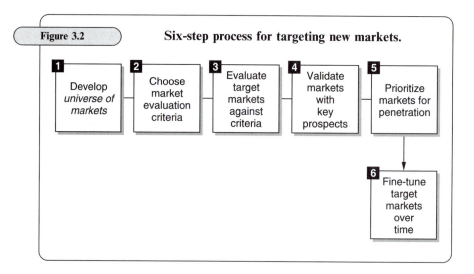

Let's take a look at each of the six steps.

1. Develop *universe of markets*

The first step is to cast a wide net for new market opportunities, in order to uncover *all* of the potential markets and segments in which you realistically could participate. The purpose is to avoid a 'rush to judgment' in which, pressured to demonstrate immediate sales results or to show some marketing activity, you jump on a sub-optimal market and miss out on better opportunities residing elsewhere.

I recommend getting started simply by generating a list of potential new markets based on what you already know or believe about market conditions. Which geographic, vertical, horizontal, consumer, or other types of markets do you think might offer good sales opportunities?

Which ones are similar to the markets in which you are already strong and successful, in terms of customer needs, industry or geography, etc.? Put them all on the list.

Then get the input of others within your company. There'll be numerous sales people, in particular, who will have valuable opinions based on their selling experiences and first-hand knowledge of current market opportunities. Ask them what they think, and add their suggested markets to the list.

Finally, just to ensure that you're considering all of the possibilities, build out the list by including additional markets that ...

■ Your consultants or market research vendors have been recommending
■ You've been reading about in the news
■ Your competitors are pursuing
■ Your partners are targeting or already doing business in
■ Could otherwise potentially make sense, based on whatever it is you are trying to sell.

Once the list has been fully built out, it's time to start narrowing it down. You may not want to give up on potential markets at this point, but eliminating the bad apples will help to focus your time and energy on the good ones. You can safely remove markets that have any of the following three characteristics:

1. *No need for your product or service*. Some markets just don't fit with some products, end of story. It's the old 'selling ice to Eskimos' issue. Sure, someone out there can do it (and that person should be hired immediately) but, generally speaking, if you sell ice, the Eskimo community is not a good target market. Similarly, you can probably rule out a whole range of markets just by thinking clearly about whether or not customers in those markets will ever need or have any interest whatsoever in your offerings.

2. *Prohibitive entry costs*. As we saw earlier in the China example, some markets have high, and even prohibitive, entry costs. Entry costs aren't just an issue in exotic markets such as China. The cost of reaching into the US small business market, for example, might exceed your budget, and penetration into a brand-new

vertical market, such as health care retail, may require excessive up-front marketing investments to establish awareness of your brand. Simply put, some markets are more expensive to enter than others. The best bet is immediately to rule out markets with start-up costs that exceed your ability or willingness to invest.

3. *Legal or regulatory restrictions.* Sometimes, entering a new market poses serious legal issues. As an extreme example, even if drug dealers desperately want to buy your product at twice the normal price, it might be better to ignore this opportunity. More commonly, the issues aren't legal, but regulatory. For example, foreign markets, particularly in developing countries, can be difficult to penetrate and supremely difficult to conduct business in, due to government restrictions and red tape. Unless you have a compelling reason to target these 'red tape' markets, it's advisable to ignore them – or to return to them *after* you've succeeded with easier opportunities in more business-friendly markets.

Once you've eliminated the bad apples based on these three considerations, you'll be left with a list of plausible markets. For example, your list might include markets such as financial services, manufacturing, and high technology. These kinds of markets are often too large, diverse and varied for efficient targeting; they contain too many customers of too many different types. If you decided to target a big market such as manufacturing, you must first divide it into discrete, smaller sub-markets, or segments, which can be targeted much more effectively and precisely. An illustration of this is shown in Table 3.1 on the page opposite.

Upon conversion of your larger markets into discrete sub-markets, you will have generated a complete *universe of markets* – a very useful list of perhaps ten to fifty markets and segments in which:

- There's at least some probability of end-user interest and demand
- You can afford to enter the market
- There are no prohibitive legal or regulatory restrictions.

You must now evaluate and compare these various markets in order to focus on the best ones. That's the subject of the next two steps.

Table 3.1 Generating segments from markets: an example

Market	Financial services	Manufacturing	High tech
	Commercial banks	Automotive	Software
	Retail banks	Aeronautic	Network service providers
	Mortgage banks	Electromechanical engineering	Hardware manufacturers
Possible sub-markets (segments)	Savings and loans	Industrial equipment	Networking equipment
	Credit unions	Consumer electronics	Optical fiber
	Brokerage firms	Discrete manufacturing	Semiconductors
	etc.	etc.	etc.

2. Choose market evaluation criteria

The purpose of this step is to establish a consistent set of criteria that can be applied across all markets, in order to evaluate and compare them in a uniform manner.

How many criteria should you use to evaluate new markets? Some organizations use twenty or more criteria, ranging from market size and international expansion potential, to average order size and transaction profitability. I believe that the use of too many criteria and conditions can lead to 'paralysis from analysis' – the inability to make a practical decision due to overwhelming amounts of data. Most companies do far better with a small, tight group of market selection criteria. As a starting point, think in terms of choosing four to six solid, useful criteria. You can always add more in the future as the need arises.

To help you choose your market evaluation criteria, the following are some of the more common ones in use at other organizations.

1. *Market size.* This usually refers to the total dollar volume that will be spent in a market for a type of product or service, in a specific year. For instance, 'Manufacturing companies are

expected to purchase $4.2 billion worth of customer relationship management software in 2003.'[62] The importance of market size, as a selection criterion, stems from the obvious fact that larger market sizes suggest larger total sales opportunities, at least for vendors who can compete successfully for share in those markets. Market size is therefore of great interest to companies seeking substantial new sources of revenue growth. Estimates of market size come from market research firms, and are widely available for many different markets and segments. However, as discussed earlier, these firms often overestimate the sizes of the markets they study. You have to be cautious.

2. *Market growth rate.* Market growth rates refer to the expected growth in purchasing volume for a type of product or service within a market, from one year to the next. For instance, 'Growth in CRM purchasing by manufacturing firms is expected to be 25 percent next year.' Market growth rates are important because they suggest the likelihood of a long-term, expanding revenue opportunity, and are therefore of particular interest to companies seeking long-term revenue growth. Like market size estimates, market growth rates usually come from market research firms – and are often similarly inflated and inaccurate.

3. *Ability to exert brand leadership.* This is a useful criterion if your goals include long-term brand building and growth. The classic example of a company that has employed this criterion very consistently is General Electric. Under former CEO Jack Welch, GE would participate only in markets in which it could be the # 1 or # 2 player. That's another way of saying that GE would only target markets in which it could exert strong brand leadership and be a dominant player. A market in which you can be the top dog is usually more attractive than a market dominated by well-entrenched, successful competitors, in which you could end up being a second-tier participant.

4. *Cost of market entry.* In the last step (generating the universe of markets), you ruled out any markets that your instincts told you would have unacceptably high costs of entry. That was just a first-cut effort to eliminate the truly obvious money-pit markets. You may now want to take it a step further by including a detailed evaluation of entry costs for markets that made it

---

[62] Market size can also refer to the total dollar volume to be spent in a specific channel, as in 'Consumers will order $26 billion worth of products online this year.'

through the initial screening. The cost of market entry is crucial and well worth a second look, particularly for companies that are concerned about profitability. Some markets have low start-up costs. For example, if you sell printing and reprographic services, you can easily and cheaply penetrate a new geographical market by mailing out brochures, calling directly on local businesses, and perhaps opening up a retail store. Other markets can have much higher costs of entry. For example, if you want to penetrate the soft drink market with a new product that competes with Coke and Pepsi, it will take many millions of dollars to establish brand awareness, generate consumer interest and demand, and build (or work your way into) an efficient distribution channel. The initial expenses associated with becoming established and successful in a market like this can eat up years of profits.[63] It can thus be crucial to consider carefully the entry costs associated with entering a new market.

5. *Cost to serve.* This refers to the cost to serve customers in the target market over time, and is another way of saying 'anticipated transaction profitability'. Cost to serve is higher (and profitability lower) when customers are difficult to reach, time-consuming and expensive to serve, or likely to purchase in small, low-dollar transactions. As an example, for most companies the SMB (small and medium business) market entails a high cost to serve, since it's difficult and expensive to do business with smaller, dispersed, and difficult-to-reach customers.[64] A high cost to serve may be a price you're willing to pay to play in a particular market. It depends on how concerned you are about profits, as opposed to the growth potential that such markets can sometimes offer.

6. *Channel availability.* Unless you plan on building a brand-new channel to serve a new target market – which is time-consuming and expensive – the availability of an existing channel to reach and serve customers can be a crucial deciding factor. For example, if you already have a sales force calling on brokerage houses in New York, it may not be much of a stretch to have them call on accounting and law firms while they're in the neighborhood: in short, you have an available sales channel that you can use to reach a new market. However, if you've identified

---

[63] There have been some notable exceptions, such as Snapple, but these are few and far between.
[64] The exception to the rule: companies that have figured out how to use low-cost channels effectively, such as the phone and Internet, have been able to serve smaller, dispersed customers profitably.

Brazilian farmers as a target market, your non-Portuguese-speaking sales force may be useless. In this case, you'll need to see whether there's another channel you can use – such as local Portuguese distributors – and whether the channel is willing and able to sell your products to the target customers. Lack of an available sales channel that can reach and serve the target market can make penetration an expensive and unsuccessful endeavor.

7. *Competitive density.* This refers to the concentration of competitors within a market. A market that you share with just a few competitors, who rarely bump into each other when pursuing sales opportunities, has a low competitive density. A market occupied by numerous entrenched players, who slug it out for each and every sale, has a high competitive density. It can be very difficult to penetrate and participate in a crowded, hotly contested market. In addition, the more competitors there are in a market, the more likely they are to use low prices in order to win new customers and sales, which pushes down margins for everyone. A clear example of this is the recent slashing of prices, and the microscopic margins, in the crowded PC (personal computer) business. Highly dense markets may not be worth the hassle, unless you can enter them on day one as a top player. For example, you would not want to enter the PC business unless you could outshine or at least stand shoulder-to-shoulder with Dell, IBM, etc., right out of the gate. While competitively dense markets are often attractive and large – after all, that's why they get all the attention from competitors – it's worth considering seriously whether you're ready and able to do battle successfully, or whether you'd be better off in a less intensely competitive environment.

8. *Strategic fit.* This refers to the long-term, strategic value of the market to your company, particularly in relation to other markets in which you are or will be participating. This criterion acknowledges that, at some companies, market selection involves more than just finding new sales opportunities; it involves the creation of a mix of markets that make sense *collectively*. For instance, if you're already strong in financial services and health care in the US, you might decide that, regardless of cost or immediate returns, you must penetrate these vertical markets in Europe and Asia, and add telecommunications and manufacturing customers too, in order to establish your credibility as a global, cross-industry brand.

What do you do with all of these potential market evaluation criteria? You are probably thinking that some are more important than others, given what you are trying to achieve. If so, then you're on the right track. If your company is heavily growth-oriented, then the size and growth rate of a new market will be more important than the costs of entry. However, if profitability is your only goal, then the cost of entry and the ongoing cost to serve will be the most important criteria and you might not care about much else. In short, there is no 'right' set of criteria for evaluating a new market; you must choose criteria that align with your business goals. Table 3.2 (overleaf) illustrates this crucial concept.

Table 3.2 is a starting point for choosing market selection criteria, but you may need to add others. The outcome of your efforts should be a tight set of criteria that enables you to evaluate and compare markets for suitability with your business goals. You might also want to classify your criteria into two groups, 'core' versus 'secondary'. This will help to clarify which of your criteria are truly the most important when looking at a new market. Once you have selected the right mix of market evaluation criteria, you're ready to move on to the evaluation of markets against those criteria.

3. Evaluate target markets against criteria

The purpose of this step is to use the market evaluation criteria that you just selected in order to assess each of your potential new markets.

Table 3.3 (see page 101) provides a simple example of how this works, for a successful company that is considering three new markets: Fortune 500, SMB, and high technology. The company, a mid-sized marketing firm seeking rapid market penetration, high revenue growth, and if possible low-cost market entry, has chosen six selection criteria in support of these goals. As the table suggests, once you've chosen a set of potential markets and good selection criteria, it's possible to compare markets and rate them against each other.

This example uses a very simple scoring system, consisting of one, two or three stars, which is more than sufficient to demonstrate that the Fortune 500 represents a far better opportunity for this firm than the SMB market. Many companies use more complicated systems, involving actual numbers (e.g. market size = $13 billion, or growth rate =

Table 3.2 Using business goals to establish your market selection criteria

Business goal	Selection criteria							
	Market size	Market growth rate	Ability to exert brand leadership	Cost of market entry	Cost to serve	Channel availability	Competitive density	Strategic fit
Long-term revenue and market share growth	✓✓	✓	✓			✓	✓✓	✓
Profitability				✓✓	✓✓	✓	✓✓	
Brand building	✓	✓	✓✓				✓	✓✓
'Quick hit' – short-term win	✓			✓		✓✓	✓	

✓✓, very important criterion; ✓, important criterion.

Table 3.3   Using evaluation criteria to rate new markets: sample, for a growth-oriented marketing and design firm

	Market evaluation criteria	Fortune 500	SMB	High tech vertical
Core criteria	Market size	***	**	**
	Market growth rate	**	***	(?)
	Channel availability	***	**	**
Secondary criteria	Competitive density	*	**	*
	Cost to serve	***	*	**
	International growth potential	***	*	**
	Overall assessment	***	**	**

***, very favorable; **, favorable; *, marginal/poor.

28 percent) and relative weightings of criteria against each other (e.g. market size is twice as important as growth rate). There's a place for that, but, for our purposes, simplicity is okay. Truthfully, for many companies, having *any* kind of tool to evaluate and compare markets would be a considerable step up in market selection capability.

Table 3.3 does highlight one of the real challenges of new market evaluation. Note that the company was unable to determine the expected growth rate for its services in the high tech market. The fact is, it is difficult to acquire all of the information that's needed to evaluate a market fully. There is rarely a single, neatly packaged source of information that will enable you to respond to each of your evaluation criteria. You will need to call on all of your resources to evaluate new markets: published research reports, consultants' studies; internal sources of information such as sales reps; customer surveys conducted in your target markets; analyses of competitors; partner interviews; and so on. Be prepared to do some fact gathering from diverse sources!

The outcome of this step should be a shortlist of perhaps five to ten markets and segments that fully or mostly meet your conditions for selection.

4. Validate markets with key prospects

The purpose of this step is to do a final vetting of your best potential markets, in order to ensure that customers in these markets will need your offerings and will actually do business with you if you target them.

There are different levels at which you can conduct a validation of new markets. At the most rigorous level, you might conduct one hundred to two hundred interviews with key prospects in each potential market to ensure, with certainty, that there is strong buying interest and demand for your offerings. At the most superficial level, you might call on a handful of prospects to perform a cursory confirmation of your assumptions about the existence of a sales opportunity.

I recommend an in-between approach – one that's practical and yet will provide you with a reasonable level of certainty regarding end-customer demand. Ask your sales organization or your partners to call on thirty customers in your prospective target markets over a three- to four-week period, just as they would call on customers in your existing markets.[65] If necessary, update their market collateral and messaging a bit to appeal to specific needs in various target markets. Then interview your reps or partners to ascertain whether there was any receptivity for your offerings in the target market, and to determine whether your reps or partners were able to make any sales.

You will learn a lot from this exercise. If you did all your homework correctly in steps 1–3, this step will just confirm what you already believe – that customers in your target markets need and will buy your product – and it will give you the confidence to move forward aggressively. However, you might find that you overestimated customer demand and interest in a particular market. It's better to find this out before you invest heavily in market penetration.

The outcome of this step is the big payoff of going through the market targeting process: namely, a group of attractive target markets that not

---

[65] Thirty is just a reasonable round number, and not necessarily a statistically valid sample size. Obviously, the more customers you call on to validate the opportunity, the better.

only meet your conditions for selection but that have also been vetted for customer receptivity and demand. At this point, you'll likely have four to eight top new opportunities to pursue.

5. Prioritize markets for penetration

Should you pursue all of your new target markets immediately? Most companies lack the resources or ability to chase half-a-dozen or more new markets at the same time. Should you target and focus on penetrating one or a couple of them? That's a more realistic approach, but which one or ones should you choose?

There are two schools of thought on this. The traditional school says to choose the market(s) that ranked highest when you evaluated them against your criteria (in step 3). Markets that met most or all of your conditions should be pursued first, since they fit best with your goals. Markets that met some but not all of your conditions should be pursued later. There's some logic in this approach, in that it ensures you pursue your 'best' markets first. However, it may not lead to the best results.

The alternative approach is to recognize that just because a market meets all your conditions does not mean it offers an immediate opportunity, and just because a market may fall short in a few areas does not mean you cannot score a big win right now. The time period in which you choose to pursue a market should be based on conditions that relate to the time and investment requirements needed to penetrate a market, which may be a little different than the criteria you used to decide whether to pursue the market in the first place. This approach is illustrated in Table 3.4.

As suggested in Table 3.4, the best markets to pursue right now are those that offer immediate sales opportunities, that you can reach with existing channels and partners, and that entail low start-up costs and few market entry hassles. Markets that offer less immediate sales opportunities, or that require more complex and expensive start-up activities, get pushed out into the future. This approach will give you an organized sequence for penetrating a range of new markets over the next eighteen months.

Table 3.4   Prioritizing your markets: 18-month plan for penetrating new market opportunities

Market characteristics	Beachhead markets	Medium-term plays	Long-term opportunities
	Next 90 days	3–12 months	12–18 months
Certainty of opportunity	High degree of certainty that strong sales opportunity exists	High to moderate degree of certainty that a strong sales opportunity exists	Sales opportunity believed to be strong, but remains to be proven
Immediacy of sales opportunity	Customers are ready to do business – immediate revenue opportunities exist in the market	Some customers may be ready to do business, but the opportunity may take 6–12 months to develop	Customers may or may not be ready to do business immediately or even in the near future
Channel-building requirements	No new channels or partners are needed. Existing channels and partners can immediately reach customers in the target market	Existing channels may be able to reach some customers, but new partners or new channels may be required to penetrate fully	Existing channels might be able to reach some customers, but substantial channel building or partner recruiting may be required
Message readiness	Can use existing marketing collateral and messaging – customers' needs and decision drivers are similar to those in existing markets	Customer needs are different than in existing markets. New messaging must be developed; new collateral will be required	Customer needs are different than in existing markets. New messaging must be developed; new collateral will be required
Market entry costs	Market can be penetrated at a low cost, which can already be covered by existing budgets	Market can be penetrated at a reasonable cost, perhaps requiring additional budget	Market may have high costs of entry, requiring substantial investment over the next year

6. Fine-tune markets over time

The one thing you can be sure of is that conditions in your markets will change over time. A market that looked great a few months ago may turn into a real disaster next year. A market that didn't seem to offer much opportunity when you evaluated it last year may explode with opportunity in six months. Markets don't stand still. You have to stay on top of them and continually keep track of where your opportunities lie.

The bottom line is that market targeting is not a one-time exercise; it's a continual 'fine-tuning' process. The world's best companies – of which we're about to look at one – take a dynamic view of their target markets, constantly revisiting their assumptions, questioning the value of their existing markets, and seeking out new markets that may only now be coming into their own as legitimate sales opportunities. If you want to benefit maximally from new market opportunities, you must make a commitment to continuous market evaluation. At a very minimum, the market targeting process described here, or something like it, should be repeated once each year to ensure that you are on top of the situation in the market place and ready to respond to new opportunities.

A MARKET-TARGETING WINNER: MARRIOTT INTERNATIONAL

When it comes to best practices in market targeting, few companies have the successful track record of Marriott International, Inc. A global leader in the hospitality industry, Marriott recorded sales of $19.8 billion in fiscal 2000 and employed over 154,000 people. The company has been studied and praised by many business leaders, consultants and academics as a leading innovator in marketing, distribution, channel integration, and customer service. It ranked last year as the # 90 company in *Fortune Magazine*'s prestigious 'Best companies to work for' list, and came in at # 186 on the Fortune 500. No flash in the pan, Marriott's stock price has appreciated at a rate of 18 percent-per-year over a period of forty-seven years.[66]

It would have been great to buy some Marriott stock back in 1953; a $1,000 investment would be worth well over $1 million today. We'll have to settle for the next best thing. Here, we'll take a look at the central role that market evaluation and targeting has played in Marriott's strategy, to see how the principles discussed earlier play out in a real live success story.

---

[66] Including reinvestment of dividends, stock splits, etc. Source: Marriott Web site: www.marriott.com. Stock appreciation figured based on 1953 to December 31, 1999. As of the writing of this book, market events have had a negative impact on the stock price compound annual growth rate (CAGR) of Marriott and many other companies.

First, a quick briefing on the Marriott empire, which is huge. The company operates and franchises a wide variety of properties, including nearly 2,400 operating units in the United States as well as fifty-nine other countries and territories. Its hotels include the familiar Marriott, the JW Marriott, The Ritz-Carlton, the Renaissance, the Residence Inn, Courtyard by Marriott, TownePlace Suites, Fairfield Inn, SpringHill Suites and Ramada International. In addition to its hotels, Marriott develops and operates vacation ownership resorts under the Marriott, Ritz-Carlton and Horizons brands; operates Marriott Executive Apartments; provides furnished corporate housing through its ExecuStay by Marriott division; and operates conference centers. Other businesses include senior living communities and services, and wholesale food distribution.

How did Marriott achieve its status as a global leader in its industry?

For starters, the company has a long track record of thoroughness and creativity in identifying a wide range of potential markets (its 'universe of markets') and serving those markets with innovative brands. Marriott recognizes that travelers are diverse and cannot be served by a one-size-fits-all brand. As a result, the company has established brands across a diverse range of market segments. These segments include, for example, economy-minded travelers on a budget (served by Fairfield Inns), well-heeled vacationers (Ritz-Carlton), executives assigned to extended out-of-town projects (Marriott Executive Apartments) or short-term assignments (Marriott ExecuStay Apartments), and normal, everyday corporate road-warriors (Marriott, JW Marriott). The company's commitment to uncovering, defining, and targeting new markets and segments is unrivaled in the industry.

As noted earlier in the chapter, defining new target market concepts is just the starting point. The real magic lies in evaluating those markets, particularly in light of their ability to support key corporate goals. Marriott has made this evaluation into a scientific process, applied to all new market and brand possibilities, in a thirteen-stage process to which it strictly and consistently adheres.[67] Once a new segment or

---

[67] Judy A. Siguawand and Cathy A. Enz, Best practices in marketing. *Cornell Hotel and Restaurant Administration Quarterly*, October 1999.

brand opportunity has been identified, the process begins with stringent research of competitors within the target segment: what are they doing and who are they targeting? What are their strategies and activities in the segment, and what can Marriott learn from them? The company then categorizes existing and future market segments – for example, identifying markets that are aging and vulnerable. Market and customer research is conducted to define how the new brand will fit into Marriott's market structure ('strategic fit') and to gauge the needs and expectations of customers in the new market.

Marriott then weighs the analysis of the new market opportunity against its corporate goals. New segments are evaluated in terms of their ability to contribute to corporate growth, their anticipated earnings-per-share (EPS), their international expansion potential, the ability of Marriott to exert brand leadership in the segment, the potential brand acceptance by customers, and the fit of the new segment with existing and future properties. Mathematical computations are used to weight each factor and score the opportunity as a whole. Applied consistently across segments, Marriott's rigorous and disciplined analysis enables the company to evaluate opportunities against each other and to focus its investments on market segments in which it knows it can win.

This 'scientific' approach to market targeting began when Marriott created Courtyard by Marriott in 1983. In the early 1980s, Marriott became increasingly concerned that it was running out of good sites to place Marriott hotels. The company decided that its future course lay in applying its hotel development and operating skills to new segments of the market.[68] To achieve this objective, Marriott commissioned a study of both business and non-business travelers, toward the purpose of creating an 'optimal' hotel.[69] The idea was to develop a brand-new property that would meet the needs of consumers who were unhappy with current offerings. Two segments were targeted; business people who travel at least six times per year and stay at mid-level hotels, and mid-tier pleasure travelers. The study was aimed at answering the

---

[68] www.marriott.com

[69] Jerry Wind, Paul E. Green, Douglas Schifflet and Marsha Scarbrough, Courtyard by Marriott: designing a hotel facility with consumer-based marketing models. *Interfaces*, January–February 1989. This is the classic study quoted in a wide variety of theses and articles concerning best practices in the hotel industry, consumer research, and target marketing. As of the writing of this book, D. K. Schifflet & Associates Ltd. was still performing consulting work for Marriott, 11 years after the original study.

following question: 'What type of hotel facilities and services should we design and offer, to attract these segments away from the competitive facilities they are currently using?'

The study included 601 customers in Atlanta, San Francisco, Dallas, and Chicago.[70] Respondents were asked about their travel frequencies, their incomes, and the types of accommodations they preferred. The most important part of the study involved a prioritization exercise, in which respondents were asked to rank the importance of various aspects of their hotel stays, such as the room itself, hotel services, and physical layout. Different combinations of amenities were presented, along with photographs and various price points. Respondents who selected combinations of amenities with unrealistically low price points were asked to try again and forego some of the amenities in order to reach a more appropriate price. In this rigorous, customer-needs-driven manner, Marriott was able to introduce the highly targeted and highly successful Courtyard by Marriott chain.

The success of the approach used to develop Courtyard by Marriott has led the company into a variety of additional market-driven brands, such as Residence Inn, Fairfield Inn, and Marriott Suites. In all of these introductions, the emphasis has been on finding good markets, and then letting the market itself drive the definition of the product. With its thirteen-step evaluation process, Marriott has avoided a problem that plagues many companies: coming up with a new product concept and then looking around for a market in which to sell it. Indeed, by the time Marriott's properties hit the street, they are already tuned precisely to the needs and expectations of its target customers.

Finally, Marriott takes a *dynamic* approach to the definition of target markets. The company continually researches and fine-tunes its target markets – and uses that information to fine-tune its offerings in order to attract and serve more customers.

For example, in 1987 Marriott introduced Fairfield Inns, a single-room (i.e. non-suite) lower–moderate (economy) hotel. In 1997

---

[70] *Ibid.*

Marriott extended the brand by introducing Fairfield Suites, an economy hotel with suites as opposed to rooms, and pleasant but few amenities. The Fairfield Suites launch was immediately followed by customer focus groups and feedback from franchisers, which suggested that customers would appreciate higher levels of amenities and would be willing to pay for them. As a result, amenities were upgraded and added, and, to ensure that this new 'upper–moderate' offering would be recognized as more upscale, it was re-branded as SpringHill Suites. Further market research indicated that a focus on a suite-only offering was missing out on an opportunity to serve customers who preferred having a choice between suites and rooms in one location. As a result, in 2000 Marriott launched a new extension of the brand, Fairfield Inn & Suites, which offers guests the choice between rooms and suites.

Similarly, Marriott recently fine-tuned its time-share (vacation ownership) offerings. This highly competitive, high-pressure market was believed by Marriott to consist primarily of upscale, well-to-do vacationers – thus explaining the average $17,500 per week cost at its Marriott Vacation Club properties. Marriott's continuing research into the market, however, suggested a large untapped opportunity: approximately half of all time-share purchasers are moderate-tier customers. To reach this segment, Marriott has introduced Horizons by Marriott Vacation Club. These new properties contain clever amenities designed to give the new target customers what they want ... while controlling costs. For example, the properties include car washes, since Marriott found that middle-tier time-share buyers tend to drive, rather than fly, to their vacation homes. Likewise, although competitors believe a two-person whirlpool in the master-suite is required to make a sale, Marriott's research suggested that as long as a whirlpool is available somewhere on the property, it doesn't have to be in the rooms. With an expected price between $11,500 and $12,000 per week, Marriott is now reaching a new target market with a well-tuned offering at a well-tuned price.

There's an important lesson in Marriott's ongoing market-tuning efforts. As noted earlier, definition of your markets is not something you can just do once. At leading companies such as Marriott, market targeting is a continuous process of rethinking and redefining target markets as they evolve over time.

SUMMARY

Without a doubt, your selection of target markets is one of the most important choices you will ever make. Choose the right markets, and you can make an awful lot of other mistakes while still coming out whole. Choose the wrong markets, and you'll be swimming upstream forever in the search for profitable business.

In this chapter we examined a number of common traps in market selection, such as an over-reliance on generic and biased market research, a tendency to chase 'blue sky' markets over proven opportunities, and a tendency to make too many assumptions with too few hard facts. Most of these pitfalls can be avoided by eliminating the guesswork, and by doing the hard work needed to convert your market targeting efforts from alchemy to science. To bring discipline and 'science' to your market targeting efforts, we examined a practical, well-organized process for uncovering and evaluating new market opportunities, which included the following steps:

1. *Develop a 'universe of markets'.* In this step, all rocks are turned over in the market place, to identify a broad range of markets that potentially could be served.
2. *Choose evaluation criteria.* Here, you develop a core set of criteria for evaluating markets, such as growth potential or cost to serve, based on your unique business objectives.
3. *Evaluate markets against the criteria.* In this step, each potential market is weighed against the criteria in order to arrive at a comparative market assessment.
4. *Validate assumptions with key prospects.* Here, markets that have basically made the cut are vetted with key prospects, to ensure that the opportunities are robust and real.
5. *Prioritize markets for penetration.* Here, markets are put on an 18-month roll-out schedule, depending on a number of factors such as the immediacy of the sales opportunities and the availability of a sales channel.
6. *Fine-tune market assumptions over time.* Once you're participating in a market, it's essential to revisit assumptions, refine the market segmentation and the offerings, and continually improve your presence over time.

Finally, we looked at a company, Marriott International, that has brought science and careful planning to the task of choosing its markets – with great success.

While market selection and targeting are crucial, don't think that choosing a market provides a complete answer to the question 'Who should I sell to?' It doesn't. All it does is point you in a general direction. To penetrate a market successfully, you must develop a deep understanding of the customers in that market – who they are, why they buy, and how they do business. It's to this topic that we turn in the next chapter.

4

Go-to-market strategy:

Aligning with your customers

T hink about any failed product, channel or marketing initiative – anything at all, from incredible yet all-too-real consumer products such as Thirsty Cat tuna-flavored bottled water, aerosol ketchup, and Gerber For Adults, to more reasonable-sounding but equally doomed offerings such as Internet home appliances, smokeless cigarettes, and Web TV.[71] To these we can add the spectacular and well-publicized product and channel failures examined in previous chapters, such as Pets.com's unsuccessful efforts to sell pet supplies over the Web, Iridium's multi-billion-dollar global cell phone fiasco, and perhaps the all-time marketing debacle, New Coke. You could probably add dozens or more of your own examples. There is a nearly unlimited supply of failed initiatives from which to choose!

I'd like to pose a simple question about products, channels and marketing initiatives that fail. They involve all sorts of different types of offerings, sold to different types of customers in different markets, through different channels – so what is it that they all have in common? What causes them to fail?

Answer: they *never* start with the customer.

They start with something else, of course. In many cases they start with the enthusiasms of engineers and technologists, convinced that they've come up with something 'cool', which people will buy just because it is, well, cool. Or they start with a well-meaning marketing group or product development team, which holds internal meetings to decide what customers want, without ever going to the source: the customers themselves. Some failed products and channels get their start with superficial customer surveys that waste so much time collecting customer satisfaction rankings and ratings that they never get around to identifying what, exactly, will satisfy customers. And, frankly, many failed initiatives are born of the arrogance of executives, who become so convinced they already know everything that they skip the part where you ask customers what they need, and then listen very, very carefully to the answers.

What failed products and channels *never* start with are the needs and actual buying behaviors of customers and prospects. How can we be

---

[71] These amusing examples are from several sources, including Susan Casey, Object-oriented: everything I ever needed to know about business I learned in the frozen food aisle. *Business 2.0*, October, 2000; and South coast today: showcase for lost products (from the web site www.s-t.com). RJ Reynold's $300 million smokeless cigarette campaign failed, interestingly, because the people who benefit from them are precisely those who don't buy them.

so sure about this? It's simple. No one would have bothered to develop tuna-flavored bottled water for cats, or Internet appliances for the kitchen, if they had first nailed down the precise needs of customers, and then designed their offerings to respond to those needs.

If you get nothing else out of this book, here is the essential, bottom-line point. The success of every go-to-market decision you make, indeed your ability to make smart go-to-market decisions at all, depends on how well you understand your customers. Their specific needs must shape and define your products and services. Their buying behaviors and preferences must set the agenda for your channel mix. Their concerns and 'pain points' must be at the root of your messaging strategy and promotion efforts. Their budgets must influence your pricing strategies. You must learn all these things about your customers, directly from them, with a minimum of guesswork and assumptions. You must build an accurate customer fact-base that clarifies and articulates who the customers are in your target markets, what they buy, why they buy it, how they buy it, how they *want* to buy it, and what would motivate them to buy more of it from you. Then you must use this fact-base to guide all of your go-to-market decisions. That is what we mean when we say, 'Go-to-market strategy must start with the customer.'

> The success of every go-to-market decision you make, and indeed your ability to make smart go-to-market decisions at all, depends on how well you understand your customers.

In this chapter, we'll examine the tools and techniques of customer alignment. We will look at the specific types of information about customers that are needed in order to make successful go-to-market decisions, and then we'll discuss how to get this information efficiently and effectively. We'll wrap up by taking a look at an example of a top-flight company that has combined thoughtful customer alignment with winning market targeting efforts, in order to drive sales growth and brand success.

GETTING STARTED WITH CUSTOMER ALIGNMENT: THE TWO TRAPS YOU ABSOLUTELY MUST AVOID

Companies that are poorly aligned with their customers fall into one of two categories. There are companies that haven't done any analysis of their customers, and therefore have no idea what their customers need or how they purchase. Then there are companies that do mind-boggling amounts of research with high-tech customer survey tools, carefully controlled focus groups, statistically valid sample sizes distributed evenly across customer segments, and automated tabulation of results, and still haven't got a clue what their customers need or how they purchase.

The 'no research' trap

Can it really be that there are companies who've done absolutely no research into their customers' needs and behaviors? You bet. There are thousands of them, and they inhabit every industry. Their product, marketing and channel decisions are driven by strong, internally held beliefs about the value and attractiveness of their products or services, and they are often accustomed to making key business decisions based on 'gut feel'. These companies may purchase some superficial third-party market research reports, which reinforce a mistaken notion that they've 'done their homework'. However, they usually don't get around to doing the *real* homework – namely, talking to their target customers and listening very carefully to learn what they want and need – until it's way too late.

Without a doubt, some of the best examples of this problem come from the late-1990s' dot.com craze. Let's take a quick look at one of them.

Furniture.com started with a hopeful vision of using the Internet to sell – you guessed it – furniture. The company's January 1999 launch was accompanied by great enthusiasm and fanfare, along with $48 million in venture capital and a $5 million national advertising campaign.

At first glance, Furniture.com seemed to have a compelling story. Its Web site provided a number of clever and intriguing features, the cornerstone of which was a design tool that enabled customers to design their own room layouts, which could then be filled with furniture selected from a very convenient – and huge – online catalog. But that was just the beginning. Site visitors could also engage in real-time chat room discussions with Furniture.com's staff of twenty-four design consultants, and could converse with these designers by email or phone as well. In addition, a unique personal shopper service was provided, in which professional consultants would suggest furnishings based on individuals' preferences, styles, needs, and budgets.[72]

In sum, not only did the Web site offer a vast collection of furniture that was larger than that offered in just about any retail store, but the variety of services, such as personal shopping assistance, design consultants, etc., was superior to that provided at most retail stores and outlets.

Sounds great, right?

There was just one problem. *People don't want to buy furniture over the Web*. They don't want to buy a couch unless they can bounce up and down on the cushions to ensure that the couch will be something they want to live with, and sit on, for the next five or ten years. That's why you rarely see mail-order catalogs for furniture. People generally want to see and touch a piece of furniture before they buy it. Furniture purchasing behavior simply did not align with Furniture.com's sales channel.

After Furniture.com's Web site went live, the company finally did get around to doing some customer analysis. An advertising agency was hired to track the behavior and site navigation habits of visitors, and to categorize those visitors along all sorts of dimensions that would help the company understand its customers' behaviors. Unfortunately, these efforts were a day late and a dollar short. No one had talked to customers *before* the site went live to determine if they would use the Web as a furniture-purchasing channel in the first place. They didn't – at least not in the kind of volume needed to sustain Furniture.com's business.

In addition to a severe mismatch between its channel and the buying behavior of its customers, Furniture.com was plagued by a host of other problems. Honorable mention must go to operational problems, such as a million dollars' worth of furniture shipped but not billed.[73] In addition, the reliability and customer service were poor, to say the least. My executive assistant Edna Carrozza, for example, an 'early

---

[72] Furniture.com press release, issued from its corporate offices, Framingham, MA, July 27, 1999.
[73] The $1million worth of unbilled merchandise was later picked up in an audit.

adopter' of this technology, ordered a china hutch (a two-piece cabinet for storing china, such as dishes) from Furniture.com. The top of the cabinet made it to her house, but the bottom piece never arrived, despite repeated phone calls. Frustrated, Edna finally visited neighborhood furniture stores and eventually found a suitable stand that would hold up the half of the china hutch. While the neighborhood store didn't offer an Internet chat room, an interior design expert, a personal shopping service, an online room layout tool, or even email support, it did offer the piece of furniture she wanted, which she was able to inspect, purchase, and carry out to her SUV.[74] Maybe that's all consumers want when they purchase furniture. It's good to find these things out before starting new companies.

Several attempts to turn around the fortunes of Furniture.com failed, including a new infusion of $27 million in cash, and an IPO filed in January 2000 but pulled in November 2000, when the company finally went bust.[75] The truth is, venture capital funding doesn't help, and neither do clever product designs and features, or anything else for that matter, if the offering and the channel are not fundamentally in alignment with the needs and buying behaviors of customers.

> Lots of organizations, across all industries, cannot state decisively what their customers need and how those customers want to do business, because they've never really asked.

There are a lot of Furniture.coms out there, and they are not just e-business companies. Lots of organizations, across all industries, cannot state decisively what their customers need and how those customers want to do business, because they've never really asked. As a result, their offerings and their channels diverge from the needs and buying behaviors of customers, leading to costly problems, up to and including total business failure.

The 'useless research' trap

A more common problem lies with companies that do tons of research and yet still understand little or nothing about the drivers of their customers' purchasing decisions. How can this be? The research that they perform goes off on all sorts of tangents, none of which includes a

---

[74] With help from her husband Al.
[75] Melanie Austria-Farmer and Greg Sandoval, Furniture.com closes doors, lays off most of staff. CNET News.com, November 6, 2000.

basic nailing down of the needs and behaviors of their target customers.

An amusing example comes to us from the researchers at Oklahoma State University, who've conducted extensive analysis to develop individually wrapped peanut butter slices, or PB Slices™ (as opposed to the familiar peanut butter in a jar that you spread with a knife). As of the writing of this book, PB Slices will soon be available in stores such as Wal-Mart, in Oklahoma, Kansas and Texas test markets. The plan is to roll the product out to other locations once it's been proven in these three geographies.

First envisaged at a brainstorming session over lunch, PB Slices were designed around the same concept as individually wrapped cheese slices. PB Slices were thought by their inventors to be the perfect solution to avoid the mangling of bread that sometimes occurs when peanut butter is spread too vigorously.

The PB Slices concept, it must be noted, was heavily tested and researched. It took over three years of development, over five hundred different formulas, and financial assistance from the Oklahoma Peanut Commission to solidify the concept into a workable product.[76] During the development stage at the University of Oklahoma's Agricultural Products Research and Technology Center, various formulations of peanut butter slices were tested for stability, texture and palatability. Statistical analysis was performed to study the effects of independent variables on the texture of the slices, and samples were analyzed at different time intervals. Taste tests were conducted on over a hundred randomly selected university staff and student volunteers, to determine the best recipe.

That is a lot of research! The big question, though, is whether prospective customers – not a group of college taste-testers, but the people who are actually expected to *buy* the product – will purchase it or even be the least bit interested in it.

There seem to be two issues here. First, does the average parent preparing Junior's school lunch think it's more convenient to unwrap a

---

[76] Brian Caulfield, The peanut butter of tomorrow. *Business 2.0*, October, 2001.

PB Slice than it is to open a jar of peanut butter and spread it with a knife? Probably not. The second issue involves the steady migration of consumer behavior toward health-oriented products – such as 100-percent natural peanut butters. PB Slices manage just to meet the minimum requirements to be called 'peanut butter' (a minimum of 90 percent peanuts). The final product, to be sold in one-ounce slices, consists of peanuts mixed with fillers such as gum and starch, then heated, poured into molds, sliced and wrapped in plastic. That doesn't seem particularly in alignment with the consumer trend toward healthier foods. My guess is, consumers don't have a major problem today with the spreading of peanut butter and will not purchase PB Slices, other than as a one-time novelty.

Of course, that's a guess, just like the guesses being made over at Oklahoma State. Verifying the needs of real live customers should have been done *before* spending time, grant money, and hundreds of pounds of peanuts to develop a product that people will probably not buy. PB Slices, just like other products developed in an absence of rigorous customer analysis, may yet succeed, but the odds are against it. Sometimes organizations get lucky without talking and listening to their potential customers, but most of the time they don't.

The moral of the story is as follows: You might already be doing a lot of 'research', but it may not be telling you what you need to know. Surveys, product testing, and even test-marketing are all useful, but none of them guarantees that you are asking the right questions or learning the right things – specifically, the things that will help you make winning decisions regarding your markets, customers, channels, products, and value propositions. So what *are* the right questions?

WHAT YOU NEED TO LEARN ABOUT YOUR CUSTOMERS TO BE A GO-TO-MARKET WINNER

What is it that you need to learn about your customers to make high-impact go-to-market decisions? In this section, we're going to answer that question. Here, we'll look at the five key types of customer information that most directly impact go-to-market decision-making, as shown in Figure 4.1.

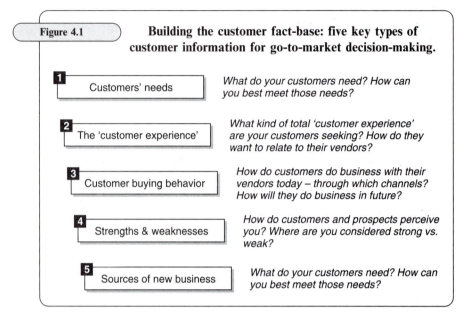

Figure 4.1   **Building the customer fact-base: five key types of customer information for go-to-market decision-making.**

1 Customers' needs — *What do your customers need? How can you best meet those needs?*

2 The 'customer experience' — *What kind of total 'customer experience' are your customers seeking? How do they want to relate to their vendors?*

3 Customer buying behavior — *How do customers do business with their vendors today – through which channels? How will they do business in future?*

4 Strengths & weaknesses — *How do customers and prospects perceive you? Where are you considered strong vs. weak?*

5 Sources of new business — *What do your customers need? How can you best meet those needs?*

You may already have some of this information. This section will help you figure out what you do know and what you don't know, so that you can develop an agenda for building (or completing) a robust customer fact-base. Let's take a look at each of the five types of customer information.

1. Customers' needs

What are the fundamental needs of your target customers? The answer will, obviously, impact your choice and design of products and services, but it will also impact your messaging and promotion strategies, your sales pitch, your choice of sales channels, and the nature and extent of post-sale support and service that you provide – in short, *everything*. Precise definition of customer needs is therefore a crucial prerequisite to any successful go-to-market strategy.

Don't be lulled into thinking that you already know enough about your customers' needs. You probably don't. Most companies think they have far more insight than they really do about the needs of their target customers. They discover too late that their offerings are based on faulty assumptions.

For example, last year I was invited to the Executive Leadership Conference of a major technology firm moving into e-business solutions, hosted lavishly for its top 150 executives at the Venetian Hotel in Las Vegas. Along with myself, the company invited five of its top customers. The six of us sat at a gold-lamé-trimmed table of honor, and for eight hours we listened to presentation after presentation about the company's new e-business solution, which combined hardware, software, and networking services into one fully-integrated 'turn-key' e-commerce solution.[77] At the end of the day, we were asked to sit as a panel and take questions from the audience. Part of the exchange went like this:

Participant: You've just listened to us talk about our new e-biz solution for the whole day. So what do you think about it?

Customer # 1: The technology speaks for itself. It's an elegant solution. I am sure there will be plenty of customers excited about this solution, although I doubt if we'd be interested in it.

Customer # 2: I don't see us moving toward a solution like this, either.

Participant: Can I ask why you're not interested?

Customer # 2: Right now, we are really trying to quantify the ROI [return on investment] of our IT projects. My sense is that it is impossible to calculate the potential return on such a complex solution. I don't believe we would invest in a new technology like this without proof of financial benefit.

Customer # 3: We are also watching our budget and we cannot get funding for anything that does not have a quantifiable ROI. I didn't hear anything today that would

---

[77] 'Turn-key' = total and complete solution, i.e. 'just buy it, and turn the key to make it work' – a phrase in use primarily in the technology industry. Needless to say, many 'turn-key' solutions have required an awful lot more than key-turning to work effectively – if they work at all.

convince me that you have figured out what the ROI is. That is a necessity in today's market.

Customer # 4:   I have a different concern – the whole notion of a totally integrated solution. We are leaning toward best-of-breed components. We try to get the best technologies from different vendors and then use an integrator to pull it all together. Nothing personal, but we don't think you have the best technology in every category.

Customer # 5:   To build on what [customer # 4] is saying, we have already made big investments in e-commerce technologies. We are interested in best-of-breed components that can be bolted onto our current platform. We are definitely not interested in starting over with a total turn-key solution.

Customer # 1:   I absolutely agree with that. Our CIO is certain that we made a big mistake by buying all-in-one solutions in the past. Now the direction is to find vendors with best-in-class solutions who can partner effectively with each other and complement our existing IT infrastructure.

Participant: That is great feedback. But don't you think that it's particularly important with complex e-business solutions to have one vendor who can bring together a whole solution, linking customers, partners, suppliers, and employees into a total e-framework? That's really our basic value proposition.

Customer # 5:   No, that's just not interesting to me. Maybe to someone else, but not to me.

Customer # 3:   I agree. That is not something we want. We are trying to get away from that.

Customer # 6:   I would just like to go back to something that someone said earlier. It is all about return on investment. We will evaluate any technology solution that has a

> definite ROI. We will no longer evaluate any tech-
> nology that does not come with a clear proof of
> concept, financially speaking.

Oops! It turned out that my client had made a big, incorrect assumption: that its customers would need, or at least view favorably, a totally
integrated e-business solution. The client was wrong. As is evident
from the dialogue, the needs of its customers are pretty clear:

■ They require a proven, quantified return on investment – a clear
  financial justification for the purchase
■ They strongly prefer best-of-breed technologies to total, integrated
  IT solutions
■ They need technologies that fit into, and complement, their existing
  IT infrastructures, not a total replacement for their current systems.

The company has now engaged in extensive repositioning, product
redesign, and development of a financial ROI white paper in order
to respond to those concerns. They are now on the right track, but it
has taken a lot of rework, time, and money. There is just no substitute
for getting to the core of customers' needs and concerns before investing heavily in new initiatives of any kind.

It's important to note that listening to customers and understanding
their needs is not just a product issue. The product you sell is just one
part of your total offering, which also includes post-sale service and
support, and, depending on your industry, configuration, installation,
training, maintenance, and ongoing counsel. All of these 'add-ons' to
the basic product must align with the needs of customers. Indeed, you
can have a great product – one that maps perfectly to the needs of your
customers – and still end up in the doghouse with your customers if
other components of the total offering fail to align with customers'
needs. Personal computer maker Gateway, a player in the PC industry
with $9.6 billion in annual sales,[78] provides an instructive example.

At the end of 2000, Gateway, historically a consumer-oriented PC
vendor with a winning product and channel model, saw its customer
satisfaction levels plummet to two-year lows. The following month,

---

[78] For calendar year 2000. Source: Hoovers.com

with computer sales in a slump, Gateway missed its already-lowered earning expectations and announced that it was laying off 10 percent of its workforce.[79] As part of a broad effort to get things back on track, CEO Jeffrey Weitzen stepped down and was replaced by the company's founder and chairman, Ted Waitt.[80]

One of Waitt's first moves was to address the ongoing decline in customer satisfaction. Topping the list of customer grievances was Gateway's policy of voiding the warranty on its computers whenever customers installed any third-party software. Yes, you read that right. If you purchased a Gateway computer in 2000, and then bought a program to make greeting cards or do spreadsheets, you'd have voided the warranty on your Gateway PC, and would not be able to get any technical support.

This policy led to immense frustration and anger on the part of Gateway's customers, and tied up the time of technical support reps, who had to explain over and over to irate customers that they had voided their warranties by loading their own software. Stunned customers simply bought their next computers from Gateway's competitors. Clearly, their service and support needs were not being met by Gateway, regardless of whether their product requirements were being met.

Once Gateway finally came around to recognizing this problem, they did away with the policy, along with a bunch of other non-customer friendly practices. As a result of this effort, Gateway immediately saw a sharp improvement in customer satisfaction, from 67 percent in February, 2001 to 76 percent by March 1.[81]

While it's important to understand the product needs of your customers, it's just as important to understand their needs when it comes to service and support, maintenance, installation, and any other factors that impact the overall experience they have with your company.

Uncovering and defining customers' needs is not rocket science, but you have to do it! If you're considering any go-to-market initiatives

---

[79] Ian Fried, Gateway chief exec steps down; former CEO returns. CNET News.com, January 29, 2001.
[80] *Ibid.*
[81] Joe Wilcox, Gateway ends stupid policies. CNET News.com, April 26, 2001.

and are not certain that you understand your customers' needs with real precision, *now* is the time to get serious about it. Figure 4.2 provides a number of useful questions that you can tweak and then use, in order to begin fleshing out your customer needs fact-base.

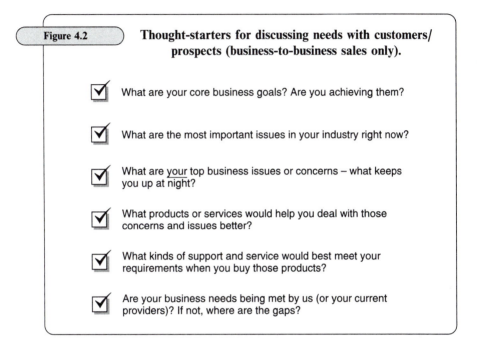

Figure 4.2   **Thought-starters for discussing needs with customers/ prospects (business-to-business sales only).**

☑ What are your core business goals? Are you achieving them?

☑ What are the most important issues in your industry right now?

☑ What are your top business issues or concerns – what keeps you up at night?

☑ What products or services would help you deal with those concerns and issues better?

☑ What kinds of support and service would best meet your requirements when you buy those products?

☑ Are your business needs being met by us (or your current providers)? If not, where are the gaps?

Whether you ask these kinds of questions in a written survey, in a face-to-face conversation, or through some other method, isn't really the issue at this point. Later, we'll discuss the strengths and weaknesses of different techniques for collecting customer information. For now, the important principle is that uncovering and defining your customers' needs is a cornerstone of good go-to-market decision-making.

2. The 'customer experience'

Determining the kind of overall *experience* that your target customers want from you is a crucial source of information for go-to-market decision-making. What kind of relationships do they want to have with their vendors? Indeed, do they want a 'relationship' at all? What sorts of things have particular value to them in the purchasing process, and what don't they care about? Figuring all this out will help you establish an overall conceptual platform for choosing your mix of channels, designing your messaging and positioning strategies, and developing your service and support policies. It may even help you understand whether your product and service offerings are fully in tune with your customers.

While there are many types of experiences that can be provided to customers, they basically fall into three groups:

1. *The efficient, low-cost transactional experience.* Some customers in some markets just want to do business efficiently, inexpensively, and with as few hassles as possible. As my colleague Neil Rackham puts it, they don't want a big, fancy mousetrap; they just want dead mice, cheap. If your target customers have this orientation, it would be misguided to offer expensive products, high-value services, and premium 'high-touch' channels, such as sales reps, which create complex relationships and time-consuming transactions. These customers want to do business efficiently and easily, without much or even any face-to-face support. A good example of a company that offers this type of customer experience in the financial services industry is E*Trade. E*Trade, which offers stock trades as low as $4.95 over the self-service-oriented Internet, has infused its offerings, its channel, and its messaging and promotion efforts with a consistent theme based on a low-cost, convenient 'do-it-yourself' customer experience.[82]

2. *The high-touch, consultative experience.* Other customers may have strong preferences and demands for 'high-touch' relationships, involving consultation and advice, frequent face-to-face interaction, and a more complete range of services. This kind of customer experience, of course, entails higher product and service costs as well as more expensive channel offerings. Yet attracting and retaining customers in search of a 'high-touch' experience is not as dependent on costs and efficiency as it is on your ability to provide the high-value services and channels that fully meet their expectations and needs. Looking again to the financial services industry, Merrill Lynch and SalomonSmithBarney are examples

---

[82] E*Trade Web site, www.Etrade.com, October 22, 2001.

of companies whose go-to-market strategies reflect an orientation toward high-touch customer experiences. A combination of high-value services, such as proprietary research and participation in Initial Public Offerings, with higher-touch channels such as face-to-face financial advisors, and higher prices, puts these two companies in a different camp – one that's aimed at different target customers seeking a different kind of experience – than E*Trade.

3. *The flexible, multi-access point experience*. In terms of customer experiences, the newest kid on the block is the flexible, multi-channel experience, or what I referred to in Chapter 1 as the *surround sound* approach. Originally developed by vendors such as Dell Computer and Charles Schwab as a means to sell to a broader base of customers at a lower cost, the model has grown enormously in popularity with customers, since it allows them to do business on their own terms, inexpensively, efficiently, and of course very flexibly. Today, many customers have become accustomed to and prefer this model, and increasingly expect to be offered multiple, flexible channels by their vendors, whether they are purchasing on company time as business people, or on their own time as consumers. In financial services, Charles Schwab is the obvious example of a provider of the flexible, multi-access point customer experience. Schwab's multi-channel model consists of retail stores, telebrokers, Web trading, partnerships with other financial service providers, and other channels. The company offers all of the convenience of the efficient, transactional providers such as E*Trade, while providing many of the value-added services of its high-touch competitors such as Merrill Lynch, while giving customers the ability to do business however, whenever and wherever they want. As a customer experience model, the multi-access point approach is tough to beat.

It's important to note that many companies provide different experiences to different customer segments. For instance, Dell Computer provides a multi-access point experience to consumers, but a high-touch, consultative experience to its top corporate customers. In the markets and segments that you are targeting, how do you determine the kinds of buying experiences desired by your customers? Ask them! Figure 4.3 suggests some questions that can help get the conversation started.

Figure 4.3

Defining the 'customer experience': some questions to explore with customers.

☑ What are the most important factors to you when purchasing products and services? What do you look for in your vendors?

☑ Which vendors do you think provide the best overall mix of products, services, channels, and support? What is it specifically that you like about their approaches?

☑ Do you always go for the lowest-cost product or service, or do you value other things besides price when you purchase? If so, what are those things?

☑ If we offered you one solid way to do business with us – say, a well-trained sales rep or a skilled reseller – would that fully meet your needs? Or is having multiple ways to do business with us a priority?

☑ How important is it to have a face-to-face relationship with your vendors? Would you be willing to do away with face-to-face interaction in order to save 5 or 10 percent of purchasing costs?

☑ Is there anything we could do right now to provide a better overall purchasing experience or create more value for you? If you could have anything you wanted from us, what would it be?

3. Customer buying behavior

Once you've developed an understanding of the kinds of experiences and relationships your customers seek, it's time to take it to a more granular level of detail by analyzing their *actual buying behaviors*.

> The days of dictating how your customers will buy are long gone. Today, customers in all markets are migrating to vendors who offer them the channels they prefer to use – and actually use.

Customer buying behavior is a crucial input to any go-to-market strategy, for a compelling reason: we live in a world in which, increasingly, customers, not vendors, decide how they will transact business. The days of dictating how your customers will buy – whether through a sales rep or a distributor, for example – are long gone. Today, customers in all markets are migrating to vendors who offer them the channels they prefer to use – and actually use. If you want to attract and sell to a group of customers, you must meet them where, when and how they want to do business, through whichever channels they prefer. In short, your go-to-market channels must closely align with the buying behaviors of your target customers.

Over the past five years, numerous companies have made increasingly off-base assumptions about customer buying behavior. Billions of dollars have been wasted building channels that no one wants, such as Web sites that no one visits or call centers that no one calls. Don't let this happen to you. You must get out there and find out how your target customers do business today, and how they want to do business in the future, before you invest time, effort and money in new go-to-market channels. Maybe your customers want to use the Web, and maybe they don't. Maybe they'd like to use the Web for some types of purchases, but not for others. Maybe they'd prefer to do business through alternative, low-cost channels such as the telephone or catalogs, or perhaps they despise low-cost channels and strongly demand and expect direct rep support. The fact is, you just don't know until you ask. Customer alignment requires a clear and accurate assessment of your target customers' buying behaviors, which you can only get by going straight to the source.

> You must get out there and find out how your target customers do business today, and how they want to do business in the future, *before* you invest time, effort, and money in new go-to-market channels.

There are three steps involved in developing an understanding of customer behavior. The first step nails down how customers *currently* do business, by investigating which channels they use today. To illustrate, I've provided an analysis of current customer behavior performed for one of my clients. The company, a $600 million manufacturer of MRO (maintenance, repair and operations) products, was deeply concerned about the impact of the Internet on its sales model. Market research reports suggested that customers in its core markets were moving toward the Internet as their primary purchasing channel. Yet the company's key executives believed that their customers strongly preferred the high-value relationships that they had with the company's dealers and its own sales reps. Confusion reigned; no one knew how best to move forward. To help sort it all out, my firm interviewed two hundred of the company's customers to determine how they were already doing business with their various vendors. Table 4.1 shows what we found.

Here's what the numbers in Table 4.1 suggest. The Internet represented a negligible percentage of *current* buying behavior by the client's customers. Just 5 percent of them purchased on the Web with any regularity ('always' or 'often'), and 72 percent of them

Table 4.1 *Current* customer channel usage (actual data from 12/00 for a $600 million manufacturing client)

How do you purchase MRO products today – through which channels?

Channel	We *always* purchase this way (%)	We *often* purchase this way (%)	We *sometimes* purchase this way (%)	We *rarely* purchase this way (%)	We *never* purchase this way (%)
Field sales rep	27	40	22	8	3
Distributor	7	35	26	14	18
Catalog (phone ordering)	3	21	29	28	19
Telephone sales call from vendor	0	7	18	30	45
Retail store	3	13	32	27	25
Fax order form	2	12	14	26	46
Internet	1	4	11	12	72

never used the Web for purchasing. Lesson # 1 for this client: don't fire the sales force just yet! However, the analysis also suggested that customers were using a variety of other channels that the client was not yet making available, such as fax ordering and catalogs. Lesson # 2: go build some new channels and you'll do more business!

Understanding current customer buying behavior is particularly important when you are seeking rapid penetration of new markets. To penetrate a new market quickly and efficiently, you must sell through the channels or partners that customers *already use* to do business. Anything else will slow you down, as you sit and wait for customers to find your new channel and decide whether they want to use it or not.

Once you've nailed down the current behavior of your customers, the second step is to assess where their buying behavior is headed in the future. It takes twelve to eighteen months to design, build and roll out new channels, so you must figure out where buying behavior will be a year or two from now. You definitely don't want to build channels that respond to current fads and enthusiasms, only to find out they are no longer 'in vogue' next year.

There is no scientific way to determine how customers will buy in the future. The best you can do is to ask your customers how they believe they will purchase in a year or two. While not quite optimal, this is actually a workable approach. In fact, it's precisely what we did for the client described earlier. We asked the same two hundred customers which channels they believed they would be using in twelve to eighteen months. The results are shown in Table 4.2.

As Table 4.2 illustrates, customers expect their usage of alternative channels, such as telephone, fax order forms, and catalogs, to be significant in the future. That information helped the client to establish its longer-term channel-building priorities.

If, as noted earlier, *current* customer behavior tells you which channels to employ for immediate, rapid market penetration, *future* (expected) channel behavior tells you which channels to start building now to achieve longer-term market penetration and sales growth over time. These worthy goals – short-term sales and longer-term penetration – require, in short, different types of information about customer buying behavior.

Table 4.2   Analysis of *changing* customer channel usage (actual data from 12/00 for a $600 million manufacturing client, continued)

How will you purchase MRO products in twelve to eighteen months?

	We will use this channel exclusively (%)	We will use this channel often (%)	We will sometimes use this channel (%)	We will rarely use this channel (%)	We will never use this channel (%)
Field sales rep	18	44	24	11	3
Distributor	9	43	32	8	8
Catalog (phone ordering)	3	29	24	28	16
Telephone sales call from vendor	1	10	21	30	38
Retail store	5	22	31	27	15
Fax order form	5	18	18	30	29
Internet	3	13	24	11	59

Finally, step 3 combines the results of current and future channel behavior to uncover *trends* in customer behavior. Table 4.3 provides an illustration of this step.

Table 4.3   Current vs. future customer behavior: the shift toward multi-channel behavior

	Present behavior (% 'always' or 'often')	Future intended behavior (% 'will use exclusively' or 'will use often')	Channel shift (growth)
Field sales rep	67	62	−8
Distributor	42	52	+24
Catalog (phone ordering)	24	32	+33
Telephone sales call from vendor	7	11	+57
Retail store	16	27	+69
Fax order form	14	23	+64
Internet	5	16	+220

The trend analysis produced some exceptionally important findings for the client:

- Customers believe they will *substantially* increase their usage of the Internet, by 200+ percent over the current year. Growth in Internet purchasing exceeds *by far* the anticipated growth of any other channel. The company's executives had been observing *current* purchasing behavior and, as a result, had been unable to see this trend with clarity.[83]
- The most important finding of all is that customers anticipate increasing their purchasing activity through *all* channels (except for field sales, which is expected to decrease slightly). Clearly, the client's customers are migrating toward multi-channel purchasing, in preference if not yet in behavior. From this simple trend analysis, the company realized that it wouldn't be good enough just to build

---

[83] However, it should be noted that the high growth is primarily due to the relatively low current usage.

a Web site, or any other single channel for that matter. Customers are seeking a multi-access point experience, requiring a surround-sound channel model. This conclusion had much broader implications for the company's overall sales approach than the findings related to any particular individual channel.

Hopefully, the value of performing a detailed analysis of customer behavior is apparent. It will help you determine how best to meet your customers in the market place, today and in the future. And it will pinpoint opportunities to align with the overall purchasing experience sought by your customers.

4. Strengths and weaknesses

Part of your customer fact-base should include an analysis of your strengths and weaknesses, as perceived by your customers. A good grasp of customers' impressions of your strengths and weaknesses can help shape every aspect of your go-to-market strategy, from your product and channel offerings, to your service and support policies and your long-term account-building efforts.

The most common approach to gap analysis, in which customers are asked to rank and rate you against your competitors, is extremely ineffective. It is highly doubtful whether 'Please rate us on a scale of 1 to 5 in service . . . Now please rate competitor # 1 on a scale of 1 to 5 . . . ' has any value whatsoever. I have seen hundreds of these surveys and, while they're sometimes interesting, I've never actually seen a single business decision made on the basis of one of them. They're a waste of time, and for something as important as uncovering your key areas for product and go-to-market improvement, you can do a lot better than 1-to-5 scales. Gap analysis should be performed as a set of in-depth qualitative conversations with key customers whom you trust and who will be completely open and honest with you. Figure 4.4 suggests a few questions to get these conversations started.

5. Sources of new business

A few years ago, a $1.5 billion high-tech company commissioned a study with my firm to develop strategies for increasing sales by 20 percent in the next year. That was the good news; the bad news was that we were given two weeks to come up with some initial strategic

---

Figure 4.4   **Exploring performance gaps with customers: sample gap analysis questions.**

 Where do you think we are particularly strong, relative to our competitors (or other vendors from whom you purchase)?

 Where do you think we are weak? What do you think we could be doing better?

 Is there anything specific that you would like to see us change, in terms of:

- Products and services
- Channel offerings (reps, partners, phone, Web, etc.)
- Pre-sales support and advice
- Post-sales support and service
- Ongoing account management

 What is the one thing we could change right now that would have the greatest impact on your impression of our company – and your desire to do business with us?

---

thought-starters. At a loss for a plan to uncover $300 million in new sales in just two weeks of analysis, we asked the company's top thirty sales reps to ask each of their customers one simple question:

What would cause you to do at least 20 percent more business with us over the next year?

Like many of the really effective tools of go-to-market improvement, this approach had the air of banal simplicity. And it worked, really well. We were deluged with over thirty specific recommendations on exactly what the company needed to do to increase its volume of business with its customers – right from the horses' mouths. Feedback ranged from advice to make sales calls on a consistent, monthly schedule, to deployment of a customer hotline, to creation of a user-accessible database of industry solutions. All of the recommendations that were affordable and mentioned by multiple customers were immediately put into effect. And *voila*! Monthly sales revenues jumped from $125 million to $140 million in four months, a gain of 12 percent. Within six months, the monthly revenue rate had increased by nearly the full 20 percent.

Since that study, I have included the incredibly simple question 'What would cause you to do a lot more business with us?' in every customer analysis. It almost always produces excellent and immediate results. This question should be put high on the agenda of your customer fact-gathering. The very least it will do is generate some new sales. It could do a lot more too, in terms of helping you to understand what your customers want from you.

HOW TO GET CUSTOMER INFORMATION EFFICIENTLY ... AND EFFECTIVELY

In the last section, we looked at *what* you need to learn about your customers in order to align with their needs and buying behaviors. We examined five basic types of customer information and, within each type, some key questions you can raise to get the facts and insight you need to make winning go-to-market decisions. If you pick and choose from all those questions, and tweak them to your own circumstances, you'll have a robust 'to-do' list of go-to-market questions to explore with your customers.

Now what? Here, we'll take a look at *how* to get answers to those questions. This section is not intended as a complete discussion of customer research techniques – far from it! You'll be shocked and amazed by the lack of depth! The fact is, there are plenty of other places to go for detailed discussions of customer survey techniques, sampling methods, and the like; this is a book on go-to-market *strategy*. So we'll just hit the high points here, to give you some basic considerations for shaping your overall data-collection approach.

The key principle is that there is no one 'right' method or tool for collecting information from customers. It all depends on what you're trying to find out, and it also depends on the size and make-up of your customer base. Over the past fifteen years I've used virtually every customer survey and research method known to mankind, and, while some work better than others, they all have their place. So let's take a look at the tools at your disposal.

Written customer surveys

By far the most common technique for collecting customer information, written surveys are also, in many instances, the most problematic and least effective approach.

Written surveys are useful for collecting simple, quantifiable information. If you want to find out how many customers bought a certain product, or how they rate your customer service reps, a written survey will do fine. Surveys also work well in consumer sales. Consumers are accustomed to filling out satisfaction cards at restaurants, after buying new cars, and so on, so it's not a stretch for them to grab a pencil and fill out yet another survey. Finally, written surveys are useful for collecting information from many respondents across a broad, dispersed customer base.

Written surveys lose their usefulness quickly when the questions become more complex, and when you're involved in business-to-business sales. For our purposes, that's a problem, because the high-impact questions of go-to-market strategy are rather complex and poorly suited to written survey tools. Take a look back at the questions suggested earlier in this chapter, such as 'What are the most important issues in your industry?' How many of these kinds of questions could you really put on a survey form? Not too many. Most customers will not take the time to answer them, and will either toss the survey in the garbage or limit their answers to the simpler 'Rate us on a scale of 1 to 5' questions. Finally, business people have been surveyed to death over the past few years. Sending surveys to corporate customers can damage your standing with them, due to general weariness with, and suspicion of, vendors' data-collection efforts.

The bottom line: written surveys are probably not the answer, unless your target customers are end-consumers and your questions are very simple.

Face-to-face interviews

A much more powerful approach is the face-to-face interview, in which you sit down with an individual customer to conduct in-depth exploration of go-to-market issues. For questions such as 'How can we significantly increase our volume of business with your organization?' and 'What are your top business concerns – what keeps you up at night?', there is just no equal to the face-to-face interview. If you have the time – and the people – to conduct face-to-face interviews, it is simply the best tool for building the customer fact-base. And it's aligned well with the business-to-business sales and the complex issues that characterize most go-to-market strategy efforts.

Unfortunately, face-to-face interviewing is time-consuming and expensive. It's an impractical tool for collecting information from more than a small number of key customers. As a result, for companies with large customer bases, face-to-face interviewing works best for analyzing customers in one or two geographically concentrated market segments, and this limitation may not be consistent with your customer fact-gathering needs. If your customer base is large or dispersed, or involves customers across a range of segments, you'll want to consider another technique that captures some of the benefits of face-to-face interviewing, but in larger numbers ... the focus group.

Focus groups

The focus group is a powerful tool for conducting observation and analysis of customers, with two key advantages. First, focus groups enable a higher 'throughput' of customers than one-on-one interviewing. Ten focus groups consisting of eight customers each will enable you to collect data efficiently from eighty customers. Focus groups are also excellent tools for seeing how customers interact with each other – to understand how perceptions of a product develop *between* customers as they evaluate the product and discuss its features and benefits. My staff have run focus groups over the years on everything from printers, copiers and computers, to political candidates and floral displays, and most of these focus groups have brought sharp definition to the roll-out of various products.

One drawback of focus groups is that they are logistically complex and take a long time to organize. Orchestrating a focus group-based study across a geographically diverse customer base is difficult. Getting customers scheduled and getting them to show up at the right place, at the right time, is complicated. Hiring a moderator, and developing an appropriate script for conducting the focus group, is expensive. A fair number of focus group efforts never get off the ground, or they get off the ground and then customers don't show up.

The larger drawback of focus groups is that they're not particularly good at collecting certain types of important go-to-market information. While it's easy to use a focus group to elicit reactions to a new product, it is much harder to use a focus group to learn about channel preferences, general positioning and messaging issues, and other go-to-market strategy concerns. The more intangible the issue, the more difficult it is to get at it effectively in a focus group.

The bottom line on focus groups is that they're an effective tool for covering more customers than one-on-one interviews, and work very well for getting feedback on tangible products and other things that customers can see and feel. They're less useful for intangible questions about customer behavior, and they are complex. If you're looking for a simpler tool that will get you the information you need, fast, then it might be better to look into telephone-based interviewing.

Telephone interviewing

A truly superior approach for building the customer fact-base, telephone interviewing combines most of the strengths of the previously-mentioned approaches, with few of the weaknesses.

Telephone interviewing permits much more complexity, in both questions and answers, than a written survey. Since phone interviews are conducted one-on-one, they permit more in-depth, confidential exploration than a focus group. Phone calls are inexpensive and can be made worldwide from a central location, so they allow for the contacting of a large, geographically dispersed customer base. Finally, the vast array of Computer Assisted Telephone Interviewing (CATI) software packages out there can help you record interview results efficiently, store them centrally, and, most importantly, perform sophisticated analysis and interpretation of results to understand subtle trends in the customer base.

Almost any go-to-market questions, from 'How satisfied are you?' to 'How can we do more business together?', can be asked over the phone. In fact, any and all of the go-to-market questions described in the last section can be raised effectively over the phone, and my teams have done so, many times. The telephone interviewing approach is so effective that we use it nearly exclusively, except in cases where a physical product must be viewed or handled in order to collect the desired information.

The bottom line: telephone interviewing is highly recommended.

The Internet

While there may be some doubt about the Internet's capabilities as a sales channel, there should be none at all about its value as a customer research tool. Use of the Web for customer research has grown dramatically over the past few years. Online customer research across twenty-nine large market research firms, for example, grew from $3.5 million in 1996 to $254.8 million in 2000.[84] The reason for this growth is simple: the Internet is an exceptionally good medium for collecting information about your customers.

At the very minimum, the Internet is a credible, low-cost replacement for traditional written customer surveys, and it is indeed replacing paper-based surveying at many leading companies. Procter & Gamble, for instance, which began dabbling in Internet research in 1998, now conducts 40 percent of its six thousand product tests and other research studies online, and claims that Web-based research has reduced its annual research costs from $140 million to $70 million.[85] Other companies are experiencing similar results. Gayle Fuguitt, vice president of consumer insights at cereal-maker General Mills, suggests that the company has reduced its survey costs by 50 percent simply by using email for customer fact-gathering.[86]

While the Web can easily replace paper-based surveying, its power as a customer research and alignment tool goes considerably further. Several companies have begun more cleverly using it to gather customer advice and feedback very early in the product development cycle, to ensure that new offerings map with greater precision than ever before to the preferences and needs of target customers. General Motors

---

[84] David J. Lipke, You've got surveys. *American Demographics Magazine*, November 1, 2000, quoting figures from the Inside Research newsletter.
[85] John Gaffnery, How do you feel about a $44 tooth-bleaching kit? *Business 2.0*, September, 2001.
[86] *Ibid.*

Corporation, for example, has worked with the Massachusetts Institute of Technology to create two Web sites that help it study 'basic vehicle architecture'. Consumers, drawn from lists provided by independent marketing firms, view architectural drawings and video streams of new convertible designs, new tailgate configurations for minivans, sunroof designs, and so on, and provide direct feedback to the manufacturer, in a sort of 'virtual focus group'. This innovative use of the Web is enabling GM to test customer receptivity for new designs *before* sending them into production.[87]

In addition to active surveying and collection of feedback, the Internet is also emerging as a powerful tool for keeping a discrete eye on customer sentiment and opinions. Bulletin boards, discussion groups, chat rooms, etc., that customers use to comment on and review various manufacturers' products and services have been identified by some companies, correctly, as gold mines of customer information. A manufacturer of luxury watches, for example, can find thousands of customer postings on www.timezone.com – everything from commentary on the watch market in general, to discussions of different brands such as Rolex, Jaeger-LeCoultre and Omega, to hundreds of posts on preferences for specific models, all the way down to opinions on individual models' bezels and dials. This kind of discussion board activity is taking place across a huge number of markets, products, and industries, and is a not-to-be-missed source of customer information.

If hanging out on discussion boards doesn't seem like your cup of tea, a new crop of software programs has been developed to collect, aggregate and report relevant customer postings across the Internet. For instance, Ford Motor Company's Lincoln Mercury division uses Intelliseek software to glean information from the Web and report car-buying trends and overall customer discussion themes.[88] Ford has already learned some useful information; for example, consumers who drive Lincoln LS Sedans like the ride but wish the car had more interior storage room.[89] That's a valuable input for product redesign. Ford likes this approach so much that the company's venture capital arm has invested in Intelliseek, and there are now over seventy companies developing software to scour the Web for customer intelligence.

---

[87] Rich Whiting, Virtual focus group. *Information Week*, July 30, 2001.
[88] David Orenstein, Hidden treasure. *Business 2.0*, July, 2001.
[89] *Ibid.*

Finally, the Internet holds out promise as a medium to collect truly 'out of the box' ideas from customers – ideas that may be difficult to collect through other methods. Soft-drink maker Coca-Cola Co., for example, is using www.ideas.com, a site that connects manufacturers with customers who are bristling with creative new ideas, as part of its effort to expand beyond carbonated soft drinks. Last September, Coca-Cola posted a notice on the site asking for ideas on how to get children to gulp more sports drinks or fruit juice. The winning idea – which earned a $5,000 prize – was a wrist-wearable package for toting the beverages. Coca-Cola is currently examining the feasibility of the concept. Expect to see continued, growing use of the Web to collect brand-new product ideas and advice from customers and prospects.

What the Internet cannot replace, of course, is a face-to-face discussion with a real live customer. For drill-down analysis of customers' deep-seated needs, their emerging buying behaviors, and their preferred total buying experiences, there is just no substitute for a face-to-face meeting, and there probably never will be. And, of course, not all customers are on the Web, so if the Internet is your only medium for collecting customer information, you may miss out on the input of important customers. However, the bottom line is that, for a vast majority of routine customer surveying, research and analysis work, as well as some newer approaches such as monitoring customer senti-ment online, the Internet is not only viable; it is a superior tool.

STAYING ON TOP OF TRENDS IN THE CUSTOMER BASE: THE CUSTOMER ADVISORY COUNCIL

Getting aligned with your customers is something you can do right now, but *staying* aligned with your customers is an ongoing process. By the time you figure out what your customers need and how best to serve them, their needs and expectations will have evolved and you must be ready to respond. There are different ways to stay on top of customer developments. Repeating any of the techniques described above – phone interviews, Web surveys, face-to-face meetings, etc. – will help. For example, an annual survey of the entire customer base, and periodic face-to-face interviews with important customers, are effective and very common. However, these are *ad-hoc* approaches that don't quite bake the feedback from customers into the organization. If you want to *institutionalize* your continual alignment with customers – and you should – the way to do it is to establish a *customer advisory council.*

Customer advisory councils have the unique strength of keeping you in ongoing contact with your most important customers, in a structured setting that ensures you get input and feedback across the full spectrum of customer and go-to-market issues. While advisory councils can have any number of customers, the trend is toward small councils consisting of one- or two-dozen key accounts. To keep things fresh, many companies now rotate customers into and out of their advisory councils on a frequent basis, e.g. once per year. Advisory councils generally meet a few times per year, supplemented by occasional *ad-hoc* meetings to discuss important new product releases and other key topics.

An excellent example of the use of a customer council comes from Symantec Corporation, the well-known maker of business and consumer software, including the familiar Norton line of security and utility products. The company, founded in 1982, has operations in thirty-seven countries and had revenues of $854 million in fiscal year 2001.[90]

Symantec's Strategic Advisory Council includes twenty-one of its top customers, across a range of industry verticals, geographies, and product experiences. Members serve two-year terms, and gather twice per year in face-to-face meetings as well as twice per year in teleconferences. In addition, members occasionally meet in *ad-hoc* focus groups when needed, and the company is currently building an online message-based forum for additional information exchange. The focus of the council is broad. Symantec gathers input and feedback from council members on its strategic and technology direction, as well as its products, support offerings, packaging, and pricing strategies.[91] In return for serving on the council and providing feedback, customers are given Beta Test versions of the latest technologies, as well as $5,000 worth of discounted product maintenance. Everybody benefits: Symantec receives ongoing feedback across the full spectrum of

---

[90] Hoovers. www.hoovers.com
[91] Symantec Web site: www.symatec.com

customer-facing issues, and its top customers get a chance to help shape new offerings – along with useful financial incentives.

If there's a pitfall with customer advisory councils, it's a tendency to use them as sales calls. The urge can be strong to use council meetings to show off new products and attempt to entice top customers toward more of your offerings. As one customer described this phenomenon to me, 'I don't go to council meetings to be sold. I was asked to provide honest feedback, and that's why I'm here. I find it offensive to show up and find out it's a big sales call.' Councils tend to succeed when the information flow is primarily from the customer to you, not from you to the customer. It's an opportunity to listen, which you can't do while you're talking.

The final word on customer advisory councils is, simply, to go start one. All you have to do is choose a dozen customers, develop an agenda of discussion topics, and get together with them. No one has ever suffered for doing that, and the return on investment can be huge.

PROCTER & GAMBLE AND IAMS: COMBINING MARKET TARGETING AND CUSTOMER ALIGNMENT TO DRIVE BRAND SUCCESS

Procter & Gamble (P&G), one of the world's most recognizable consumer brands, provides an excellent example of how the principles discussed in this chapter can be combined with the market targeting principles discussed in Chapter 3 to create a big success story in the market place.

P&G started out humbly in 1837 when William Procter and James Gamble began making soap and candles. The two men, married to sisters, were convinced by their father-in-law to go into business together, and grew their company to eighty employees and $1 million in sales by 1859. That was just a beginning. P&G has since grown into a $30 billion global powerhouse and now ranks at # 31 on the Fortune 500. With operating units in fifty countries, P&G sells in more than 140 countries and has a broad array of 'household name' brands such as Oil of Olay, Ivory soap, Tide detergent, Covergirl and Max Factor cosmetics, Crest toothpaste, Pringles, and Pampers.

Procter & Gamble enjoys a special status among many business analysts and academic observers as one of the world's top marketers and brand builders. The company's leadership in marketing goes back at least to 1924 when, in one of the seminal events in marketing history, P&G created the first market research department tasked with studying consumer buying habits and preferences. The sophistication of P&G's research methodology has increased steadily over the years, and most recently includes extensive use of the Internet for customer fact-gathering. Today, P&G is considered by many to be the standard benchmark for best practices in marketing, branding and customer research.

It would take an entire book (or more) to examine P&G's marketing strategies and practices, and indeed several have been written.[92] Here, we have a more limited objective: to get a glimpse into how P&G uses market targeting and customer alignment *together* in order to create successes in the market place. Let's take a look at one recent – and very important – example.

In June 1999, P&G announced a massive reorganization and a focus on acquiring new brands that would contribute to the company's growth. Key criteria for new acquisitions included all the usual suspects, such as access to large markets and growth potential. Of particular importance to P&G was the strategic fit of a new brand within the context of the company's existing product lines, established distribution networks and channels, and focus on higher-end, premium offerings.

P&G's Corporate New Ventures group, tasked with finding new areas of business, identified Iams, a player in the pet food market, as a ripe candidate for acquisition. As a potential target market, the pet food business fit extremely well with P&G's criteria. A huge $30+ billion per year market, it is growing modestly but consistently at 3–4 percent per year. As noted in Chapter 2, over 70 percent of US families own a total of over 136 million cats and dogs, each of which gobbles up an average of $366 worth of food per year.[93] These pets all have to eat,

---

[92] Several books on P&G can easily be found by visiting Amazon.com and entering 'Procter & Gamble' or 'P&G' in the Search box. These books vary widely in quality.
[93] See Pets.com discussion in Chapter 2, Third Commandment.

regardless of overall economic conditions, providing stability and predictability to the pet food business.

Within the pet food 'space', Iams was singled out as a particularly attractive candidate. Recognized as a leader in premium pet food, Iams had sales of $800 million in 1998 and had grown at an average of 16 percent per year over the previous four years.[94] Iams and its super-premium brand Eukanuba were trusted and respected high-end products, which fit well with P&G's own product lines. Iam's emphasis on health-oriented products fit well with P&G's own expertise in health and nutrition. Iam's relatively high 2 percent investment of revenues into research and development equaled P&G's own above-average R&D investments. Most importantly, Iams would immediately establish P&G as a serious contender in the huge pet food market.

As a result of this strong strategic fit, in August 1999, just two months after announcing its intent to acquire new brands, P&G announced its decision to enter the pet food business by acquiring Iams.[95] The acquisition was completed in just sixty days, in a $2.3 billion cash transaction – the largest in P&G's history.

P&G recognized right out of the gate that a better understanding of Iams' customers and an improved alignment with their needs and buying behaviors would produce immediate gains in sales. Prior to the acquisition, Iams' products had been available only in specialty pet retail stores, a limitation seen by both P&G and Iams executives as a disadvantage.[96] To solve this problem, after the acquisition was completed P&G and Iams combined forces to examine the needs and buying behaviors of Iams' customers. Research was conducted among both current and potential Iams customers using several techniques, including a Web-based survey and telephone interviews conducted by Iams' customer service reps. Results from one thousand pet owners were conclusive: lack of access to Iams products was the most

---

[94] Tim Tresslar, Iams: a year after the sale. *Dayton Daily News*, August 6, 2000.
[95] New York Time News Service, Procter & Gamble to buy Iams, pet food maker for $2.3 billion; premium line added to accelerate growth via diversification. *The Baltimore Sun*, August 12, 1999.
[96] Indeed, prior to the acquisition Iams had begun pondering new channel possibilities to increase its customer reach.

frequent issue. The ability to find and buy Iams products in more convenient places was the most frequent and important suggestion.

P&G acted decisively. A few months after the acquisition was completed in January 2000, the company announced that Iams would branch out from its specialty retail channels to grocery chains and mass merchandiser outlets. In March, P&G rolled out Iams Pet Food products in 25,000 new supermarkets, superstores, and other mass market channels – the largest single-day roll-out of any P&G brand.[97] It was an immediate hit. Iams' products fit right into P&G's established distribution network in these channels, and this gave Iams' customers exactly what they wanted.

Within just three months, Iams' dollar share of the dog and cat food market in grocery, club and mass merchandise stores went from 0 to 7.2 percent.[98] Iams' revenues grew 50 percent from $800 million to $1.2 billion in the first two years after acquisition, and its share of the premium pet food market has increased from 10 to 27 percent. Its success has helped P&G's Health Care Division, of which Iams is a part, to post robust revenue growth of 16 per cent,[99] at a time in which P&G announced its first quarterly loss in eight years, due primarily to restructuring costs from its poorly performing food, fabric-care, and cosmetics lines.[100] These are impressive results, and they were achieved by realigning the go-to-market strategy with the carefully-researched behaviors and needs of customers.

Following its initial successes, Iams continues to focus on staying aligned with its customers. Visitors to the company's Web site are asked preference questions in a series of ongoing pet-related surveys and sweepstakes. The company has also launched other initiatives to get closer to its customers. A massive direct mail campaign has brought the Iams name to millions of new customers, who are encouraged to call the company with questions. For real pet enthusiasts, Iams provides the opportunity to post pet pictures on its Web site. It's a little unconventional, perhaps, but Iams has learned that increased contact

---

[97] Patrick Lawson, A year after buy, P&G muscle pushes Iams. *The Cincinnati Post*, August 23, 2000.
[98] *Ibid*. Iams also produces Eukanuba brand pet food, its 'super-premium' brand. P&G decided to leave its distribution channels alone for Eukanuba. This was a wise choice, as it helped to assuage, at least to some extent, the discontent among specialty retailers that Iams was deserting or competing with its established channel.
[99] Year-over-year.
[100] P&G suffers loss, first in 8 years, on revamp costs. *Investors Business Daily*, August 8, 2001.

frequency and interaction with its customers can help the company understand their preferences and behaviors, and make high-impact, growth-generating business decisions.

In sum, P&G's acquisition of Iams has positioned it well in a large, growing market. By identifying the right new market for penetration, finding a strong acquisition candidate in the market, and aligning its channels with the needs and buying behaviors of customers, P&G has covered all the bases and, apparently, hit a home run.

SUMMARY

All go-to-market activities, initiatives and tactics must begin with the needs and buying behaviors of customers. We encountered this crucial concept earlier in the book as the First Commandment of Going to Market ('Go-to-market strategy must start with the customer'), but here we took it a big step further.

We began the chapter by looking at two common customer alignment traps: first, a failure to conduct *any* meaningful customer analysis, and second, the more insidious and frequent tendency to conduct a lot of useless research without learning the right things about your target customers.

Next, we examined the five fundamental components of a robust customer fact-base, including:

1. *Customer needs*. What business needs do the target customers have? What is it that they want in general, and what is it that they want from *you*?
2. *The customer experience*. What kind of experiences are your target customers seeking from their vendors? Do they just want simple, efficient transactions? Do they seek high-value, high-touch personal relationships with their vendors? Or do they particularly value flexibility when purchasing from their vendors?
3. *Customer buying behavior*. How do customers do business today with their vendors? Which channels do they use, and which ones are likely to increase in importance in the future?

4. *Current gaps.* Where are you strong in meeting customers' needs? Where are you weak? What do you need to fix in order to align better with the expectations of your target customers?

5. *Sources of increased business.* What would lead to increased purchasing volume with your company? What could you do *today* – right now – to increase sales volume, in your customers' own words?

We looked at a number of tools for getting answers to these questions, ranging from traditional surveys and focus groups, to the very effective phone interviewing approach, to newer tools such as Web-based data gathering. We also discussed the importance of staying on top of trends and changes in the customer base over time, and the valuable role that a customer advisory council can play in helping to do this.

Finally, we looked at the customer-focused approach of Procter & Gamble in acquiring pet food maker Iams. P&G's purchase of Iams provides an excellent example of a company that has successfully combined market targeting with customer alignment to identify new channels that could better meet the needs of their target customers. It's a helpful example of the tangible payoff of getting serious about customer alignment.

The P&G-Iams case also illustrates another important point. Ultimately, the outcome of good market targeting and customer alignment is the definition of how best to reach out to and serve a group of target customers . . . i.e. through channels. Choosing the right channels to 'cover' a market is, of course, at the very core of a winning go-to-market strategy, and in fact it's what most people have in mind when they talk about 'go-to-market strategy'. In the next chapter, we'll examine the issues involved in developing your own channel coverage model.

5

Go-to-market strategy:

Choosing the right channels and partners

C ompanies large and small, across all industries, are facing crucial strategic questions such as these:

■ Can we reduce sales costs, and increase profits, by using alternative, low-cost channels? How much savings can we expect?
■ What should we be doing on the Internet – and are we doing the right things today?
■ What is the right partnering model for our company? Are we making the best use of our business partners? Do we need more of them, less of them, or different ones?
■ What should we do with the sales force? Leave it as is? Focus its efforts on big-ticket accounts, and use other channels to capture smaller deals? Downsize it? Grow it?
■ Should we have an 'integrated multi-channel model'? What's the payoff – and how do you build one?

These are all *channel* questions, and they are now 'top of mind' concerns at many companies. When my last book *The Channel Advantage* came out three years ago, few people were paying attention to sales channels.[101] Today, scores of marketing firms, strategy consultants, and IT software and services vendors have sprung up to advise companies on their channel models, and major consulting firms such as McKinsey & Company have started up entire channel strategy practice groups. A recent online search on the phrase 'marketing channel' turned up over 76,000 responses, and 'sales channel' turned up 49,100.[102] Channels in general, and the Internet channel in particular, are the most widespread and persistent topics at industry and company conferences. Why all the sudden interest? There are basically three reasons.

First, over the past ten years the benefits of channel expansion have become increasingly evident. A decade ago, you could go whole years without encountering the word 'channel'. Companies basically took their products or services, and stuffed them into whatever channel they already were using – in many cases, the same ones they'd been using since the day they went into business. Little if any time was spent thinking about new or different ways to go to market. Alternative

---

[101] Lawrence G. Friedman and Timothy R. Furey, *The Channel Advantage*. Butterworth-Heinemann, 1999.
[102] Search on www.google.com with the phrases 'marketing channel' and 'sales channel', November 6, 2001.

channels of any type were rarely used, and the Internet hadn't yet been used for a single commercial transaction. People now look at channels very differently, to say the least! Today, you cannot get past the first page of the *Wall Street Journal*, or read any business magazine, without encountering some company whose clever channel approach has produced enormous financial gains and competitive advantage. Widely-publicized go-to-market successes from the likes of Dell Computer, Charles Schwab, Marriott, Wal-Mart, Lands' End, and Cisco Systems have demonstrated that thoughtful multi-channel models can reach far more customers, in more markets, to do more business, at a much lower cost, than traditional, single-channel approaches. Channels have become credible and widely recognized sources of competitive advantage – crucial differentiators between profitable, growing companies and their struggling, slow-growth, low-margin competitors.

Second, many executives have realized that an effective multi-channel model is not a 'nice-to-have' but an absolute business requirement. The reason boils down to an enormous change in customer behavior over the past decade. In the old days customers basically did business however they were told. If you did business through sales reps, or retail stores, well, that's how you did business, and customers who wanted your products used whatever channels you made available to them. Today, the notion that you can force customers to use the channels you want them to use seems ridiculous. Customers increasingly 'surf' across channels at will, using whatever combination of sales reps, partners, telechannels, and the Internet that suits their purposes. They might call a sales rep if they feel like it, or they might just as easily get on the Web to research a product, then pick up the phone to gather further information, and then visit a distributor or retail store to place their order. Increasingly they stick with vendors who make it easy to do business how *they* want to do business, and dismiss vendors who don't. This is as true today in traditional manufacturing markets as it is in the fast-paced technology and media industries. Put simply, we live in an age of 'customer choice', and companies are scrambling to respond with flexible, customer-centric channel models.

Finally, newer channels such as the Web, partners, and business-to-business telesales have created a lot of interest, but also a lot of confusion. Alternative channels sound great in theory, but on a practical level they raise a lot of challenging questions. Which channels are optimal for your unique business, and why? How and where should you use these channels? How do you make them work *together* with each other and with your existing sales resources? What do you do about channel conflict, and particularly, the serious conflicts arising between new direct-to-customer channels and your distributors or sales reps? These are tough questions, and executives are not at all convinced that they have the whole 'channel thing' figured out. In a recent survey by my firm, The Sales Strategy Institute, just four out of fifty companies voiced strong confidence in their channel models, and over half admitted that they had little idea whether or not they were on the right track. To many executives, building a coherent channel strategy appears to be a Herculean task.

The good news is that you really don't have to be Hercules to put together a winning channel model. You just have to know the right questions to ask, the right things to do, and the right steps to follow – and you have to be willing to 'get outside the box' a little and think creatively. That's what we're going to focus on in this chapter. Here, we'll look at the basics of sales channels:

■ What channels are
■ How to choose the right ones for your business
■ How to build a *market coverage model* that assigns channels to the right markets and segments.

Later on, in Chapter 7, we'll examine the more complicated challenge of pulling all of your markets, products and channels together into a high-performance, *integrated* multi-channel system. But first things first! Before you can build an integrated multi-channel model, you must choose the right channels and determine where they will participate in your markets. So let's get started.

CHANNELS 101: WHAT IS A 'CHANNEL'?

What is a 'channel'? Ask ten different people, and you'll get ten different answers. To some, a channel is any alternative to a field sales rep, as in 'direct mail channel' or 'retail channel'. To others, a channel is a group of business partners, as in 'We're going to sell the new product through our distributor channel.' Some industries have come up with their own homegrown definitions for channels. In the technology business, for example, 'the channel' refers to a network of IT resellers, and has become so entrenched in the industry's go-to-market awareness that it has become a proper noun, as in 'Let's get the new computer into *the channel* by March.'

These various definitions of channels have two problems. First, they are all different! How can you develop a sound channel model if you cannot even agree on what a channel is? More importantly, they are all very limited in scope and narrowly defined, most often around specific types of partners. If a 'channel' is a type of partner, then what do you call an extranet? Would you even think to use an extranet if you hadn't identified it as a potential channel? How can you take a wide view of your full range of channel options, and make creative choices, if your definition of channels excludes many of your best go-to-market options? You can't.

That's why you need a broad, inclusive definition of channels, one that captures the full range of sales alternatives available to your organization. Here is the broadest and most useful definition of all: *A channel is any pipe that you can use to connect your products and services with your target customers.* Further, a channel, unlike an advertising medium such as a radio advertisement or highway bill-board, enables information to flow *both ways* between buyer and seller, thus making sales transactions possible. This view of channels is depicted in Figure 5.1 on the page opposite.

As illustrated in the figure, channels are the pipes, or routes, that you establish between your company and the customers in your target markets in order to do business (that's why channels are sometimes referred to as *routes to market*). Any and all of the pipes that you could use to do business with your customers are channels, whether they are sales forces, high-volume distributors, the telephone, the Internet, or even your Mom selling your products out of the back of a minivan. Yes, your Mom could be a channel, if she's willing to get out there and sell!

In sum, defining the word 'channel' narrowly – nit-picking about whether a 'channel' is a reseller or a field sales rep or a Web site – is a complete waste of time. Narrow definitions get in the way of

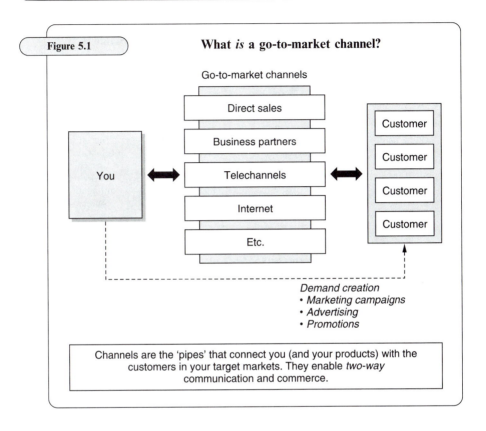

Figure 5.1   **What *is* a go-to-market channel?**

Go-to-market channels

Direct sales

Business partners

You   Telechannels   Customer / Customer / Customer / Customer

Internet

Etc.

Demand creation
• Marketing campaigns
• Advertising
• Promotions

Channels are the 'pipes' that connect you (and your products) with the customers in your target markets. They enable *two-way* communication and commerce.

the creative thinking needed to identify new channel opportunities. To reach, attract, and serve your target customers, you must build good pipes that connect you with your customers so you can do business efficiently and effectively, and channels are *all* of those pipes.

While there are many types of channels, they do fall into a few major categories. These categories are important, because channels within a particular category tend to offer similar benefits – and also similar disadvantages. The three categories are *direct sales channels, indirect channels*, and *direct-to-customer channels*, as shown in Table 5.1.

Let's take a look at each of the three channel types, focusing on their role within a multi-channel mix. (For a much more detailed discussion of individual channels, go get a copy of *The Channel Advantage*!)

Table 5.1   The three categories of go-to-market channels

	Direct sales channel	Indirect channels (partners)	Direct-to-customer channels
Purpose	• Complex sales • Control over sales process in key accounts • 'High-touch' service	• Lower-cost sales • Complete 'solutions' • Local customer support and care • Expanded geographic and vertical market 'reach'	• Lowest-cost sales • Maximum market 'reach' and penetration • Efficient transactions for simpler items and automatic repurchases by existing customers
Major types	• Field sales reps – Global account managers (GAMs) – Key account managers (KAMs) – Corporate account managers (CAMs) – Senior account executives – Account executives – Technical reps – etc.	• Distributors • Resellers – Volume resellers – Value-added resellers (VARs) • Service and support partners • Retail stores (partner-owned) • Mass merchants • Manufacturer's agents, reps and brokers • Integrators and aggregators	• Telechannels – Telemarketing – Telesales – Telecoverage • Internet and e-commerce – Public Web site – Proprietary Web sites (extranets, Web EDI, etc.) – E-marketplaces • Direct mail (e.g. catalogs) • Retail (company-owned) stores

The direct sales channel (field sales force)

The direct channel, or field sales force, is a company-owned, company-paid organization that sells products and services directly to end-customers. It is the traditional route to market that has existed, in one form or another, for thousands of years.

In recent years, rumors have persisted about the imminent death of field sales forces, due to the growth of alternative channels. The logic has gone something like this: who needs costly, labor-intensive sales forces, now that alternative channels are available to reach customers less expensively? This kind of thinking has led to some massive sales force down-sizings, particularly in the past few years, as executives have gotten on board with the benefits and proven performance of low-cost channels. There is good reason, in some larger, bloated companies, to question the continued dominance and size of field sales forces. However, the rumors of the death of sales forces, to paraphrase Mark Twain, have been greatly exaggerated.

The fact is, most companies still have field sales organizations, and they will continue to have them. A company-owned, operated, compensated, and trained sales force is still the most knowledgeable and trustworthy representative of its products and services in the market place. For certain types of transactions – particularly those involving higher-value products and services sold into key, strategic accounts – there is no equal to a good field sales rep. Sales reps provide the 'high-touch' hand-holding, service, support, and account management that customers expect and often demand in big-ticket, complex deals. And that's precisely why field sales forces have stubbornly survived and persisted in the face of lower-cost alternative channels.

Despite their obvious capabilities in high-end sales, field sales forces do have some real disadvantages when compared with other channels. First and foremost, a sales force is the most expensive way to sell; all other channels provide lower-cost alternatives. Direct sales reps, often running $60,000 to $300,000 apiece (depending on industry), are just not cost-effective for selling lower-priced offerings or serving lower-end accounts. In addition, sales forces lack 'leverage', the ability to cover and penetrate a broad market place. No one can afford to put enough sales reps into the field to access the full range of potential target markets. As a result, reliance solely on field sales reps implicitly involves writing off some markets – usually, the small-to-mid sized markets that represent the fastest-growth opportunities. To access these markets, even companies long associated with large field sales organizations, such as IBM and Xerox, have had to migrate sales to new low-cost channels.

To sum it all up, there is still a role for field sales, but it is becoming a more limited and specialized – and yet also more valuable – role than in the past. Today, in most companies the direct sales channel should be used solely to do what it does best: acquire large strategic accounts, and make complex, big-ticket sales. Other channels are readily available to handle smaller deals and less strategic accounts, and they can do so much more efficiently. Using a highly focused sales force to serve the very top end of the market, and using a mix of other channels to serve the rest of the market, is the emerging 'best practice' in business-to-business sales. It is an indisputably powerful channel model.

Indirect channels (business partners)

An indirect channel is any intermediary that sits between you and the end-customer. This category includes manufacturers' reps; agents; brokers; resellers; local, national, and global distributors; consultants; integrators; and a variety of industry-specific partner types. To get a sense of how important indirect channels really are, consider that distributors and other types of partners constitute the largest category of employment in the US, providing jobs to over fourteen million people.[103] In some business-to-business markets, such as technology, over 80 percent of all revenue is sold through business partners. In some consumer markets it's 100 percent. Indirect channels are serious business, and will remain so.

Like field sales forces, indirect channels were written off – very prematurely – when direct-to-customer channels such as the Internet and telephone exploded onto the scene in the 1990s. Successes at companies such as personal computer maker Dell Computer, which mauled its partner-oriented competitors such as Compaq with efficient Web and telephone channels, convinced many people that indirect partners represented an unnecessary expense – an inefficiency in the sales process whose time had passed. The idea quickly took hold that the 'middleman' could be completely eliminated by selling directly to end-customers, and that the cash that was previously paid out to distributors and resellers could be pocketed (or shared with customers, in the form of lower prices).

However, what works in a simple commodity sale, such as a personal computer, doesn't necessarily work with other types of products and services. Lots of products and services require customization, configuration, installation, support, and guidance in the sales process, and all of these are services that business partners are, in most cases, much better equipped to provide than are low-cost, alternative channels.

---

[103] I'm not sure what the source is on that number, but I've heard it at least a dozen times, so I'm sticking to it.

Partners also offer the ability to reach and penetrate broad, dispersed markets. If the goal is to sell across a wide range of geographies or industries, business partners may well be the most effective and efficient way to do it. Partners offer much broader coverage characteristics than field sales organizations, and have an understanding of local market conditions, as well as local account penetration, that often cannot be equaled by any other channel.

In addition, partners also bring significant cost savings over direct sales channels. Compared with a sales force, an efficient, well-run partner channel can slice 40–60 percent off of selling costs (depending on the type of partner). That's a pretty significant number. On a $10,000 sale, that'll put an extra $1,000 to $1,500 in your pocket, for overall margin increases of 10–15 percent, with little or no decrease in service levels.[104]

In short, partners offer the opportunity to cover more markets and customers at a lower cost than field sales forces, while providing higher levels of service and support than alternative channels such as the phone or Web.

Finally, business partners can do something that no other channel can do: combine your offerings with those of other companies to create complete solutions. This has been particularly important in the financial services and technology industries, where vendors' offerings are generally less desirable as stand-alone products or services than when they are combined with the offerings of other firms. For example, mutual fund aggregators such as Charles Schwab and Fidelity Investments, who combine the funds of numerous providers into one total-choice solution, have given themselves and their partners a much stronger value proposition. They've encouraged customers to move money into whichever mutual funds they prefer, in one convenient place, thus increasing total inflows into mutual funds and making the pie bigger for everyone. Likewise, in the technology industry, software and hardware vendors have discovered that by partnering with each other, they can present more compelling, complete offerings to customers that benefit everyone – the customers,

---

[104] Based on an assumed 25 percent cost-of-sales for the direct sales channel. On a $10,000 product, a 25 percent cost of sales would be $2,500. A 40–60 percent savings would therefore be $1,000 to $1,500, or 10 to 15 percent of revenues.

and the vendors who sell in higher volumes as a result of a stronger overall value proposition.

While there are many types of partner channels, they basically fall into four categories:

1. *Volume-oriented partners.* These include corporate resellers, high-volume distributors, and others who sell products in large quantities to corporate accounts or to other distributors and resellers.[105] Services provided by these partners are often limited, and tend to focus on financing and efficient distribution. Volume-oriented partners are optimal for companies with off-the-rack products who are seeking high-volume sales. They are not as suitable for companies whose products require customization or local service in the sales process. Many of these companies, such as $5 billion MRO[106] distributor Grainger, offer extensive online product catalogs and other channels, enabling you to kill two birds with one stone – enlist a strong business partner, and gain access to alternative channels at the same time.

2. *Value-oriented partners.* These include value-added distributors and resellers, local consultants and integrators, and many smaller partners such as local manufacturers' reps. They often combine the products they resell with a variety of their own services, such as product configuration and customization, installation, training, and customer care. They are ideal for companies with more complex offerings, and particularly those whose offerings require local customer service in face-to-face relationships.

3. *Service and support partners.* These specialized partners do not sell, but rather come in after the sales transaction to provide customer support and service. They're hot right now, due to the large number of companies that have moved to direct-to-customer channels and who must rely on service and support partners to take care of customers after products have been sold over the phone or Web. Dell Computer, for example, one of the leading direct-to-customer companies, uses support partners such as Unisys to support its mid-market corporate customers. The use of service and support partners will continue

---

[105] Distributors who sell to other distributors: 'two-tier distribution'.
[106] MRO = Maintenance, Repair and Operations.

to grow as companies migrate more and more sales over to the Web and phone. Service and support partnering also remains a common model for manufacturing firms whose products must be serviced locally. For example, companies in consumer electronics, household appliances, and business systems use authorized service centers and third-party customer support networks to provide the post-sale services that neither they nor their sales distributors want to provide.

4. *Solution partners.* As the name implies, these are partners – often high-end, prestigious companies – that combine the offerings of multiple vendors into total, integrated solutions. They come in different flavors, such as *integrators* and *aggregators*, and primarily inhabit technology markets, where heavy-duty integration of multiple vendors is required. They include firms such as Accenture and PriceWaterhouseCoopers at the national and global levels, and thousands of local integrators and solution providers at the local level. Good solution partners have dominant presence in their markets and C-level relationships with customers, due to the impact of the total solutions they sell.[107] That's the good news. The bad news is that they are highly sought after and courted by the vast throngs of vendors who see them as attractive entry-points into key accounts. Good luck getting on the radar screens of top-of-the-line solution partners! To do so, you must have something very compelling to sell – something that also fits well within their product and service portfolios.

To sum up the situation with indirect channels, they are powerful tools for accessing large and dispersed markets, providing high-value services and capabilities that exceed those of any alternative channel, while costing considerably less than a field sales force. As a result, most companies would do well to consider where and when they can use business partners – or use them further – to increase their market reach and leverage. However, business partners are not the lowest-cost channels, and they don't necessarily reach as many customers as some alternative channels. If you really want to achieve the highest possible market reach at the lowest possible cost, you have to look to *direct-to-customer channels.*

---

[107] C-level = CEO, CIO, CMO, CTO, CFO, COO, etc. Very important customers, in short.

Direct-to-customer channels

A direct-to-customer channel is any channel, other than a field sales force, that you can use to sell *directly* to end-customers (i.e. without an intermediary such as a distributor or reseller). The three main types of direct-to-customer channels are the telephone, the Internet, and direct mail.[108] These channels have been growing rapidly in recent years, and now outpace the revenue growth coming from all other types of channels.

The increasing usage of direct-to-customer channels is due to three advantages over other types of channels. The first is that they are *very* low-cost. For example, a transaction that would cost $1,000 to make through a field sales rep or $400–600 through a partner might cost as little as $50–150 over the phone, and even less over the Web. The cost-savings are really that dramatic. Companies that have been aggressive in deploying direct-to-customer channels have seen their selling costs plummet and their profits increase. If margins are a big issue, you simply cannot afford to ignore the profit advantages of a direct-to-customer channel model.

> If margins are a big issue, you simply cannot afford to ignore the profit advantages of a direct-to-customer channel model.

The second benefit is *reach*. All direct-to-customer channels offer a superior ability to reach markets efficiently, regardless of how geographically dispersed these markets are or how many customers you must contact in them. The Web, to take the extreme example, can reach every single customer on the planet who has an Internet connection (provided that they know about and visit your Web site – not always an easy task). Even the telephone and mail-order channels can reach many more customers in more markets, much more efficiently and cost-effectively than traditional channels, and get your company and its offerings in front of millions of customers all over the world.

The third benefit is the fit between direct-to-customer channels and today's customer preferences. In an increasing number of markets,

---

[108] In addition, in consumer markets, retail stores and outlets would constitute a fourth type of direct-to-customer channel.

both business and consumer, customers actively use these channels and like them. They appreciate the convenience, low cost, lack of hassles and sales pressure, and efficiency of doing business directly with a supplier through a direct channel. They particularly like using direct-to-customer channels for the purchase of simpler, 'off-the-rack' products, and for automatic repurchases (i.e. replenishment of supplies, such as toner cartridges and paper, once a supplier relationship has been established). In short, direct-to-customer channels can help you align better with the expectations and channel preferences of customers in your target markets.

The downside of direct-to-customer channels is that they generally have a limited ability to provide customer service and support. The Internet hasn't yet proven itself as a service channel, and it may never do so. The telephone, while able to handle many routine customer problems, is no substitute in a complex sale for the face-to-face support provided by a field sales rep or business partner. As a result, direct-to-customer channels must be combined with a separate service channel for offerings of any significant complexity.

Beyond customer support, there is the issue of *customization*. While some products are sold 'off the rack', many others require customization to unique specifications, particularly in business-to-business sales. Direct-to-customer channels can handle a limited amount of product customization. They're actually quite good at handling 'customization lite' – for example, letting customers use drop-down menu boxes on Web sites to custom-configure personal computers, gift baskets, and even cars. However, these channels do not offer the heavy-duty configuration and design assistance of a sales rep or partner. As a result, direct-to-customer channels tend to work best with lightly customized or off-the-rack products, and with automatic repurchases of products and supplies following a sale made initially by a field rep or partner. These limitations are not showstoppers, but they do suggest that you cannot necessarily sell everything to everyone through direct-to-customer channels.

Let's take a quick look at the three major types of direct-to-customer channels.

The telephone

Many still think of the telephone as a low-end channel for selling to consumers, and have not taken it very seriously as a core go-to-market alternative. That's a big mistake. Teleselling is a huge channel success story. Telechannels account for over $669 billion in transactions per year in the US alone, a number that's expected to grow 9 percent per year over the next five years.[109] Today there are well over 565,000 firms involved in teleselling, up from just 1,500 in 1980,[110] and an astounding 250,000 US companies use telemarketing services.[111] While the telephone has long been accepted as a good channel for reaching consumers, it has really taken off in the last five years as a credible and important business-to-business (B2B) channel, with B2B revenues exceeding $392 billion, or 59 percent of total telechannel revenues.[112] At a number of leading global companies such as IBM, telechannel sales account for well over 15 percent of worldwide revenues, including the sales of relatively complex products and services such as AS/400 computers.

The telephone is not one type of channel, but three, and the differences between them are crucial. First there's *telesales*, in which the telephone is used to make outbound sales, and for which the goal is deal-closure right over the phone at the conclusion of the call. Telesales is effective primarily for selling simple, off-the-rack (non-customized) products, such as long-distance service, and much less effective or common for selling complex, customized offerings.

A second, and very different, usage of the telechannel is *telemarketing*. In telemarketing, the telephone is used to generate leads for follow-up and closure by another channel, such as a sales rep or business partner. Here, the goal is not to get a sale, but rather just to open doors, qualify prospects, and create initial interest to 'warm up' an opportunity for another channel. Telemarketing is very effective in complex, high-price-point sales, and is therefore very useful in business-to-business selling. I have not yet seen a product or

---

[109] Source: Direct Marketing Association.
[110] Sandra Herman, Magic beans and has beens ... embracing relationship management. *DM News*, March, 1998.
[111] Source: Omni Telemarketing. For more information: www.callomni.com.
[112] Source: Direct Marketing Association.

service that couldn't successfully be promoted through telemarketing to generate good leads for other channels, regardless of complexity or price. In fact, the more complex and difficult the product or service, the more likely it is that telemarketing can help in the sales process.

Finally, the telephone can be used as a powerful tool for existing-customer growth and retention. In a *telecoverage* channel, phone reps are assigned to call existing customers on a regular schedule (e.g. once every three to six months), in order to discuss their issues and needs and see if there are any areas for add-on sales. Telecoverage is a very attractive addition to a go-to-market strategy. Disciplined, regular calling by telecoverage reps to key customers often has a dramatic impact on account growth, contributing double-digit gains in sales and similar improvements in share-of-customer. The increased frequency and regularity of contact that telecoverage reps provide also improves customer retention, and dramatically reduces customer defection rates.

In sum, telechannels offer a number of different possibilities, depending on what you sell. Companies that sell simple, off-the-rack products, particularly to consumers, can use telesales to increase sales revenues at a fairly low cost. Companies that sell more complex offerings into businesses probably should not look to telesales. For these companies, it will probably be more appropriate to use the phone to generate leads for other channels (telemarketing) or to keep in touch with existing accounts and seek out incremental new sales (telecoverage).

The Internet

The Internet has gradually come into its own as a go-to-market channel, although it is still far from clear how it will actually end up being used at most companies. While skepticism is very appropriate in the face of all the relentless Internet hype, there is no question that people are doing more and more business over the Web.

Estimates for total Internet transaction volume vary wildly. Gartner Group's estimate of $433 billion for worldwide business-to-business Internet commerce in 2000 is in between the various high and low estimates and therefore may be a reasonable figure – but no one really knows![113] More important than the numbers is the fact that the Internet continues to become part of the everyday process of doing business – just the way many of us buy things, as consumers and as business people. Indeed, the recent *ennui* surrounding the Internet is a sign of its increasing normalcy and its institutionalization as an accepted medium of information and commercial exchange, not its rejection. Today, there are few companies that aren't on the Web, and most of the ones that aren't are in real trouble, because that's the very first place many customers now go to research, learn, evaluate vendors, and make their buying decisions – regardless of whether they ultimately complete their transactions in another channel.

There is no easy way to get your arms around the Internet as a sales channel, given its newness and lack of clear direction. However, it is useful to think of the Internet as being divided into three different channel opportunities:

1. *Public Web sites*. These are the familiar, now common corporate Web sites, accessible by anyone with a computer, which provide company information, product and service descriptions, and a variety of other content, up to and including the ability to purchase products online. Increasingly, public Web sites are the first stops for prospects seeking out new vendors and products. As a result, it is essential to have a clean, professional, easily navigable Web site that clearly articulates what your company is all about and entices customers to do business over the Web or contact you for follow-up through another channel. A poor or mediocre Web site will cost you lots of lost prospects – and you won't even know you lost them, because they'll have never made contact with you.

2. *Proprietary Web sites*. When Dell Computer came out with its *Premier Pages* a few years ago, people were stunned. Accustomed to thinking about the Web in terms of public access and information sharing, analysts and customers couldn't get over the cleverness of Dell's *Premier Page* 'extranets', which were private, password-controlled sites customized to the unique specifications and needs of over *ten thousand* individual

---

[113] Gartner Group press release: Worldwide business-to-business Internet commerce to reach $8.5 trillion in 2005. March 13, 2001.

corporate accounts. The *Premier Pages* enabled commercial and governmental institutions to pre-select their computer hardware configurations, thus letting customers' main offices set IT standards (e.g. specific models, RAM and hard disk sizes, etc.) which local offices would then automatically use when visiting their *Premier Pages*. The privacy of the premier pages also enabled Dell to set up pre-negotiated, preferential pricing structures.

The private-site model is currently one of the most important developments taking place on the Internet. Today, companies from General Electric, Motorola and Square D in manufacturing, to IT vendors such as Cisco, IBM and Microsoft, have built private-access Web sites to communicate and transact business with their customers, suppliers and partners.

Once you've established a private Web space, you can move all sorts of proprietary information and processes to the Web – such as purchase orders, inventory management, confidential product descriptions, pricing specifications, collaboration areas and joint design tools. Private Web sites, and private Web-based systems such as Web EDI, have enabled companies simultaneously to reduce the transaction and processing costs of working with customers and partners, as well as to improve the effectiveness of communication and add more value in the sales process. Private Web capabilities bring many of the benefits of one-on-one business relationships to the low-cost, efficient Internet.

3. *E-marketplaces*. A significant and highly publicized part of the emerging Internet story is the *e-marketplace*, or e-exchange. Originally conceived by some very clever people at start-up companies such as Ventro, CommerceOne and VerticalNet, the basic principle was to connect a wide variety of sellers and buyers in one place on the Web so they could do business together more efficiently. Some e-marketplace entrepreneurs envisioned gigantic industry or even multi-industry hubs where buyers and sellers of all sorts of products and services would congregate, paying a percentage of sales to the 'market maker' – the Web-site operator.

That model didn't work out so well, and many of the early e-marketplace sites have since gone belly-up. Even technology leader Dell Computer pulled the plug early in 2001 on its e-marketplace for small businesses, Dellmarketplace.com, citing a lack of interest among customers and suppliers.[114] Dell's experience has been mirrored in the poor performance of highly-touted e-marketplaces such as e-Chemicals and PlasticsNet. Why have many e-marketplaces failed? It's simple. Businesses did not see a compelling reason to pay hefty transaction fees to Web-site operators, fees that often exceeded the cost of buying and selling through other channels.

It would be a mistake, however, to write off e-marketplaces and to ignore their potential role in your channel mix. First, while there have been a lot of false starts and failures, there are also plenty of e-marketplaces that are succeeding, such as General Electric's Global eXchange Services – which, as noted in Chapter 1, handles $1 trillion dollars per year in transactions for more than 100,000 trading partners. The range of e-marketplaces that are still around and serving various industries and communities is huge, from $1 billion-per-year e-Steel.com, to lawcommerce.com[sm] ('The online center for the legal profession'), to the US Commercial Service's buyUSA.com's site, which provides export and global trading services to over sixteen thousand member companies.

In addition, the e-marketplace model is evolving, and is moving quickly in new directions that bode well for its long-term success. The most important direction is the development of private, proprietary e-marketplaces, such as Siemens' *click2procure* site for global procurement management, which enables the company to manage relationships with its supplier partners all over the world. Private e-marketplaces don't have objectionable transaction fees paid to Web-site operators. Absent the transaction fees, e-marketplaces offer attractive, efficient, and cost-effective ways to do business with customers, partners and suppliers. This model will only get better with time, and will eventually constitute a significant percentage of business-to-business transactions, regardless of some recent growing pains.

You will probably not adopt the e-marketplace as your sole go-to-market channel. But with well over $1 trillion already being transacted through this new medium, it is worth taking seriously. Let your competitors scoff at the twenty-somethings who blew millions creating generic multi-industry hubs on the Web. As

---

[114] Alorie Gilbert, Leading companies pull e-marketplace plugs. *Information Week: Com News*, February 26, 2001.

e-marketplaces increasingly prove their financial benefits, they will become viable parts of the go-to-market mix.

Direct mail

The direct-mail channel includes all direct-response communications sent through postal mail (or private delivery services), and includes catalogs as well other media such as letters, brochures, cards, videos, computer disks, etc. The defining characteristic of 'direct mail', as opposed to an advertising campaign, is that the purpose of direct mail is to sell a product immediately through 'direct response', generate an inbound telesales lead, or push traffic to another channel such as a partner or retail store. That's what makes direct mail a *channel* – it establishes a two-way communication between seller and buyer so that a sales transaction can be consummated.

Direct mail is big business, with US-only revenues in 2001 of $580.3 billion, of which $225 billion, or 39 percent, were business-to-business sales.[115] That makes direct mail in the US just a little smaller in revenue production than telechannels, and competitive with Internet commerce (for the time being). This should be enlightening to the many skeptics who've been questioning the viability of paper-based mailings in an increasingly electronic economy. The fact is, direct mail is alive and well. Direct mail revenues are expected to increase 9.3 percent per year over the next five years, in line with the anticipated growth in telephone-based sales.[116]

As a channel, direct mail has many similar characteristics, and limitations, to telechannels. Like telechannels, direct mail is used both to complete deals on the spot (by having customers fill out order forms and mail or fax them back) as well as to push customers into other channels, such as a Web site, retail store, or telephone. And like telechannels, direct mail tends to work best with simpler, off-the-rack or lightly customized offerings. This channel is not well suited to complex offerings that require extensive customization or hand-holding in the sales process, unless the goal is just to get the customer over to another channel such as a field sales rep or partner.

---

[115] Source: Direct Marketing Association.
[116] *Ibid.*

Today, over 97 percent of all of traditional direct mail catalog firms are online, and their Internet sales already account for 13 percent of total revenues.[117] What this says is that the line between offline and online catalog sales is becoming blurry, as customers migrate back and forth at will between paper-based and electronic channel offerings.

Channel convergence

The point made above represents a crucial development in direct-to-customer marketing as a whole. Increasingly, customers use *all* of their vendors' direct-to-customer channels *together* when they purchase. For example, they may glance at a brochure that they receive in the mail, then go to the Web to perform more detailed research, and finally pick up the phone or visit a store when they are ready to place an order. This channel-surfing behavior on the part of customers has led some to speak in terms of *channel convergence* and of '*teleweb*' and *catalog/retail/web* channels, new phrases that acknowledge the thinning borders between direct-to-customer channels, if indeed these borders still exist at all. Channel convergence cannot be ignored; it is only going to increase over the coming years. Companies that have built one direct-to-customer channel while ignoring or avoiding others have experienced poor results. For example, many of the early Internet firms made it intentionally difficult to contact them over the phone. It didn't work, and most of these companies have paid a heavy price in customer dissatisfaction and lost sales. Likewise, many traditional direct mail catalogers were slow to realize the importance of the Web, and left their customers looking around for Internet sites that didn't exist. They too paid a heavy price.

It is wise to view the telephone, the Internet, and direct mail as different sides of the same direct-to-customer capability. This is certainly the approach of the world's leading direct marketers, such as Lands' End. Traditionally a mail-order catalog firm, Lands' End has gradually built a complete suite of direct-to-customer channels that customers can, and do, use interchangeably and seamlessly. In addition to the 269 million catalogs distributed by the company in 2001 (Lands' End catalog, Lands' End Kids, Lands' End Corporate Sales, etc.), today Lands' End has the largest apparel Web site, representing its entire

---

[117] Source: Direct Marketing Association.

consumer and corporate product lines. Its inbound telesales call centers receive an average of 40,000–50,000 calls per day, 364 days each year. The company also responded to each and every one of 231,000 emails last year, and has opened 16 retail stores. Wherever you want to buy clothes, Lands' End is there – and that, increasingly, is the successful model for going directly to customers. Anything less is likely to leave customers dissatisfied, as they become more and more accustomed to multi-channel models that offer them 'do business however you want' channel models.

To conclude our overview of channels, there are a lot of channels, and their numbers are growing. If anything characterizes the overall direction of go-to-market strategy today, it is *channel proliferation*, the steady increase in the numbers and types of channels, both indirect (partners), and direct (Web, phone, etc.). Industries that had two or three main channels to market a decade ago now have six or eight; industries that had ten choices in 1990 now have fifteen or more. All of this begs the question, 'Given all these channels, which ones should we use?' Let's take a look at the tools needed to answer that question.

CHANNEL AND PARTNER SELECTION

Unless you're starting up a whole new company, the fact is that you already use sales channels. After all, you *are* going to market today, whether it's through traditional sales reps, distributors, or the Web! The question is whether you have the *right* sales channels. In this section, we're going to look at a well-tested process for evaluating your current and potential channels, choosing the best ones for your business, and aligning them with the right opportunities in the market place. The process is shown in Figure 5.2 overleaf.

Let's take a look at each of the steps.

1. Build the Universe of Channels

If there's a common characteristic of companies that have limited, and limiting, channel models, it's that they fail to consider the full range of channel opportunities available to them. You don't want to make that mistake! You want to look into every feasible channel opportunity,

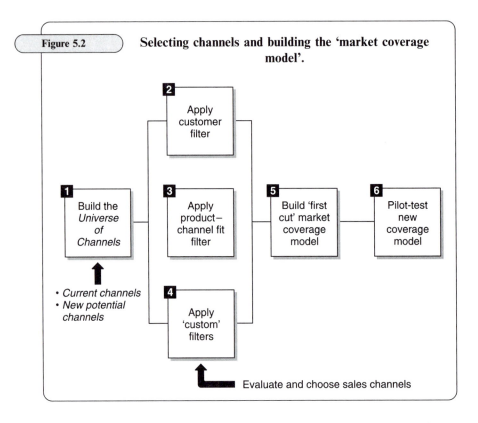

Figure 5.2 **Selecting channels and building the 'market coverage model'.**

and then carefully select the right ones. To do this, you must begin with a *Universe of Channels*, a master list of *all* of the channel options available to your organization, from which you can then make the best choices.

Start your Universe of Channels by identifying all of the channels that you use today for lead generation, sales, support, service, and account management. You might, for example, include your field sales force, your Web site, and your inside sales organization – or whatever mix of channels you already have in place.

Now for a more complex and difficult, but very rewarding, task. Build out the Universe of Channels by identifying all of the channels used by your direct competitors, as well as by other vendors and partners participating in your target markets. Examine their use (or lack of use) of all of the basic channel types: field sales reps, volume-oriented distributors and resellers, value-added partners, service and support partners, solution partners, telesales, telemarketing, telecoverage, public Web sites, private sites (extranets, intranets, etc.), digital market places, and direct mail. In addition, some of these channel types may need to be further subdivided in order to develop an accurate picture of channel activity in your markets. For example, in helping a printer manufacturer identify its potential channels to enter the commercial printing market, my firm, The Sales Strategy Institute, uncovered twelve separate types of local distributors actively serving the commercial printing space. Most markets are served by a wide variety of industry-specific partners, who must be identified beyond the superficial level of 'resellers and distributors'.

How deeply must you delve into the use of channels by competitors and other vendors in your markets? A good guideline is that, to develop a complete Universe of Channels, you should obtain answers to the following five questions:[118]

1. Which channels are our competitors (and others in our markets) using today?
2. What do they use those channels for – e.g. lead generation, sales, customer service and support?
3. Who do they use those channels to serve – do all channels serve all customers, or are some channels used just to cover certain types of customers?
4. How well are their channels working – which ones are providing the biggest 'bang for the buck' in terms of margins and in terms of new sales?
5. What new channels are they now building or considering for the future?

Once you've uncovered and analyzed the channels used by others in your target markets, it's time to engage in some 'out of the box' thinking. This is a crucial part of the Universe of Channels approach. After all, today's channel innovators and leaders didn't get where they are just by emulating the strategies of competitors. No amount of 'copycat' channel development would have led to Dell's decision to sell PCs over the telephone and Web, or to Schwab's development of a teleweb-retail 'surround sound' channel model. If you want to exert

---

[118] Through detailed competitive benchmarking, whether performed in-house or, more likely, through a research or strategy consultant.

leadership in your markets, and squeeze out big gains from your channels, you must take a fresh and creative look at new ways to connect with your target customers.

So what does 'out of the box' channel thinking look like? It can come in many forms, such as the deployment of a channel used successfully in another industry or another set of markets but not yet prevalent in your own. Or it can involve an entirely new approach, such as the use of competitors and their company-owned channels as your own routes to market. If partnering with the competition, and using their channels to sell your own products, sounds flighty or even ridiculous, consider a very real example from two of the toughest direct competitors you'll find anywhere: the United States Postal Service (USPS) and its ambitious, tough-as-nails competitor, FedEx.

The United States Postal Service delivered over 207 billion pieces of mail and generated revenues of $64.48 billion in 2000.[119] Those numbers make the USPS larger in revenues than all but ten companies in the US.[120] But profits are another story. In 1983 the USPS stopped receiving tax dollars to cover its operating losses, and it has increasingly faced economic hardship, with an estimated $2–3 billion shortfall for 2001.[121] High on the USPS' priority list are new strategies and tactics for achieving significant cost savings.

In another quarter of the ultra-competitive shipping business, Federal Express burst onto the US domestic scene in 1971. Using a 'central hub' package distribution model first envisioned in a business school paper (and awarded a low grade), the company has since grown into a $20 billion premier provider of transportation, e-commerce, and supply chain management services. Throughout its thirty-one-year history FedEx has become synonymous with overnight, guaranteed delivery – taking some of the most profitable shipping transactions away from none other than the USPS.

While the USPS is concerned about its bottom line, FedEx is concerned with capturing a larger share of business from small companies and

---

[119] Source: www.postalfacts.com
[120] Based on the Forbes 500 list. Source: www.forbes.com. The USPS ranks just ahead of Philip Morris ($63.28 billion) and behind Verizon ($64.7 billion).
[121] John Dimsdale, US postal service forms business partnership with FedEx. *Marketplace* (radio program), August 27, 2001.

today to purchase similar products. The results are shown in Table 5.3.

From this simple analysis, we were able to draw three important conclusions:

1. The national/regional distributor channel, while common for the purchase of 'off-the-rack' food preparation equipment, turned out to be used far less often for the purchase of specialty products such as those offered by G. Dobson. Just a third of the target customers 'always' or 'often' purchased specialty products through distributors, and over 40 percent rarely or never bought specialty products this way.
2. Independent manufacturers' reps – a channel that G. Dobson barely used and rarely thought about – had strong, dominant presence for specialty product sales in Dobson's target markets, with well over four customers in five 'sometimes', 'often' or 'always' purchasing specialty products from manufacturers' reps.

Table 5.3   Customer channel behavior analysis: G. Dobson & Son Manufacturing, Buffalo, NY
Please describe for us the channels that you use to purchase specialty *food preparation equipment such as pasta makers, smokers, and tortilla machines.*

Channel	We use this channel exclusively (%)	We use this channel often (%)	We use this channel sometimes (%)	We use this channel rarely (%)	We never use this channel (%)
Sales executive	2	8	12	57	21
National/regional distributor	10	25	21	26	17
Manufacturer's rep	14	46	27	12	1
Telephone sales call from manufacturer	0	2	12	58	28
Public Web site	0	4	5	30	61
Private Web site (e.g. extranet, EDI, etc.)	0	0	1	4	95
E-marketplace	0	1	4	3	92
Direct mail	0	0	4	17	79

3. The Internet, while certainly offering future possibilities, did not seem to be of much current interest to G. Dobson's target customers.

We then proceeded to ask the same customers how they planned to buy in the future. The enlightening results are shown below in Table 5.4.

The results – and one in particular – could not have been more important! Of G. Dobson's target customers, 40 percent intended do business 'often' or 'sometimes' over the Web. And while intended purchasing behavior on the Web was high across all customer groups, major hotel and restaurant chains, which were highly coveted by G. Dobson, planned to buy from vendors over both industry and private e-marketplaces as well.[128]

Table 5.4   Customer channel behavior: G. Dobson & Son Manufacturing, Buffalo, NY

Please describe for us the channels that you believe you will use in twelve to eighteen months to purchase specialty food preparation equipment such as pasta makers, smokers, and tortilla machines.

Channel	We will use this channel exclusively (%)	We will use this channel often (%)	We will use this channel sometimes (%)	We will use this channel rarely (%)	We will never use this channel (%)
Sales executive	2	7	15	53	23
National/regional distributor	9	18	21	31	21
Manufacturer's rep	12	48	25	14	1
Telephone sales call from manufacturer	0	3	12	61	24
Public Web site	0	14	26	32	28
Private Web site (e.g. extranet, EDI, etc.)	0	2	5	8	85
E-marketplace	0	5	12	22	61
Direct mail	0	0	5	19	76

[128] The data was collected, and analyzed, by type of customer (e.g. national hotel chains, restaurants, specialty grocers, etc.).

From the analysis of current and future (intended) channel behavior, G. Dobson was able to narrow its Universe of Channels down to a few key opportunities. The company focused *immediately* on building a strong manufacturers' rep channel to penetrate and serve its new target markets, and earmarked budget for the coming year to invest heavily in its Web site and in its participation in hospitality industry e-market-places. Other initiatives the company had been considering, such as expansion of the field sales organization and more emphasis on distributors, were scaled back for the time being.

As the example suggests, an analysis of customers' channel behaviors – both current and intended – can be a precise tool for narrowing your Universe of Channels to a core group that fits best with your target customers.

3. Apply product–channel fit filter

In the Third Commandment of Going to Market – all the way back in Chapter 2 – we discussed the fundamental go-to-market principle that:

> **How you sell has to fit with**
> **what you are selling.**

That's another way of saying that the channels you choose must fit with the products and services you sell. Sometimes the fit is obvious. For example, if you sell expensive consulting services, you'll probably want to sell them through well-trained, company-owned sales reps, but if you sell office supplies, you'd be better off with a lower-cost, high-reach channel such as a distribution network, catalog or Web site.

Sometimes, however, the fit between products and channels is more elusive and fuzzy. Let's say you sell computer software to help companies control expenses and monitor employee spending. Should you sell this product over the Web? Through partners? If so, what kinds of partners – high-volume distributors? Value-added resellers? All of the above? It isn't always so easy to decide which channels represent the best fit with your products and services!

In this step, we'll make the task easier by looking at four effective ways to evaluate product–channel fit in order to narrow down your Universe of Channels:

1. Product complexity and customization
2. Clarity of benefits
3. Risk and uncertainty
4. Negotiation.

Product complexity and customization

First and foremost, the complexity of your offerings – and the extent to which they must be customized and configured in the sales process – will greatly impact your channel choices.

Complex, highly-customized products usually require extensive configuration, design, training, support, and advice in the sales process. As a result, these offerings must often be sold through 'high-touch' channels, such as field sales reps and value-added partners, who can provide face-to-face interaction and guidance in the sales process.

Conversely, simpler products that require little if any customization, training, support, or advice in the sales process can usually be sold through 'low-touch' channels, which, as their name implies, offer little or no face-to-face support and interaction. Low-touch channels are preferable – *if they can handle your products and services* – because they can reach more customers at a lower cost. Figure 5.3 below suggests how channels line up in terms of the amount of 'touch' that they provide in the sales process.

A great example of the importance of channel touch comes from the software industry, where a friend of mine, the CEO of an independent software vendor – the one I mentioned earlier, that sells expense control and employee monitoring software – truly blew it in choosing a new go-to-market channel.

Pressured by his board of directors to get the company into 'hyper-growth' mode so it could go public, the CEO approached a number of leading high-volume corporate software distributors (a mid-touch channel; see Figure 5.3). The great thing about high-volume distributors is that they can move a *lot* of product – indeed, tens of thousands

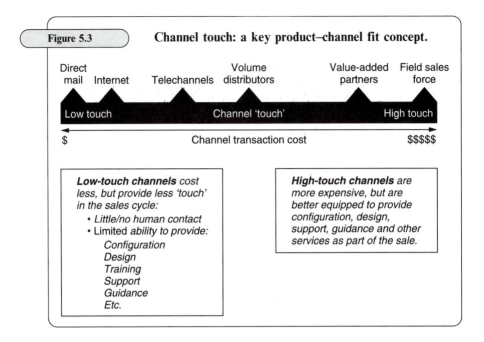

Figure 5.3 **Channel touch: a key product–channel fit concept.**

of copies or licenses of software programs. The downside is that this channel sells either 'shrink-wrapped boxes', or products that require so little tweaking that customers can do it themselves as part of a routine software installation process.

My friend's product fit that description, to some extent. You could load it on a computer, install it, and run it without any vendor support. However, all of the 'goodies' that made the program worthwhile required customization, by software engineers, to unique customer specifications. For instance, one module compared employee expense charges against lists of prohibited, controlled, and freely approved items by title, department, and division, and produced sharp-looking reports detailing compliance with both company spending guidelines and tax regulations. Without customization, that module couldn't be used appropriately, and the product became just another expense reporting program, which are a dime a dozen. As a result, the product flopped in the high-volume distributor channel, since these partners don't have software engineers on staff to work one-on-one with customers. Belatedly, my CEO friend realized that he needed 'higher-touch' partners – value-added resellers who, while selling in lower volumes, could provide the on-site customization that made the product compelling.

Low-cost channels, such as volume-oriented distributors, the Web, and telesales, are always appealing, because they cost less and reach more customers. The question is, are they suitable for your product or service? If your product is complex or requires configuration and customization in the sale, you may need to use more expensive 'higher-touch' channels. Or you may want to rethink the product so that it fits with a lower-touch channel, a topic we'll come back to in Chapter 6.

Clarity of benefits

Some products sell themselves; they provide obvious benefits and solve easily recognized problems. For example, do you need to print documents? Go buy a laser printer! You don't need to be told what a laser printer is or why you should buy one. No one has to 'sell' you on the idea. And that makes the laser printer an excellent candidate for a low-touch, low-cost channel such as the Web, which provides transaction processing without the 'overhead' of face-to-face interaction needed to convince someone that they should buy the product. And the Web is, in fact, a channel through which millions of laser printers are sold, directly to end-customers by manufacturers such as Hewlett-Packard, and indirectly through resellers such as CDW (a leading Web and telesales reseller).

Conversely, let's consider customer relationship management (CRM) software for the enterprise. Hey, what is that, anyway? How many people outside of the IT industry can really describe the benefits of an enterprise CRM software program? Come to think of it, how many people *inside* the IT industry can describe the benefits? Needless to say, such programs aren't frequently sold over the Web or telephone. The product itself, and its business benefits, must be articulated and described in a series of face-to-face sales calls.

Products and services with unclear or difficult-to-articulate benefits aren't bad products and services. They're often just new, or too complex to explain quickly and easily. These products are almost always sold by high-touch channels, such as field sales forces, that can patiently and carefully explain their benefits to customers. Other products, with clearer benefits and self-explanatory purposes, can usually be sold in lower-touch, lower-cost channels.

Risk and uncertainty

Did you worry the last time you bought a shirt, a coffee mug, or even a cell phone? Probably not. If any of these products didn't work, you could just throw them out and replace them. They pose no risk. As a result, you probably wouldn't mind saving some money by purchasing them through a low-cost channel such as the Internet, even if you didn't know whether the seller was reliable or likely to be in business ten years from now.

However, other offerings pose considerable, and even massive, risk – large, complex computer systems; expensive contracts for management consulting services; construction of a new office building; brain surgery. With these kinds of products and services, if something goes wrong you'll lose more than a lot of money. They pose high risk. You are not going to purchase these products and services through an impersonal channel. You are going to demand a face-to-face interaction – a high-touch channel.

The higher the risk involved in purchasing the product or service, the further up the channel touch continuum the sales will probably have to be made. If your offerings are risky to customers, you'd have to think very carefully before pushing them down the continuum to lower-touch channels.

Negotiation

Many products have fixed prices, standard terms and conditions, and absolutely no room for negotiation. These include many routine business purchases, and most lower-priced consumer items too. Needless to say, the absence of anything to negotiate about fits well with low-touch channels, which don't provide the people needed to negotiate!

On the other hand, not every product or service fits that description. In consumer sales, more expensive offerings such as cars, houses, and jewelry all involve heavy-duty negotiation as part of the sales process. In business-to-business sales, many higher-priced products and services, as well as any high-quantity purchase of even the simplest commodities, involve substantial negotiation of prices and terms. Who, exactly, is supposed to do the negotiating from the seller's side if the seller chooses a low-touch channel? While some developments with the Internet have been encouraging, in terms of accommodating negotiation (e.g. auction sites, e-marketplaces, etc.), the truth is that we still live in a world in which serious negotiation is still done face to face. If your products and services have negotiable prices or terms, or other variable components that must be worked out one-on-one with customers, you'll find it very difficult to move your sales to low-touch channels.

In sum, the channels you choose must fit well with your products and services. Complex, risky, or negotiated offerings, or offerings that must be explained in the sales process, tend to require higher-touch channels. Simple, low-risk, fixed-price products can be sold through any channel, and are ideal for low-cost, high-reach channels.

4. Apply 'custom' filters

Once you've assessed your Universe of Channels against your customers and products, the next step is to consider whether your organization has any unique goals or requirements that would create a need for special additional filters.

What kind of custom filters should you consider? The most common two filters are *profitability* and *time-to-market*.

Profitability

If higher profits are a key corporate goal, then channel transaction costs will be an essential filter for your Universe of Channels. Channels vary wildly in their costs-to-serve, and therefore have a huge impact on overall company margins. Let's take a look again at relative channel costs, using a figure first shown in Chapter 2 but reprinted here for convenience as Figure 5.4.

As Figure 5.4 illustrates, direct-to-customer channels such as the Web and telephone are the least expensive way to sell, but volume distributors can also be effective in reducing the cost-to-serve. Higher-touch channels, on the other hand, such as value-added partners and especially field sales reps, do not fit well with a goal of increased profitability. That's precisely why so many companies today are attempting to migrate from high-touch channels to lower-touch channels. Depending on the importance of profitability to your company, a

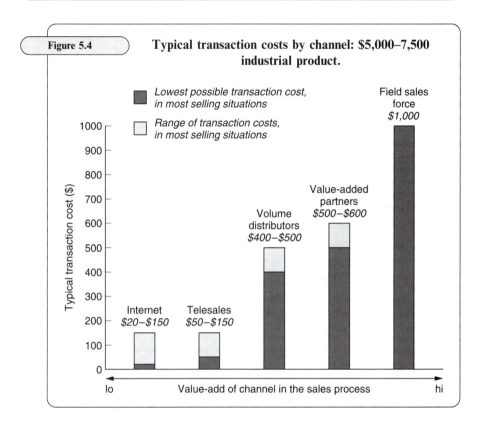

Figure 5.4   **Typical transaction costs by channel: $5,000–7,500 industrial product.**

channel cost-to-serve filter may be an essential part of your channel evaluation process.

Time-to-market

For some companies, the goal of a channel initiative is to sell more products and services *quickly*. If you share this goal, then you will definitely want to include a time-to-market filter.

Simply put, some channels provide faster times-to-market than others. For example, you could get a small, internally staffed tele-marketing operation up and running within a week. You could also hire more sales reps within a month. And while prestigious, high-end partners can take a long time to recruit, local, regional partners may be readily available to help you sell into new markets. These chan-nels stand in contrast to the long lead-times needed to build complex Internet channels – and to get customers to go to them. Technology-based channels are not usually the quickest routes to immediate sales – a useful consideration if short-term results are a priority in your organization.

Other filters

Your company may have other goals that create the need for additional custom filters. For instance, companies with exclusive, high-end products may want to put channels through a 'prestige filter' that vets potential partners for the ability to represent a high-end brand effectively in the market place, thus eliminating mass-market distributors and other 'low-end' resellers. To take another example, some companies seek partners with specific post-sale support capabilities, such as the presence of a full-time technical service representative trained and certified in their product offerings. Any unique goals held by your organization, such as these, can be translated into a channel filter against which to evaluate your Universe of Channels.

In all, then, you've got three types of filters to consider – customers' needs and behaviors, product–channel fit, and custom filters needed to align your choice of sales channels with your company's goals. Let's take a look at how these three filters can quickly bring shape and clarity to a channel selection initiative. Figure 5.5 (opposite) shows how a fairly extensive Universe of Channels has been put through all the filters to result in a basic two-channel offering.

Of course, once you've settled on a group of sales channels, you still have to decide what to do with them. And that brings us to the next step, development of the *market coverage model*.

5. Build 'first cut' market coverage model

A *market coverage model* answers the question, 'Which channels will sell which products to which customers?' Put another way, it defines how each of the sales channels that passed your various filter tests will be applied to your target markets.

There are different approaches for building a market coverage model. To take one example, you could serve your smallest customers with low-cost channels such as a Web site or call center, your medium-sized customers with business partners, and your largest accounts with field

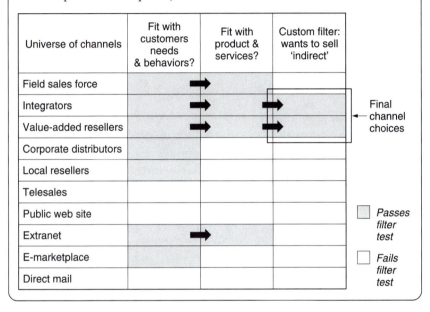

Figure 5.5 **Applying channel 'filters' to the Universe of Channels (example).**

A high-end manufacturer of customized workstations has vetted its universe of channels against customer behaviors and product–channel fit. It has one final, 'custom' filter: it wants to sell through indirect channels so that it can refocus its efforts on product development, not sales.

sales reps. A very different approach would be to let all customers do business with you however they want – through whichever channels they prefer. As a third alternative, you could reserve a special high-touch channel, such as your field sales force, for a small number of key accounts, while serving the remainder of your customers with a blend of lower-cost, higher-reach channels. Each of these three basic approaches, which we'll look at in a moment, have their advantages and disadvantages. What you *don't* want is to have all of your channels haphazardly 'out there' in the market place, competing against each other and creating havoc. Avoiding that situation is the purpose of building a market coverage model.

In developing an *initial* market coverage model, perfection isn't necessary, because the coverage model will evolve over time in any event as you and your channels adapt to market conditions, and as you learn what works and what doesn't. The goal should be just to develop a sound, workable channel coverage concept that will get you out in front of a lot of target customers, cost-effectively. Let's take a look at the three basic ways to do that.

Option 1: Selective market coverage

Selective market coverage refers to an approach common in the past but less popular today, in which you assign each of your different sales channels to discrete markets and segments, thus minimizing or even eliminating the overlap between channels as they pursue sales opportunities. This approach is illustrated in Figure 5.6.

As the figure suggests, in selective market coverage you begin by dividing your overall market into discrete 'product-markets' such as 'off-the-rack products sold to large corporate accounts' and 'complex solutions sold into the middle market'. Next, you assign each channel to serve a different product market. In Figure 5.6, for example, field sales reps are tasked with selling complex solutions into large, enterprise accounts, while mail-order catalogs are used to reach and serve small businesses with simple or mass-customized products. The idea behind selective market coverage is to keep each channel in its own 'silo', serving a discrete and unique group of customers on its own.

This approach has two notable strengths, and two significant disadvantages. Its first strength is that it minimizes conflict between chan-

Figure 5.6   **Market coverage example: selective market coverage.**

Markets / Products	Simple, 'off-the-rack' products	Mass-customized products	Complex, unique solutions
Large, enterprise customers	Corporate resellers	Field sales reps	Field sales reps
Mid-sized accounts	Corporate resellers	Solution partners	Solution partners
Small office/home office	Mail order catalog	Mail order catalog	(unserved space)

nels. For example, you don't have to worry too much about your mail order catalog channel stealing sales from resellers, or resellers bumping up against your field sales reps in accounts, as long as you keep these channels pointed at different sectors of the market. Minimization of channel conflict tends to keep partners happy and margins high. A second strength is that this type of coverage model is relatively easy to manage. For example, it is easy to monitor the performance and sales activity of individual channels when each of them is assigned to a discrete market. You can easily count the sales of specific products sold into specific markets, and credit those sales to the channels assigned to those product-markets – something that you cannot do as easily, or at all, when multiple channels sell lots of different products into the same market segments.

But make no mistake about it: selective market coverage is a model with significant disadvantages. First, there is a difference between designing a coverage model on paper and making it work in the market place. Real channels working in real markets do not perform 'to specifications'. Resellers assigned to certain products or to smaller accounts may covet larger opportunities and pursue customers they are supposed to avoid – as they often do. Customers assigned to one channel, such as resellers, may use other channels, such as the Web or the telephone, thus breeding resentment among channel partners who were promised a certain group of markets for their own. In the end, it usually proves impossible to engineer a strict separation of channels.

The second disadvantage is that the assignment of individual channels to discrete markets is often at odds with customer buying preferences. Customers do not like being forced into one channel or another; they strongly prefer to have options. Attempts to force them into a particular channel usually fail. They either go to the channel(s) they prefer, or they go over to a competitor. You can tell your own sales reps where to sell, and sometimes you can even tell your partners where to sell, but you can't tell customers where to buy. That, in a nutshell, is why highly engineered, carefully constructed selective market coverage models tend to fall apart as soon as they're deployed in the market place.

> You can tell your own sales reps where to sell, and sometimes you can even tell your partners where to sell, but you can't tell your customers where to buy.

Option 2: Intensive market coverage

In intensive market coverage, all channels sell most or all products to all customers. It is the 'maximum flexibility' model, designed to let all customers do business however they want, whenever they want, wherever they want. This approach is illustrated in Figure 5.7.

Intensive market coverage has genuine appeal, in that it responds *completely* to the trends of customer choice and channel convergence. It meets customers on their own terms, and lets them migrate to their preferred channels. As a result, a 'conventional wisdom' has taken hold that this is the coverage model of the future: the approach that all companies will use just as soon as they figure out that anyone should be able to buy anything, anywhere.

Unfortunately, it is also a model that works much better on paper than it does in real markets with real partners and customers. For one thing, oversaturation of markets by multiple channels, particularly when partners compete against both field sales reps and direct-to-customer channels, results in high levels of channel conflict, leading to eroded margins and defection of the best partners. For another, providing a huge inventory of channels to cover the same segments is not exactly a cost-effective approach. All of those channels must be built, maintained and managed, which costs money. No one can afford to give every customer everything.

Figure 5.7   **Market coverage example: intensive market coverage.**

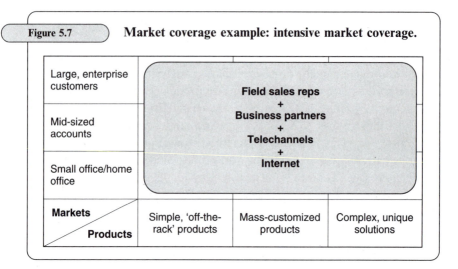

Perhaps most importantly, as discussed in Chapter 2, every company has premium customers who deserve and expect high-end, differentiated services. No one can afford to ignore top-tier customers' valid expectations for special offerings, including channel offerings. Giving every customer every channel implicitly involves writing off the opportunity to give extra special treatment to a crucial subset of top-of-the-line customers. As we noted in Chapter 2, for this very reason, despite all the hype regarding 'let anyone do business anywhere', few if any companies actually use pure intensive market coverage.

Option 3: Hybrid market coverage

In a hybrid market coverage model, a core, select group of premium customers is provided with high-touch, premium channels, while the remainder of the market is offered a convenient, but lower cost, multiple-channel mix. There are many varieties of hybrid coverage models. For instance, in a 'three tier' model, you might cover your top twenty-five global accounts with global account managers from the sales force (tier 1), another hundred or so key accounts with high-end solution partners (tier 2), and the remainder of the market with a mix of direct-to-customer channels (tier 3). In a simpler, two-tier approach, you might cover your top global accounts with field sales reps, and all other customers with a mix of partners and low-cost alternative channels. This approach is illustrated in Figure 5.8.

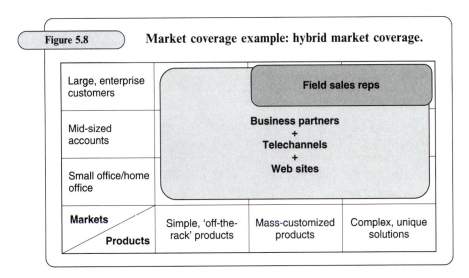

Figure 5.8 **Market coverage example: hybrid market coverage.**

Markets \ Products	Simple, 'off-the-rack' products	Mass-customized products	Complex, unique solutions
Large, enterprise customers		Field sales reps	
Mid-sized accounts		Business partners + Telechannels + Web sites	
Small office/home office			

Hybrid market coverage has real advantages. It uses an aggressive mix of alternative channels to extend penetration and 'reach' into the smaller and middle markets, giving customers in those markets what they want – a flexible set of purchasing options. At the same time it also carves off a top-end segment of the market to be served by premium, higher-touch channels – thus giving exclusive customers what they want and expect. Hybrid coverage does have some of the same problems as other models, such as channel conflict in the middle market (where multiple channels and partners compete for sales), as well as higher sales costs than a pure alternative-channel model. Yet, in situations in which customers demand lots of choices, but also where a select group of premium customers must be coddled and protected, hybrid coverage is best able to accommodate these different and competing interests. Hybrid coverage is the model used by most of the channel innovators described in this book, such as Dell Computer and Charles Schwab & Company, and is a highly recommended approach in most circumstances.

Whichever approach you choose, the important thing is to put a market coverage model down on paper and get on with it! For many companies, the real risk in market coverage isn't the development of a bad model, but the development of no model at all. Insistent on micro-engineering every last detail of the coverage model, managers spend months and months poring over documents, making slide presentations, and debating whether this-or-that type of channel or partner can best serve this-or-that type of market, while sales go over to competitors and potential partners lose interest. The best approach is to develop a 'first cut', and probably imperfect, coverage model, and then to go test it in the market place – the subject of the next step.

6. Pilot-test new market coverage model

A new market coverage model should be 'pilot-tested' before it is deployed fully in the market place. A pilot-test is a carefully controlled test run of a new coverage model in a managed, low-risk environment, to ensure that it works prior to making a large commitment and investment.

Pilot-testing is much wiser than bringing a new market coverage model to market all at once. The fact is, new market coverage concepts often miss the mark on the first attempt. For example, you may decide to add a call center or a certain type of reseller to your existing sales force coverage of a vertical market. Despite the best efforts to anticipate and avoid potential issues, either of these channels may meet with customer resistance or even outright rejection. Alternatively, these channels may be accepted by customers and work fine on their own, but they may collide and compete with your sales force or with each other, creating channel conflict and customer confusion. When covering a market with a new mix of channels, it's better to uncover these kinds of problems in a controlled and low-cost pilot-test before taking the model 'live' to the broader market place.

So what should a pilot-test look like? The most effective approach is to introduce simple, 'first cut' channels into small, targeted market segments. This may involve something as straightforward as hiring a telemarketing firm for two months to generate middle-market leads, in order to test your hypothesis that these customers will be receptive to an eventual full-blown, in-house call center. Or it could involve the recruitment of five or ten resellers for a regional market such as Georgia/Northern Florida, prior to a larger intended recruitment effort of 150 resellers in this region – and then observing how the five or ten resellers perform. As another example, it could involve putting up a simple extranet for your existing insurance customers, to see how, and how often, they use it before making a big investment in feature-rich private Web sites for these customers and for customers in your other vertical markets.

Your market coverage pilot-test should be based on the following three principles.

1. *Representative, but low-risk, markets.* The pilot-test should be conducted in a geographical or industry/vertical market that is representative of your markets as a whole, yet non-mission-critical. For example, if your company sells mostly to manufacturing customers, then a manufacturing segment is the appropriate place for a pilot-test. However, within manufacturing, a non-essential segment should be chosen. So if electronics and equipment manufacturers are your high priority segments, it would be better to pilot-test your coverage model in another, non-vital manufacturing vertical such as apparel or steel. In so doing, you'll get a sense for whether your coverage model is on track without putting an important target market at risk.

2. *One or two new channels*. Your channel selection process may lead you toward three types of partners and three or four direct-to-customer channels. That's all well and good for the long run, but for the purpose of a pilot-test, it's too much. You'll end up with a slew of confusing findings. For example, let's say you introduce a call center, a reseller channel, some solution partners, a direct mail campaign, and a Web site into the small-company market, and sales go up 15 percent. Which channel would you say produced the results? You just won't know. As a result, you won't be able to decide which channels should be built out and which, if any, should be eliminated. A pilot-test should consist, at most, of one indirect and one direct-to-customer channel. You might, for instance, introduce a call center to create new leads (telemarketing), while adding in some local VARs. After these two new channels have proven themselves, there will be plenty of time later to introduce more new channels to the mix.

3. *Results monitoring*. It's crucial to monitor key performance indicators (KPIs), both before and after the pilot-test. Otherwise, your pilot-test will produce inconclusive or fuzzy findings. Revenues, margins, customer satisfaction and loyalty, channel transaction costs, or whatever is important to your organization, should be assessed prior to the pilot-test and then ninety days into the pilot-test, to see what differences your new coverage approach made.[129] Only a careful analysis of post-pilot results, measured against pre-pilot performance, will provide you with the certainty you need to take a new coverage model to your broader base of customers. Figure 5.9 suggests some of the important things to look for at the ninety-day mark of the pilot-test.

Once your pilot-test is complete, and you've carefully analyzed the results, you'll be able to make an informed decision as to whether your new-and-improved coverage model is ready for 'prime time' across your markets. Most likely, a fair amount of 'tuning' will be required. The pilot-test will uncover the kinks in the system and point you in the direction of a smooth-running channel model. At that point, you will be ready for the remaining two challenges of go-to-market strategy: ensuring that you have the right products and

---

[129] Don't expect results in less than ninety days. It takes ninety days at a minimum to see the results of a new market coverage model.

| Figure 5.9 | **Assessing the pilot-test: six areas to explore, ninety days into the pilot-test.** |

☑ **Sales from new channels**: How much sales revenue has been generated by each of the new channel(s) introduced to the target market? Did new channels meet sales expectations or fall short of expectations?

☑ **Channel shift vs. lift**: Have sales revenues generated by new channels been 'stolen' from channels that were already serving the target market prior to the pilot-test ('channel shift'), or do they represent legitimate new sales ('channel lift')?

☑ **Reach & penetration**: Is the new coverage model reaching the customers it is supposed to reach? How effective has it been in deepening penetration in the target market? Are the right new customers being captured and served?

☑ **Selling margins**: Have total selling costs to serve the target market gone up or down? Is the new coverage model delivering improvements in profitability?

☑ **Customer satisfaction**: Has customer satisfaction increased or decreased? Are customers happier – or less happy – with the new coverage model than they were with the old coverage model?

☑ **Channel conflict**: Is there conflict between channels serving the target market? If so, is it a tolerable amount of confict, or is it a problem that must be fixed?

---

value propositions for your channels, and figuring out how those channels should work *together* in the sales process – the subject of Chapters 6 and 7.

SUMMARY

We covered a lot of ground in this chapter! Channel selection and strategy is a large and complex body of knowledge, and not an easy one to put into a neat and tidy box or a set of simple definitions. After all, we are talking here about the entire range of issues involved in taking your products and services to customers, in every possible way! While we didn't cover every possible facet of sales channels, we did take a good stab at the overall set of issues involved in identifying, evaluating and selecting them.

We started off with a simple but inclusive definition of sales channels: they are the 'pipes' that enable two-way communication and commerce between sellers and buyers. We then discussed the three basic types of channels:

1. *Direct sales channel.* This type of channel consists of all varieties of company-employed sales reps, such as national account managers and account executives. In a multi-channel system, the challenge is to focus sales force activity on complex sales and key accounts, while migrating other types of sales to lower-cost channels.

2. *Indirect channels.* Indirect channels consist of all shapes and sizes of intermediaries, or business partners. The four major categories are *volume partners, value partners, solution partners,* and *service partners.* Partners can play a valuable role in a multi-channel mix, providing similar or even better levels of service and hand-holding as field sales reps, at a much lower cost. They are very effective at reaching and serving dispersed geographical markets, and providing local support to customers.

3. *Direct-to-customer channels.* These are channels, other than a field sales force, that enable you to do business directly with customers, i.e. without intermediaries such as distributors or resellers. The three major types are telechannels, the Internet, and direct mail. The key advantage of direct-to-customer channels is that they provide the ability to sell 'off-the-rack' or lightly customized products at a very low cost.

Next, we looked at a robust six-step process for selecting sales channels and assigning them to 'cover' the market place. The steps included the following:

1. *Build the Universe of Channels.* The purpose of this step is to identify *all* the possible channels that can connect you with your target customers.

2. *Apply customer filter.* In this step, you carefully prune your Universe of Channels to select only those channels that fit with the needs and buying behaviors of your target customers.

3. *Apply product–channel fit filter.* Here, channels that fit poorly with your products and services are eliminated from the mix.

4. *Apply 'custom' filters.* In this step, you identify and apply additional filters to ensure that your channel choices align with your own goals and business needs.

5. *Build 'first cut' market coverage model.* Here, the channels that have made it through your various filters are assigned to 'product-markets'. The recommended model, for most companies, is hybrid coverage, in which a premium channel is offered

to top-end customers, while a mix of convenient, lower-cost channels is offered to the rest of the market.

6. *Pilot-test market coverage model.* In this final step, the new market coverage map is pilot-tested in a low-risk geography or vertical market, in order to assess its effectiveness prior to going 'live' in the overall market.

Now that you have a channel coverage model – a group of sales channels, and a game plan for applying them against market opportunities – it's time to ensure that you have the right things to put into those channels. Channels must be filled with the right products and services, as well as the right 'message' – a compelling value proposition that motivates buyers toward purchasing activity. Filling your channels with the right products and messages is the subject of Chapter 6.

6

Go-to-market strategy:

Rethinking your products and value proposition

I t may seem strange to have a chapter on products in a book on go-to-market strategy. After all, Chapters 3–5 dealt with 'marketing' issues, and you would expect to find them in a book on go-to-market strategy, whereas products are, well, 'product' issues. In many organizations, marketing and product development have been kept separate over the years, with the general view being that some people make stuff, while others sell it. Marketing types worry about things like market segmentation and branding, while engineers and technologists worry about things like product features and functionality. This is an age-old and fundamental distinction. The gap between the two, at many companies, is one through which you could drive a truck, and in which some of the least effective of all internal communication takes place. So what on earth is a chapter on products doing in a book on go-to-market strategy?

Put simply, the separation of marketing and products does not work anymore. Something very significant has changed, and it has radically impacted the ability of companies to put marketing issues and product issues into separate silos.

In the old days, you first made a product and then you gave that product to your channel – your sales force or distributors – to sell. *How* you sold the product had little or no impact on the product itself. Why would it? The very idea of designing a product to fit with a certain sales strategy had little relevance in a world dominated by field sales forces and distributors.

That, however, is no longer the world in which we live. Our world consists of multiple types of channels, including newer direct-to-customer channels. These channels can have a dramatic and crucial impact on your choice of *what* to sell. Planning to sell over the telephone or Web? Then you are definitely going to have to rethink your products and develop versions of them that can be sold effectively through those low-touch channels. You'll have to reconsider how they are priced, configured and packaged, because newer channels, and the new customers who purchase through these channels, require different products than older 'high-touch' channels and the customers who buy through them. As a result, a modern go-to-market strategy initiative, particularly one that involves the use of low-cost channels, must include an evaluation and in some cases even a redesign of your products.

In this chapter, we will take a straightforward look at products, focusing on the impact of go-to-market change on their design. We'll focus on three key topics:

1. *The impact of market and customer change on products.* Part of almost every go-to-market initiative involves the targeting of new markets and customers. When you target new markets and customers, you must address some key questions. Do new customers have the same needs and buying expectations as your existing ones? Do they want to buy the same kinds of products that you've been selling to your traditional customers? Or do they require something *different*? If you are planning to target new markets and customers, you may have to rethink your offerings, or at least develop new versions of them. What you *don't* want to do is to go into a new market with a product that's poorly tuned to the needs of new target customers just because these products have sold well elsewhere. Whenever new markets and new customers are involved, there is just no escaping the need to take a cold, hard look at your offerings. In this chapter, we'll take a look at the impact of new market and customer initiatives on your product design efforts.

2. *The impact of channel change on products.* As noted earlier, the deployment of new sales channels will impact on your offerings. Products that sell well in some channels may sell poorly in others. In particular, products that sell well in high-touch face-to-face channels, such as field sales reps, often flop or fail to generate customer demand in lower-cost, lower-touch channels. Depending on your intended mix of sales channels, you may have to redesign your offerings to ensure they are suited to the channels that you intend to use. In this chapter, we will look at the issues involved in redesigning or reconfiguring a product to fit with a new channel strategy.

3. *Rethinking the 'value proposition'.* With go-to-market change comes a need to rethink not only your offerings, but also the messages and communication that accompanies those offerings – your *value proposition*. Market, customer or channel change can dramatically impact your messaging strategy. For example, a message that compelled buying activity from large corporate accounts when delivered through field sales reps may be meaningless or even harmful when delivered to small business customers by direct-to-customer channels. Just like products, your

value proposition must be 'tuned' to fit with a new go-to-market strategy. Later on in this chapter, we'll take a look at some of the basic issues involved in tuning the message to a new set of market, customer and channel parameters.

Let's get started by looking at the impact on your offerings of new market and customer initiatives.

THE IMPACT OF MARKET AND CUSTOMER CHANGE

Most go-to-market initiatives include the targeting of new markets, or, at the least, the targeting of new groups or segments of customers within existing markets. For example, your go-to-market initiative may involve the penetration of a whole new vertical market, or may focus more narrowly on acquiring mid-market customers within an existing vertical market. Either way, you'll be selling to new people. In addition, even if your go-to-market initiative is basically focused not on markets but on channel expansion – such as the deployment of an e-business capability – the odds are high that you are building this new channel in order to reach new customers.

That's important, because new customers will have different needs than your existing customers. They will have different expectations and requirements, and you must be prepared to respond with new products, or at the least updated configurations of your existing products. Your offerings will have to be priced, configured, and packaged correctly for your new customers. Failure to ensure a strong fit between your products and your new target customers can have very bad consequences for the overall success of a go-to-market initiative.

As an example, consider the experience of Rothstein Travis, an $80 million computer consulting and services firm based in my neck of the woods, northern Virginia.[130] A provider of high-end business intelligence software, the company focused from its inception on acquiring and serving large, Fortune 500 customers. It was a good strategy for nearly a decade, but by the middle of 2000 Rothstein Travis concluded that it was tapped out in the 'enterprise' market (i.e. Fortune 500), and

---

[130] A pseudonym, at the request of the company.

that intense competition from the likes of Cognos, Oracle, and SAS Institute in this space would not let up anytime soon. The company's executives decided that it would be preferable to be a large fish in a smaller pond, and in early 2001 Rothstein Travis embarked on an ambitious new strategy to reach middle-market customers, which they defined as companies with $500 million to $3 billion in annual revenues. Often under-served by the larger players, these customers were believed to represent a better opportunity for business expansion and growth.

To get the new initiative off the ground, Rothstein Travis began with an analysis of the purchasing behaviors of its new target customers, which led to the conclusion that many of the smaller ones would consider renting software over the Web through Application Service Providers (ASPs). Larger customers – those closer to $3 billion than $500 million in sales – expected and demanded direct field rep support. Based on this analysis, Rothstein Travis decided to partner with a few key ASPs while expanding its sales force. Deals were made with three leading ASPs, and fifteen new sales reps were hired. Off into the market place it went.

There was just one problem. Rothstein Travis had done an admirable job of uncovering a new market opportunity, and a decent job of identifying the right channel mix to serve this market. However, the company never thought to re-evaluate its product in light of its new go-to-market initiative. The 'product' turned out to be Rothstein Travis' Achilles' heel. It consisted of a $175,000 business intelligence software platform combined with $200,000–350,000 in customization to unique customer specifications, and twelve-month support agreements in the $100,000 range. With a total package price of $475,000–625,000, the offering exceeded by far the typical budget of a mid-market customer. It was also far too complex, and required more in-house maintenance and IT expertise than a typical mid-market customer had or would want to get.

As a result, the initiative bombed. The company acquired just six new accounts over a period of four months, and all of them were right around the $3 billion mark – just below the cutoff of the Fortune 500. In fact, all of them could have been reached simply by extending the traditional focus from the Fortune 500 to the Fortune 600, without doing any new market or channel development. Smaller customers had

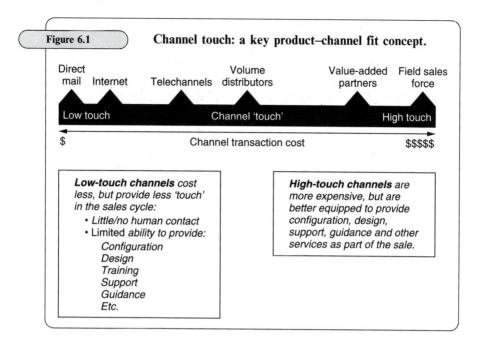

Figure 6.1 **Channel touch: a key product–channel fit concept.**

etc., in the sales process, then they may not be suitable *in their current form* for new lower-cost channels. If your go-to-market objective is to make more or better use of low-cost channels, then you will need to take a good, hard look at your products to determine whether they fit with these new channels. If they've traditionally been sold through high-touch channels, the odds are high that they'll need to be rethought and redesigned to work with your new channel mix. Beyond a *requirement* to redesign your products to fit with new low-cost channels, you may *choose* to develop new versions of existing products in order to take full advantage of the potential reach of low-cost channels. Even if you could, in theory, sell a complex offering through a channel such as the Web, you might well choose to develop a simplified version of it in order to extract the maximum possible sales potential out of this new medium.

An excellent example of an entire industry that has gone through several major product redesigns, in order to succeed in new low-cost sales channels, is the personal computer (PC) business.

Personal computer manufacturers started out in the late 1970s selling temperamental, crash-prone, highly-customized PCs through high-cost specialty retail shops, such as Apple Computer stores. Salespeople in these stores were able to provide the substantial customer hand-holding, training, configuration, and customization that was required to sell first-generation personal computers. By the 1980s, however, PC manufacturers realized that low-volume specialty shops lacked the ability to reach a mass market of consumers, and were therefore a drag on revenue growth. As a result, PC makers looked to mass-market distributors such as CompUSA and Best Buy in order to take their products to the broader mass of potential consumers. It was good thinking, and was probably more responsible for the wide-scale consumer adoption of computers than any other factor. However, to make the PC sale work in this new channel, the product had to be 'dumbed down' from a complex, custom sale to a relatively standard box offered in a smaller number of configurations. PCs that were basically built from scratch evolved into relatively standard offerings that came in a few different flavors (e.g. different hard disk size, processor speed, screen size and resolution, etc.)

Over the past six or seven years, PC manufacturers have taken their efforts to go 'mass market' to the next level, by selling PCs and laptops over new direct-to-customer channels such as the telephone and Web. These channels, with virtually unlimited reach across the globe, have finally given PC manufacturers the ability to realize Bill Gates' long-standing vision of 'a computer in every home'. However, these new low-touch channels have very limited ability to provide support and guidance in the sales process. To make the PC sale a success in these channels, PC manufacturers again had to redesign the product, this time by bundling in some product training on compact disks, standardizing the PC to a smaller number of easily understood configurations, reducing the complexity of features, simplifying the price points, and preloading the system and application software so that inexperienced users could buy a PC, turn it on, and get to work. All of these design elements were required to make the PC into a product that consumers would be able and willing to purchase without any face-to-face guidance in the sales process. Today's mass-customized Web-purchased PC or laptop bears little resemblance to the fussy, totally customized boxes sold in computer stores nearly twenty years ago.

In sum, PC manufacturers have migrated, over a period of two decades, from high-touch to low-touch channels, and have had to rethink and redesign their products every step of the way in order to make sure those products were ready for their new channels.

You, too, may need to revisit your offering if you want to sell through new channels, and particularly if you want to take advantage of low-cost direct-to-customer channels. You will need to ensure that your offering is 'channel ready'. The tools at your disposal include the following:

1. *Product standardization and product line reduction.* Many companies have bloated product catalogs, with hundreds or even thousands of products spread across dozens of product lines. While there is no *technical* reason why you cannot sell all of those products through a low-cost channel, the fact is that an overwhelming product catalog tends to confuse customers; it often requires the presence of a face-to-face rep to explain the applicability of different products to different purchasing situations. When using a channel that doesn't provide face-to-face interaction, it's important to present a comprehensible product line from which customers can make the right choices without a lot of support. That's why you see companies increasingly offering just a subset of products through their alternative channels, while keeping the larger product line in reserve for face-to-face selling to key corporate customers.

2. *Feature simplification.* The more confused a prospect becomes in evaluating a product, and the more the prospect believes that advice is needed in the sale, the less likely he or she is to complete the transaction in a low-cost, alternative channel. Complex, feature-laden products sell poorly through channels such as the Web, telephone, or direct mail for just this reason; these channels are far more successful with products that have been streamlined and simplified. As a result, along with reducing the sheer quantity of products offered, it's important to simplify those products so they can be sold effectively through alternative channels.

3. *Pricing simplification – and reduction.* Products with complicated pricing schemes, such as licensing fees, complicated discount formulae, or negotiation, tend to require face-to-face discussion, and therefore work poorly in alternative channels. If you want to make use of these channels, you'll need to revisit your pricing strategy and ensure that it is clear, simple, and suitable for impersonal channels. In addition, customers will expect a financial incentive for doing business through alternative channels, in the form of lower prices. Unless you have a specific reason for maintaining high prices in a low-cost channel, such as the need to

avoid conflict with resellers, it's wise to pass along some of the cost-savings to your customers. Lower prices create much stronger customer acceptance of alternative channels.

4. *Bundled training and procedures.* An inherent weakness of most low-cost channels is their inability to provide the quality of training and instruction that's possible with a face-to-face channel such as a field sales force. Despite the recent enthusiasm for Web-based training, no low-cost channel has yet equaled the effectiveness of human experts in instructing customers in the use of a product. This will be a significant issue if your offering requires a lot of training, and may impede your ability to sell it through low-cost channels. To get around this issue, you may have to bundle in your training materials and manuals with the product itself, and you may need to upgrade the quality and comprehensiveness of those materials significantly.

5. *Standardization of terms and conditions.* Products with customized, 'one-off' terms and conditions fare *very* poorly in alternative channels. In fact, it is virtually impossible to negotiate individual terms and conditions through a low-cost channel. To succeed in these channels, you must develop a standard 'term sheet' that applies to *any* customer doing business through the channel.

6. *Streamlining of financial terms and processes.* While some products can be paid for with a credit card, many others require financing and financial support in the sale. If your products require complex financing, financial applications, and approvals, you will need to think carefully about how all of this can be simplified. Customers will fill out credit applications over the phone or Web, but they will not be patient with complex and time-consuming financial application processes. You will have to find a way to boil down the financial component of your sale to simple forms and processes that will meet the needs of customers – and with which they will be willing to comply.

7. *'Support' channel.* Finally, most products require some kind of support after the sale, such as problem resolution, the fixing or replacement of malfunctioning products, and the answering of general customer inquiries and questions. Some of this can be done in low-cost channels, but the truth is, you will probably have to provide a secondary 'support' channel to make it all work effectively. These channels can range from third-party support partners to the availability of face-to-face reps to deal with particularly difficult problems. Identifying and building an effec-

tive post-sale support channel can mean the difference between success and failure in getting a new low-cost channel to work effectively in selling to customers.

In the end, there is little doubt that you will have to rethink and redesign your offering if you want it to succeed in new channels, and particularly in low-cost, low-touch channels. You have a variety of tools at your disposal to do this, which are summarized in Figure 6.2.

Figure 6.2	**Summary of tools to make a product 'channel-ready' for sale through lower-cost channels.**	
☑	Product standardization	*Reduction of product line to a smaller number of standardized, 'off-the-rack' offerings*
☑	Feature simplification	*Reduction in the number and complexity of product features and functions*
☑	Pricing simplification – and reduction factor	*Simplification of pricing model – and passing on of some cost-saving to customers in the form of lower prices*
☑	Bundled training and procedures	*Inclusion of straightforward, 'self-education' training and procedures with the product itself*
☑	Standardization of terms and conditions	*Development of simple, 'off-the-rack' terms of sale and conditions of purchase*
☑	Streamlining of financial terms and processes	*Simplification of financial terms, and access to streamlined financial application and approval processes*
☑	'Support' channel	*Development or recruitment of a channel to provide support and care after the sale*

RETHINKING THE PRODUCT TO FIT WITH NEW MARKET, CUSTOMER AND CHANNEL INITIATIVES: AN EXAMPLE

Herman Miller, the second largest furniture manufacturer in the US, with $2.24 billion in sales in 2001, provides an excellent example of the impact of new market, customer and channel initiatives on the design of a product line.

Herman Miller has for seventy-five years sold furniture to large corporate customers through a carefully cultivated network of independent dealers. By the mid-1990s, however, the company realized that its existing sales approach was unable efficiently to reach and serve customers in the SOHO ('Small Office, Home Office') market, a space occupied by retailers such as Office Depot and Office Max. This was a big problem. As Herman Miller brand manager Greg Clark noted, 'Fifty percent of people employed in America are employed by small businesses, and that's a market that Herman Miller wasn't reaching.'[131] To gain access to this market, the company decided to try out a number of new initiatives.

In 1995, the company introduced the SQA ('simple, quick and affordable') product line, geared to SOHO customers and marketed through Herman Miller SQA Small Business Dealers. The SQA line offered customers a limited version of Herman Miller's existing product line, and it promised quick delivery (within two weeks, compared to the several months required for large corporate orders) as well as lower prices.[132] In 1998, Herman Miller pulled open the curtains on Herman Miller for the Home, selling furniture directly online to residential customers. Successes from these initiatives helped establish the fact that the SOHO and consumer market as well as an alternative channel model was a real opportunity, and paved the way for the creation of a whole new division within Herman Miller: Herman Miller Red.

The idea behind Red was to reach the broad base of smaller customers primarily through the Internet,[133] by focusing on channel-ready, reasonably priced 'hip, affordable designs'. For example, Red's online catalog contains an ultra-ergonomic (and award-winning) Aeron work chair and Red Clover desk for less than $1,000. There's also the $395 Red Grasshopper Storage Unit 3 High. For customers seeking some drama and willing to pay a little extra for it, there is the $2,549 Nelson Marshmallow Sofa, with multi-colored vinyl cushions attached to a tubular steel frame with satin black legs.

---

[131] Interview with Karen Raugust. Herman Miller Red: Greg Clark. *Advertising Age*, October 8, 2001.
[132] Chuck Moozakis, Herman Miller builds three-pronged strategy – furniture company tailors Web efforts to size of customer. *Internet Week*, June 11, 2001.
[133] Interview with Karen Raugust. Herman Miller Red: Greg Clark. *Advertising Age*, October 8, 2001.

What's most important about the Red product line is that its design has been shaped fundamentally by the use of the Web as its primary sales channel. Red furniture was designed not just to meet the dynamic but limited work environments of its new SOHO customers, but also around the clear recognition that the Internet imposes important constraints on the products that are sold through this medium.

Basically, Herman Miller realized that for Red to work over the Web, the product line would have to be able to survive outside of Herman Miller's network of technically skilled dealers. The longstanding role of these dealers has been to work closely with customers, all the way from the highly consultative process of selecting and configuring office systems through to the eventual stages of assembly, installation and maintenance of those systems. Herman Miller Red sought to create designs that could exist without the hand-holding that its dealers provide – thus making the Web a viable channel.

Working with independent industrial designers to ensure that Red products would fit the new sales channel, Herman Miller developed products that were quite different from the highly-customized 'office systems' familiar to Herman Miller's base of large, Fortune 1000 corporate clients. For one thing, Red presented furniture that was easy to set up. According to one report, Red furniture requiring assembly could be put together in 20 minutes or so by a single person.[134] In addition, by offering freestanding 'mix and match' pieces, Red gave customers the flexibility to move things around and reconfigure their floor plans without having to call a local dealer for advice and assistance.

Finally, Red products were designed from the outset to be 'UPS-able', meaning that they could be shipped efficiently and affordably. Wherever possible, Herman Miller worked with designers to develop furniture that was consistent with the dimensions of a standard UPS box.[135] In addition, the company focused on the use of lightweight materials that cost less to ship. For example, many Red products used

---

[134] Elaine Louie, Together in 20 minutes, they say, with nary a part left over. *New York Times*, July 5, 2001. In fact, the company ran assembly tests by pulling in workers from other divisions, timing the process from the moment they opened the box, reported Rhoda Miel in 'Herman Miller's red line aims for start-ups'. *Plastics News*, August 13, 2001.

[135] Chuck Moozakis, Herman Miller builds three-pronged strategy – furniture company tailors Web efforts to size of customer. *Internet Week*, June 11, 2001.

structural foam molding, the same lightweight material found inside a boogie board.[136] This kind of innovation enabled Red to control the shipping costs associated with online ordering, and to ensure fast turnaround time. Red, in fact, ships within 48 hours of an order – a vast improvement on the months that it usually takes to get custom-ordered office furniture.[137]

So what kind of impact has this clever product rethinking had for Herman Miller? In spite of a difficult economic environment confronting all manufacturers today, Herman Miller Red has been a success. In October 2001, *Advertising Age* reported that the Business & Institutional Furniture Manufacturers Association forecast a 4.4 percent decline in the US office furniture market for 2001, but Red has defied the trend. As of June 2001, estimates of its sales growth have ranged from 7 percent over the previous quarter to week-over-week figures of 5–7 percent.[138] Herman Miller Red is an excellent example of a company that took advantage of new market and channel opportunities by rethinking its products and ensuring that they were both market-ready and channel-ready.

THE VALUE PROPOSITION

So far we've been focusing on the *product*. We've looked at the need to align the product with the other components of a go-to-market strategy, such as the markets in which the product will be sold, the customers to whom it is directed, and the channels that will have to sell it. Redesigning the product to fit with the rest of the strategy is smart and necessary, but is it sufficient? Are you done with your work once you've tweaked or redesigned your offerings to fit with new market, customer or channel initiatives?

The answer, of course, is 'No'. It isn't good enough just to have the right product. The product must be combined with a winning value proposition – a core message – that compels customer interest and purchasing activity. Without a value proposition to communicate to customers, your offering is just a widget or gadget sitting in a corner

---

[136] Rhoda Miel, Herman Miller's red line aims for start-ups. *Plastics News*, August 13, 2001.
[137] *Ibid.*
[138] Karen Raugust, Herman Miller Red. *Advertising Age*, October 8, 2001.

and waiting for potential buyers magically to come to the conclusion that they need it. That isn't going to cut it. You must have a clear, winning message that you can promote through various media such as brochures, Web sites, and other forms of advertising. An appealing, winning value proposition is just as important to a go-to-market strategy as an appealing, winning product. The message gets your offering, and the value of your offering, out in front of potential customers.

Doesn't everyone know that they need a 'message'? Isn't it really too elementary to suggest that your go-to-market strategy requires a good sales pitch? It's probably true that everyone knows they need some sort of message about their company and their offerings, and has one, in one form or another. The problem is, most of these messages are awful and border on being complete gibberish. Consider the following value propositions, all of them real, from actual companies existing at the time of this writing.

[Our] idea will be to deliver life-cycle centric solutions directly into customer's value chain, with special focus on obtaining improved knowledge and workflow management. The business idea is based on the following vision: 'To provide our customers with life-cycle centric solutions to design, strength assessment, risk, and knowledge management.'

What?!

Let's look at a few more ...

At [company] we assist our clients to align their organizations with the needs and expectations of their customers and employees. These two groups decide the ultimate success or failure of your business. The closer the alignment, the better your competitive advantage.

You will experience a drastic reduction in the time required for competent performance at scale.

Our vision is to be proactive, anticipating the needs of our customers so that they will continue to be leaders in their respective fields. The opportunity to work with our clients is a privilege, we realize that, and we do all that is humanly and professionally possible to maintain that privilege.

Do you have any idea what any of these companies do or make? I sure don't!

One last example, from a high-tech company that's taken the 'buzz-word thing' to a whole new level:

> [Company] is the world's first company dedicated to using the science of experience strategy, design, and technology to create extraordinary results for our clients. Our entire team is committed to transforming our clients' businesses through the creation of multi-channel experiences that inspire and strengthen dynamic connections among people, businesses, channels, and communities.

You get my point, I'm sure. The fact is, we've all been so pummeled over the last decade with the boring, meaningless lexicon of management buzzwords – phrases that could be random-generated by a computer – that we can no longer see how ineffective they are in promoting a product or service. Come to think of it, whatever happened to subtle, powerful value propositions that communicate core positioning in the market place and the value of doing business with a particular vendor, such as IBM's famous message 'No one ever got fired for buying IBM', and my all-time favorite, from the same company: 'Buy IBM, and you can sleep at night.' For anxious IT buyers in the 1970s and 1980s, evaluating numerous brands and vendors, unsure of how to proceed, and concerned about the risks of new technology, IBM hit it right on the mark.

You may not be able to get your value proposition down to something as straightforward as 'You can sleep at night', but you can do much, much better than the linguistic gobblygook appearing these days in brochures, Web sites and print advertisements. Your goal, after all, is to sell lots of products, and anyone who's sold anything knows that confusing, fuzzy messages do not generate sales. The goal should be to develop a tight, crisp message that, regardless of the media through which it is promoted, contributes to tangible sales success. With that in mind, let's take a look at some useful guidelines for creating a strong value proposition (Table 6.1).

Table 6.1   Characteristics of *winning* value propositions

Simple	Clear and concise ... easy to understand. Absence of buzzwords and techno-gibberish
Compelling	Strong, bold statement that motivates customers to evaluate and eventually to purchase
Believable	Makes claims that are reasonable and believable
Attractive to the *right* customers	Targeted at the specific needs and interests of the right customers in the right markets

Let's take a brief look at each of the characteristics.

1. *Simple.* A good value proposition is clear and concise, to the point, and easy for customers to understand. It communicates the basic value inherent in doing business with you and in purchasing your product or solution. A few sentences should be enough to communicate this message. The goal, after all, should be to clarify the value in doing business with you, not to confuse the prospect.

2. *Compelling.* A good value proposition is also compelling. It doesn't ramble on about 'creating unusual results and amazing returns for stakeholders, partners, customers, employees, distributors ...', but, rather, explains why someone should actually be interested in buying stuff from you. The best method for communicating value is to put it in financial terms. That's the only thing a business customer cares about; the rest is just fluff. To take another example from my favorite value proposition company, IBM: '[Business intelligence has a] 43 percent annual growth rate, worth an estimated $148 billion by 2003.[139] If you're not part of it yet, you definitely want to jump aboard.' That's pretty compelling if you're a reseller trying to figure out who to partner with – which happens to IBM's target market in this case. Don't lose the opportunity to put some real numbers in the value proposition. That will make it much more compelling both to customers and partners.

---

[139] Source: www.ibm.com

3. *Believable.* The more compelling you make your value proposition, the less believable it may become. Claims of hundreds of millions of dollars saved or countless new customers acquired are compelling only if customers believe them. Today's typical value propositions, with their hyperbolic claims of outrageous shareholder value created by products as mundane as small software programs and routine business services, are simply not credible, and probably do more harm than good. A strong value proposition tempers the drive to be compelling with claims that are realistic, honest and believable. And it certainly doesn't hurt to have detailed customer reference cases to back up your claims.

4. *Attractive to the* right *customers.* Finally, a value proposition must be targeted at the right customers – specifically, the customers that you are now attempting to acquire. In fact, if you are trying to reach and penetrate new customers, it's likely that whatever message you have today is outdated. A message that compelled purchasing activity by Fortune 500 buyers, for example, may fall flat or even alienate middle-market buyers. The customers in the middle market have different interests, needs, budgets, and tolerance for dealing with complex products and solutions. As you move into new markets, you will have to revisit your value proposition to ensure that it is attractive to your new target customers and compels them to take a serious look at your company and offerings.

A cautionary note is to avoid the tendency to develop a value proposition in a vacuum. Like any other component of a go-to-market strategy, a strong value proposition must originate with real live customers, and therefore cannot be designed in a conference room with the door shut. You may think you know what will resonate 'out there', but you must take the value proposition to customers and prospects and verify with them that you have a powerful, winning message. When my firm, The Sales Strategy Institute, performs value proposition development and testing for our clients, for example, we begin with a very simple message and take it out to the client's customer and prospect base. Running it by dozens or sometimes hundreds of prospects in a set of target markets, we gradually refine and bring shape to the message by getting direct feedback from key prospects. They tell us what excites them – and what bores them – and that is the only sound basis for developing a strong message. The odds of developing a powerful, resonant message by asking key customers and prospects what they like and don't like are fairly high. On the other hand, the odds of developing a winning message through internal meetings and sheer cleverness are abysmally low.

Finally, it is important to have a solid value proposition for your customers, but it may be even more important to have a winning value proposition for your partners. After all, if your partners don't sell your products, you may be out of business. The value of doing business with you and of representing your products aggressively in the market place should be clear. You must develop a clear, compelling and believable message for partners that focuses on the business benefit to them of taking you seriously and, as IBM put it earlier, getting aboard. Particularly with partners, the message must emphasize the direct, tangible financial gains to be had from working with you.

In the end, no customer is going to purchase your products, and no partner is going to sell them on your behalf, unless you communicate to them what's compelling about those products and what's 'in it for them'. You must develop a value proposition for both customers and partners that is simple, compelling, believable, and targeted directly at their interests and needs.

SUMMARY

Products and markets have long been thought of as being fundamentally different issues, dealt with by different people within an organization, often with poor communication between the two groups. In recent years, however, the boundaries between products and markets have become thinner and thinner. New, low-cost channels have forced companies to rethink their products and value propositions and redesign them to fit with new market, customer and channel assumptions. Rethinking your products and value propositions is very much at the core of a winning go-to-market strategy.

We began the chapter by looking at the impact of new markets and customers on products. New customers will have different needs and expectations than your existing customers. As a result, if your go-to-market initiative involves reaching and penetrating new markets or customers – and it probably does – then you will have to rethink and perhaps redesign your products to attract and penetrate those customers. You cannot assume that a product that works well in an existing customer base will work as well in a new one.

We then looked at the impact of new channels on products, focusing particularly on the impact that low-cost alternative channels can have on product design. Since lower-cost channels tend to be 'lower touch', they require a different kind of product – a simpler, streamlined offering. We looked at a number of tools, or approaches, for getting a product to fit well with these new channels, such as product standardization, feature simplification, and the standardization of terms and conditions. The bottom line is that to sell through simpler channels, the product itself may have to be simplified.

Finally, we looked at the importance of developing a winning value proposition. It is not good enough just to have a good product; you must be able to promote and articulate that product to new customers and partners. While most companies already have some kind of value proposition, those value propositions are often confusing, buzzword-y, and unlikely to compel any real buying interest. The first order of business with the value proposition is to make sure that you have a message that is simple, compelling, and believable. As importantly, any change to a go-to-market system will definitely create a need to rethink the message. New customers in new markets will have different needs than your existing customers, and your message must be designed to appeal to those customers. It is well worth taking the time to ensure that your message is in tune with the needs and interests of your *new* target customers.

With this discussion of products and the value proposition, we have now covered all five major components of a go-to-market initiative: markets, customers, channels, products, and the value proposition. As we discussed way, way back in Chapter 1, it's when all five of these components come together and work together cooperatively that you get something powerful, something that will win in the market place. While that may have been a conceptual stretch back in Chapter 1, at this point the importance of making all five components work together in one go-to-market *system* should be apparent. Your channels must reach the right customers in the right markets. Your products and value proposition must fit with your markets, customers and channels.

In the next chapter, we will take the whole idea of cooperation between go-to-market components to the next level. It's one thing to choose markets, customers, channels, products and messages that fit together – that's certainly a good start. To bring out the full power of a go-to-market strategy, though, you must develop a fully integrated model that brings everything together *within a coordinated sales cycle* to serve your customers. That is the subject of Chapter 7.

7

Go-to-market strategy:

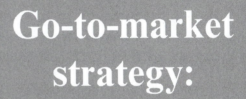

Putting it all together: the integrated multi-channel model

T oday, scores of leading companies have built *integrated multi-channel models* and – you heard it here first – hundreds or thousands more will jump on the bandwagon in the next two to three years. The integrated multi-channel model has become the Holy Grail for sales and marketing executives, the 'end game' of go-to-market strategy to which an increasing number of companies aspire. The reason is simple. It's an enormously beneficial and battle-tested, proven approach in which multiple channels work *cooperatively* in the sales process to increase profits, revenues, market coverage, and customer loyalty, all at the same time.

That all sounds great in theory, but for every company that has built a successful, winning integrated multi-channel model – the Charles Schwabs and Dell Computers and Marriotts – there are many others that have struggled with the concept and fallen flat. Like Lancelot, who searched far and wide for the Holy Grail but who came up short in the end, many have sought the elusive winning multi-channel model and found only customer confusion, channel conflict, and lower margins. Of course, Lancelot didn't have a business consultant to break the search down into a set of practical steps and processes; that would have ruined the story or certainly reduced its poetic value. We have no such limitation here. In this chapter, we will examine the nuts and bolts involved in developing a robust, customer-focused, and *winning* integrated multi-channel model.

Let's get started by defining what this approach is all about. Integrated multi-channel models have four basic characteristics, as follows:

1. *Multiple channels work* together *to make sales.* The defining characteristic of an integrated multi-channel model is that multiple channels, such as field reps, partners, call centers and the Web, work *together* to generate leads, close deals, and serve customers.
2. *Channels take on* specific roles *within the sales cycle.* In an integrated model, each channel takes on a specialized sales role, such as lead generation, negotiation, or post-sale support.[140] In other words, not every channel performs every selling task; rather,

---

[140] In many multi-channel models, individual channels take on more than one role within the sales process, a topic we'll return to later.

individual channels are assigned to the specific tasks that they are best-suited to perform.

3. *Channel integration is achieved through information systems.* Because integrated multi-channel models use different channels to perform different selling tasks, there is always the potential for chaos and poor coordination at the interfaces between channels. The outcome can involve lost or mishandled sales leads, conflict between channels, problems with customer service, and so on. To prevent these kinds of problems, companies that use multi-channel models almost always employ IT systems to coordinate the activity of their channels, in order to ensure a smooth sales cycle and make possible a seamless, 'channel-transparent' customer experience. In today's markets, which are filled with customers who expect immediate access to accurate and up-to-date account information in whatever channels they choose to use, integrated multi-channel models not supported by information systems are rare indeed. Within a few years, they will be extinct.

4. *Multi-channel models usually serve a targeted market or group of markets – not* all *of a company's markets.* Despite the fact that we hear so much today about Schwab's or Dell's or Marriott's 'integrated multi-channel model', the use of one comprehensive multi-channel model across all markets is very rare, and certainly is not descriptive of any of these go-to-market leaders' approaches. The simple reason is that different markets usually require different channel mixes, and therefore any company that sells into a variety of markets will require different multi-channel models to serve those markets. For example, let's say that you cover top, strategic accounts with field reps and partners, and the middle market through partners (perhaps even the same partners), the Web and the telephone. You'd clearly have to develop two distinct multi-channel approaches to sell into these two different markets. Though the notion of a company-wide multi-channel model may be intellectually appealing, it's a realistic approach only when all markets and customers will be covered in exactly the same way.

So what exactly does an integrated multi-channel model look like? These models come in many flavors. Some companies use simple models, in which a low-cost channel, such as the Web or a mail-order catalog, is used to generate inbound sales leads for a 'main' channel such as a sales force or retail store. A more complex approach, which is closer to the model used by Dell Computer to serve the small business market, involves the use of direct mail to generate inbound leads to call centers and Web sites, followed by sales closure over the telephone, an extranet, or a public Web site, then by post-sale support provided by business partners, and finally, by customer care provided over the Web and telephone.

There are many other variants, in both business-to-business and consumer retail sales. For example, retailer J.C. Penney uses a 'threetailing' approach. The company lets its customers shop at retail stores, on the Web, or by telephone – so far, pretty standard fare. But J.C. Penney also lets its customers combine all three channels in the purchasing process, by visiting a retail store to touch and feel the products, then using an in-store phone to place an order from a catalog, and then taking in-store or at-home delivery. To get just a taste of the benefits of integrated multi-channel selling, J.C. Penney's average sales-per-customer are $194 per year for in-store purchasers, $242 for catalog shoppers, and $1,050 for customers that use all three channels together.[141] Put another way, this company's multi-channel users do over 300 percent more business per customer than single-channel users. That says something important about the impact of an integrated multi-channel model on customer behavior and sales results.

We will explore a variety of integrated multi-channel models in this chapter, suitable to different market conditions and business goals. Despite the wide variety of approaches, however, all integrated multi-channel models are aimed at achieving a mix of four key business benefits:

1. *Increased sales.* As in the case of J.C. Penney, integrated multi-channel models can produce significant gains in total revenues as well as revenues-per-customer (which are the most profitable types of new revenues, since the cost of customer acquisition has already been paid). Multi-channel models increase sales revenues in several ways: by using low-cost channels to reach more customers early in the sales process, by providing a more flexible customer experience that makes it easier and more convenient for

---

[141] Multi-channel advantage. *Chain Store Age Executive with Shopping Center* Age, December1, 2000.

more customers to do more business, and, in the case of business-to-business sales, by freeing up the time of high-value channels, such as sales forces, to focus on closing larger deals in strategic accounts. Estimates vary, but most companies that move from a single channel model to an integrated multi-channel model achieve overall sales increases of 15–20 percent or more within twelve to eighteen months of implementation. That may sound dramatic – especially for companies in mature, slow-growth markets – but it's quite typical, and in this chapter we'll look at how to do it.

2. *Increased profits.* An integrated multi-channel model is perhaps the single most effective tool available to you for increasing company profitability. Why? Because this approach enables you to 'offload' expensive sales tasks to lower-cost channels, thus decreasing the overall cost of sales. Many companies achieve a 20–25 percent reduction in selling costs within a year or two of implementing an efficient multi-channel model, and I've never seen a company achieve less than a 10 percent cost reduction. That's a lot of money! *How* a multi-channel system actually generates cost-savings – and how *you* can achieve real cost savings and margin improvement – is something we'll look at in this chapter.

3. *Increased coverage and market share.* A third benefit of an integrated multi-channel model is that it makes possible a deeper penetration and coverage of a market or group of markets. Multiple channels working together cooperatively can *always* cover more customers, more thoroughly, than a single-channel approach, or even an approach in which multiple channels exist but operate more-or-less independently of each other. The reason is that channels operating on their own have limitations that aren't present in an integrated multi-channel model. Low-cost, low-touch channels such as the phone and mail order are great for reaching customers, but poor at negotiating and closing complex deals. Expensive high-touch channels such as sales forces and business partners can handle very complex transactions, but cannot reach as many customers, due to their high costs. When low-cost and high-touch channels are combined, however, every single customer in a target market can be reached, penetrated and served. As a result, an integrated multi-channel model is *always* the most effective way to deepen penetration and increase share within a market.

4. *Increased customer loyalty and retention.* Finally – and perhaps most importantly – integrated multi-channel models can have a huge impact on customer satisfaction, retention, and longer-term loyalty. The reason is that multi-channel systems align well with how customers prefer to do business. This approach gives them the right channels at the right 'touch points' in the buying process, more purchasing options, more efficient service, and often lower prices as a result of the decreased cost-of-sales. What customer wouldn't want that? Companies have seen their customer satisfaction rates increase by double digits, and loss rates (i.e. percentage of customers defecting to competitors) decline by 40 percent or more, within a year of implementing an integrated multi-channel model.

In short, there are lots of sound business reasons to take your go-to-market efforts to the next level by building integrated multi-channel models to penetrate and serve your key markets. In this chapter, we'll look at how to do that, by focusing on four key design tasks:

1. Constructing an integrated multi-channel model that will support your business goals and align with your customers' buying behaviors
2. Ensuring a 'seamless' customer experience through channel coordination and information technology
3. Anticipating and managing potential channel conflict issues
4. Designing performance metrics to encourage the right channels to do the right things in the sales cycle.

CONSTRUCTING THE INTEGRATED MULTI-CHANNEL MODEL

The defining characteristic of an integrated multi-channel model is that different channels do different things within a single sale. For instance, you might use a call center to generate leads, a group of distributors to close deals, and a Web site to provide post-sale support. There are lots of other possibilities, but before you can even begin to think about how you will assign sales tasks to different channels, you must first determine what those tasks are – in other words, you must define your sales cycle.

In most companies, the sales cycle consists of four to nine tasks, starting with lead generation and ending with the support and long-term care of customers. Every company's sales cycle is different, so for illustrative purposes I've provided a pretty typical, everyday business-to-business sales cycle, consisting of six steps, as shown in Figure 7.1. (We will use this six-step sales model throughout the chapter to discuss various multi-channel integration approaches and issues.)

While selling tasks will be familiar to most readers, it's worth taking a moment to define each of the tasks in the figure, since they're used throughout the chapter.

1. *Lead generation.* In the lead generation task, the goal is to establish initial contact between you and a prospect (i.e. a potential customer). This can result from outbound selling activity, such as a sales call, as well as inbound activity, such as a prospect's completion of a request-for-information form on a Web site.
2. *Lead qualification.* In this step, sales leads are 'qualified', or vetted for probability of eventually closing. Lead qualification usually involves confirming four things: the prospect's need for your product or service, buying interest, funding, and timeframe

Figure 7.1   **Typical sales cycle: tasks performed throughout the sales process.**

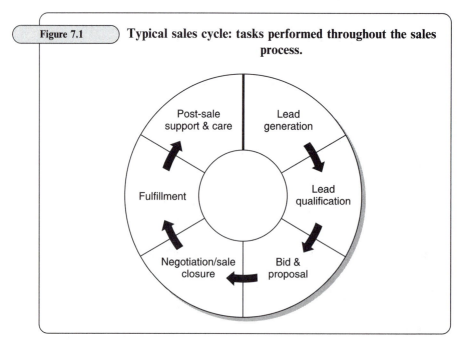

for making a purchase. 'Qualified' leads are those in which the prospect has a need, an interest, the funds or credit to make the purchase, and the intent to purchase within a reasonable timeframe such as thirty or sixty days.[142] Leads failing any of these four tests are usually considered 'unqualified', and are either dropped or back-burnered for follow-up at another time.

3. *Bid and proposal.* Bidding and proposing includes all of the tasks needed to convert a qualified lead into a ready-to-close sale. In simple consumer sales, there may not be much of a bidding and proposing task. However, in more complex business sales, the preparation of bids and proposals can be the most time-consuming and complex part of the entire sales cycle, involving activities such as rigorous customer requirements definition, development of specifications, and the preparation of written proposals with extensive supporting documentation. Long ago, when I was an executive in Accenture's systems integration practice, for example, I worked on a twelve-person team that developed a 1,600-page proposal over a period of seven months![143]

4. *Negotiation and sale closure.* This task includes the negotiation of prices, terms and conditions, followed by finalization and confirmation of the order. This task is complete when goods and payments have been exchanged, or, at a minimum, when a binding contract for their exchange has been signed.

5. *Fulfillment.* In sales of simple commodity products, fulfillment may consist just of shipment and delivery of the product to the customer. However, in more complex sales, fulfillment can be a major component of the sales cycle, involving extensive configuration, customization, and installation. As companies have focused increasingly on selling more complex 'solutions', rather than simple products, the task of fulfillment has become more complex, leading to fulfillment teams that specialize solely in coming in after the sale to configure, install and test solutions.

6. *Customer care and support.* Separate from fulfillment, which is aimed at finishing the sale, customer care and support is aimed at long-term customer retention, loyalty and growth. As a result, while this task does include immediate post-sale problem resolution, customer guidance, and training, its longer-term focus is

---

[142] In the cases of longer sales cycles, the timeframe may be considerably longer. In the case of shorter sales cycles, the timeframe may be much shorter. For example, car dealers seeking same-day sales may consider any customer who walks off the lot after a test-drive (i.e. a non-immediate timeframe) to be an unqualified lead.

[143] Back when it was called Andersen Consulting. We won, by the way.

often on maintaining ongoing contact with customers and ensuring that their needs over time continue to be addressed and met.

Once you have defined your sales cycle – and the tasks that comprise it – the next step is to map *current* channel usage against that sales cycle. To illustrate this step, let's take the simplest of all possible examples: a company that performs all selling tasks through a field sales force. This approach is illustrated in Figure 7.2.

As Figure 7.2 shows, in this example the field sales organization is assigned to *every* task in the sales cycle, from the generation of sales leads all the way through to customer care and support. That is the traditional and familiar *direct sales model*, which we encountered and discussed earlier in Chapter 5, and which was employed until recently at large corporations such as Xerox and IBM.

Importantly, note how the *multi-channel integration map* in Figure 7.2 suggests the fundamental problem with the single-channel direct sales approach. By arranging channels from top to bottom in terms of their relative cost-of-sales (see the far left side of the figure), the integration map provides a graphic depiction of selling costs, which in the direct

Figure 7.2   **Multi-channel integration map: single-channel (field sales) model.**

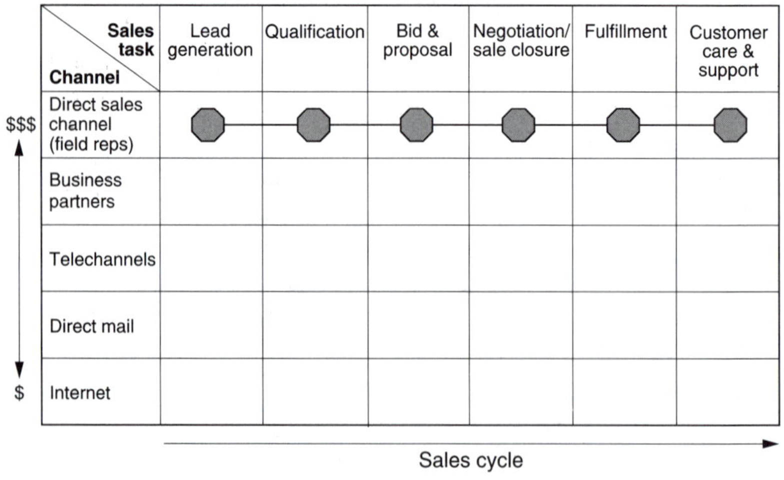

Channel \ Sales task	Lead generation	Qualification	Bid & proposal	Negotiation/ sale closure	Fulfillment	Customer care & support
Direct sales channel (field reps)	⬢	⬢	⬢	⬢	⬢	⬢
Business partners						
Telechannels						
Direct mail						
Internet						

$$$ ↑   ↓ $

Sales cycle →

somewhat independently; for instance, business partners create some of their own leads and follow these leads to the end of the sale, but also get supplemental sales leads from a call center. Meanwhile, the call center refers smaller customers to a Web site, which is itself independently generating and closing deals.

Needless to say, this is a very aggressive channel approach, aimed not at simplicity or the lowest-possible selling costs, but at the highest possible top-line results.

An excellent example of a company that uses a maximum-growth integrated multi-channel model, in retail/consumer markets, is Salton, Inc., a $792 million designer, marketer and distributor of small kitchen and personal care appliances. Salton's well-recognized brands include Salton, Breadman, Juiceman, and a brand familiar to any insomniac viewer of infomercials, George Foreman Grills. Salton has the leading US domestic market share for indoor grills, toasters, breadmakers, and juicers, and sells everything from ice-cream makers and pizza makers to flatware and china. Salton is a high-growth story, one of just fifteen companies that have made it onto Fortune's Fastest-Growing Companies list for all three years of the list's existence. Salton's net sales grew 65.4 percent in 2000, due to the company's 'overriding focus on growth', as described in its annual report.

To feed and sustain its growth engine, Salton offers its products through an expansive and integrated mix of sales channels and partners. In North America, the company sells its products to distributors through a direct sales force as well as a network of independent sales reps. In addition, the company has an outlet store in Gurnee, Illinois. Salton's other channels include retail stores such as Wal-Mart, Target, Kmart, Sears, Saks and Costco, through which it markets its own products as well as separately-branded offerings under names such as White-Westinghouse®, Kenmore®, and Magic Chef®. Salton also sells to mail-order catalog companies, and to consumers through half-hour television infomercials and well as through its own Internet Web site. The Web site offers Salton products and the offerings of a wide variety of partners such as Melitta (coffee makers and espresso machines) and Farberware® (kitchen appliances). Customers can use channels independently or in combination. For example, customers visiting the Salton Web site can place orders over the Web, or be connected to a live operator via VoIP (voice over Internet protocol), or go to a retail store. Salton is currently exploring a variety of new sales channels, such as grocery stores and e-commerce outlets.

An aggressive multi-channel mix, as used by Salton and others with fast-growth objectives, will undoubtedly capture the maximum number of sales transactions and revenues. But this is not a channel model for dilettantes and armchair strategists. It is the most complicated of all integrated multi-channel approaches, opening up the possibility – indeed the probability – of channel conflict and reduced margins. After all, it takes great effort and costs lots of money to build all those channels and to keep them working together effectively. It may well be worth the effort and cost if maximum growth is the most important go-to-market goal.

Summary: maximum-growth model

- As the name implies, this is a model for companies primarily concerned with maximum revenue growth
- Difficult to design and implement – lots of room for channel conflict and confusion
- Maximum flexibility for customers
- Not the most profitable way to sell
- Revenue growth through this approach can be dramatic

So there you have it: four 'archetypes' of integrated multi-channel models. Your choice of model will depend on whether your goal is a low-risk, low-hassle increase in sales leads, maximum margins, maximum market coverage, or maximum revenue growth. These four different approaches demonstrate the importance of thinking through what you're really trying to accomplish *before* developing an integrated multi-channel model, since different models will contribute to some business goals and detract from others.

> You must consider carefully the impact that a new model will have on your customers, and ensure that the model gives them what they want at each step in the sales cycle.

When constructing an integrated multi-channel model, is there anything you need to take into account besides your own goals? You bet there is. You must consider carefully the impact that a new model will have on your customers, and ensure that the model gives them what they want at each step in the sales cycle. As you push sales tasks down to alternative channels, you are also pushing *customers* down to alternative channels. Will they accept that change? They may, or they may not. If they don't, your model can cause confusion and anger in the customer base and fall flat on its face. Let's take a closer look at this crucial issue.

Aligning the model with your customers: channel coercion vs. migration

Implementing a new integrated multi-channel model means requiring – or at least asking – customers to do business differently. You will be suggesting that they use Channel B for a certain purchasing task, when they've been accustomed to using Channel A. For example, your new model may offer them the phone for pre-sales support, whereas they previously had access to sales reps or partners. Or it may require them to go to the Web for post-sale problem resolution, where they previously had access to phone reps.

If you've done your homework correctly in choosing your sales channels, as described in Chapter 5, your channels will generally meet the needs of customers and fit with their buying behaviors. But that doesn't mean the *specific tasks* to which your channels are assigned in an integrated multi-channel model will map correctly to their behaviors and preferences. For example, they may like the idea of being able to make purchases over the phone when they want, but may resent being told to use only the phone if there's a problem after the sale, rather than being able to meet with a sales rep.

One way to avoid customer fit problems is to ask your customers how they want to interact with you at each 'touch point' in their purchasing processes – such as product evaluation, the actual purchase, and post-sale support – and then map your channels to those preferences. For example, if your target customers like to use the Web to evaluate vendors, but hate using it to purchase, then give them a Web site to evaluate your company but provide another channel to complete transactions. While this is good common sense, it does assume that you have no influence over your customers' use of channels, which isn't the case. You *do* have influence, and you can certainly try to move customers into new channels at various points in the sales cycle. Whether you succeed depends, in large part, on how you approach it. You basically have two choices: sticks and carrots.

The 'stick' approach, or *channel coercion*, involves forcing customers to do business in a new way, either by taking away their preferred channel or by making it too costly to continue using their preferred channel. A useful example of channel coercion comes from the manufacturing industry, where one of my clients, a $2.4 billion manufacturer of industrial systems and components, last year deployed a new model aimed at getting its customers to use its Web site rather than its call center for routine post-sale support issues. Why? The company had taken over 110,000 inbound post-sale support calls in the past year, most of which in no way required real-time dialogue over the phone (e.g. 'Did you plug the machine in?'). The client finally decided that enough was enough. Customers, in its view, were abusing its provision of lifetime toll-free support calls, which created an enormous and unfair expense – namely, the people required to staff enough phones to handle 110,000 calls per year. The company sent out letters to all of its customers informing them that, from this day forward, there would be a $15 fee per phone call, but that a full-featured Web site was now available to handle their basic questions and problems.

Over the next two months, irate customers flooded the company with over four thousand angry letters, many of which informed my client that it had permanently alienated them by charging a fee for what was perceived as an integral part of the relationship. It seemed relevant to the company that it had a good Web site, but that was irrelevant to its customers. Customers wanted access to their traditional telesupport channel, and deeply resented being asked to pay for what was, in the past, a free service.

Channel coercion of this sort rarely produces the desired results. It's difficult to force customers to use channels that they don't want or, especially, to abandon channels that they like and to which they feel entitled.

The 'carrot' approach, or *channel migration*, can produce much better results. This approach uses incentives, promotions and the fine-tuning of benefits across channels, in order to encourage customers to make a new channel their 'own' – by choice. The idea is not to coerce customers into your new channels by force, but to effect shifts in customer behavior that fit with your own channel preferences.

An enlightening example comes from a group of companies that tried at first to coerce customers into low-cost channels, such as the Internet and ATMs,[146] and hit stiff resistance. These companies were forced to back off, and to prod customers into these channels more gently through incentives and improved features, which in the end got them what they wanted: customer acceptance of new low-cost channels. I speak, of course, of the retail banking industry. Let's take a look.

By the mid 1990s, major retail banks, facing lower profits in increasingly crowded and competitive markets, realized that they had to get customers out of 'walk-in' retail bank branches and into alternative channels such as phone banking, Internet banking, and ATMs. The reason is easy enough to understand. A retail branch transaction costs a typical retail bank around $1.07 per transaction, telephone banking about $0.55, ATM banking $0.27 per transaction, and Internet banking approximately $0.01 per transaction.[147]

To increase margins, banks used every means imaginable to force customers out of their walk-in retail branches and into lower-cost alternative channels. Hundreds of retail branches were shuttered, and fees were charged to customers who insisted on going to the remaining ones – as high as $3 per teller-based transaction at banks such as Wells Fargo and Bank of America. By 1996, a number of banks offered fee-based Internet and private dial-up banking as an alternative to branch banking, which they felt would be readily accepted by customers due to the rapid adoption of home PCs. But the migration to new banking channels was slow and painful. Customers deeply resented the new fees put on walk-in branch banking, and refused to be forced into other channels that, themselves, had yet more fees. Many customers went over to other banks, which would have evened out over time and been acceptable to the retail banking industry as a whole. However, millions of others defected entirely from their retail banks by moving over to brokerage houses, such as

---

[146] ATM = Automated Teller Machines.
[147] The Federal Reserve Bank of Chicago. *Chicago Fed Letter*, March 2001, number 163.

Charles Schwab, which began offering convenient banking services with flexible channels and no transaction fees.

Retail banks were forced to recognize the failure of channel coercion and fundamentally to rethink their approach. In a word, they went from sticks to carrots. Internet banking, phone banking, and ATM fees were reduced at many banks and eliminated entirely at others. New features and improved functionality were added to their Web sites, such as bill pay; and new channels such as supermarket banking with evening hours were thrown into the mix (the 'carrots'). Meanwhile, noxious fees charged to walk-in branch users were eliminated (the 'stick'), allowing customers to visit a local bank teller when they want – which many no longer do, since they've become accustomed to Web, phone, supermarket, and ATM banking. By using incentives rather than penalties to get customers into the right low-cost channels, many banks have now overcome the initial reluctance and hostility of their customers; indeed, major banks now sport millions of active Internet, phone and ATM banking users. They are finally getting what they wanted in the first place: a migration of customers out of the branch offices and into lower-cost alternative channels.[148]

The moral of the story should be obvious. You must ultimately give customers what they want at each step in the sales process. If you want to migrate customers into lower-cost channels, then you'll have to do just that: *migrate* them, not *coerce* them. Channel migration requires tuning the relative benefits and incentives of different channels to elicit high customer acceptance for new channels. Coercing customers into new channels by removing a channel they already prefer, or by penalizing them for using that channel with new fees, rarely works.[149]

So there you have it: a basic framework for constructing an integrated multi-channel model that:

■ Breaks down your sales cycle into discrete tasks, and assigns channels to each of those tasks

---

[148] Having finally gotten customers to do their banking at ATMs, supermarkets and on the Web, many banks are discovering that it's one of those cases of 'Be careful what you wish for'. Customers – many of whom never go to retail branches anymore – are no longer readily available to the banks; thus making it impossible to cross-sell them the wide portfolios of financial services that banks now want to sell.

[149] An exception might be the computer software business, where companies routinely charge for customer support calls that were free not too long ago. To some extent, this policy has been accepted in the customer base. Whether this policy has had a cost in terms of customer loyalty and satisfaction is another story.

- Provides a number of different multi-channel approaches, each of which is aimed at a different mix of business benefits
- Ensures that the new model will win customer acceptance, by moving customers into new channels through incentives rather than coercion.

The basic integrated multi-channel model, as just described, is a starting point. Once you have a basic model in place, you must address the crucial issue of channel coordination within the sales process – of making multiple channels work together as a unified system to deliver a seamless customer experience.

ENSURING A 'SEAMLESS' CUSTOMER EXPERIENCE THROUGH CHANNEL COORDINATION

The first thing that becomes apparent in implementing an integrated multi-channel model is that there's a lot that can go wrong. Compared with a single-channel selling approach, a multi-channel model is a minefield of potential customer confusion and dissatisfaction, as well as lost sales opportunities. With any multi-channel model, be prepared to address some real channel coordination issues.

The basic challenge involves managing the hand-offs, or transitions, *between* channels. These hand-offs don't exist in a single-channel model, since one channel performs all tasks in the sales cycle, but they exist in abundance in a multi-channel model. For example, the profit-oriented multi-channel model that we looked at earlier has at least *six* channel hand-offs. Take a look at Figure 7.8 to see why.

Each and every one of the channel hand-offs in Figure 7.8 presents a real challenge for channel coordination.

For example, leads generated by the Web or through direct mail could fail to make it to the telechannel. Next, leads qualified by the telechannel and appropriate for hand-off to field reps could be lost, ignored by field sales, or followed up improperly by field sales – particularly if sales reps get incomplete information or the wrong information from call center reps. That explains why 40–50 percent of all sales leads typically disappear in an integrated multi-channel system

Figure 7.8   **Channel hand-offs in the sales cycle.**

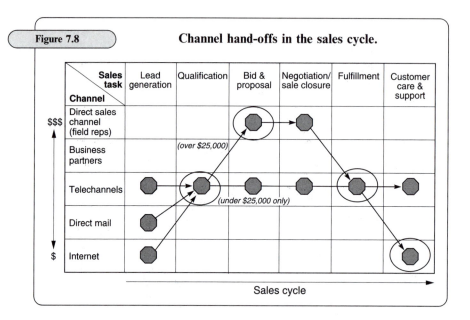

that isn't backed up by an IT system to track and monitor lead progress. You read that right: 40–50 percent of all sales leads disappear. They come out of a lead-generating channel and go off into never-never land, never to be seen again. That's a lot of lost leads. But that's just the beginning of the sales cycle. After sales closure, field reps can mis-record, or not record at all, pertinent customer information that's needed for telesupport reps to do their jobs effectively. Telesupport reps can route customers to the Web without recording the customer status information needed for the Web to present updated and complete account histories, leading to low customer acceptance or even rejection.

That's a lot of potential problems, each and every one of which occurs daily in a poorly coordinated multi-channel model. To avoid these problems, first and foremost the hand-offs between channels must be designed and 'baked' into the model. Specifically, the following questions must be answered:

1. What are all of the sales cycle tasks that involve hand-offs from one channel to another?
2. When is each task considered 'complete'? For example, at what exact point is a lead considered 'qualified' and therefore ready for hand-off to another channel?

3. What information must be transmitted from one channel to another once it has completed its task(s)? For example, is just simple lead information to be transmitted, or is there an entire customer history that must be moved from channel to channel throughout the sales cycle?
4. How will the hand-offs actually be performed? Will telereps physically hand leads to field reps, email those leads, or call reps on the phone with them? After the sale, will customers be told to call telereps for support, or will those telereps make immediately outbound contact after the sale to introduce themselves? All of these questions must be answered before going 'live' with an integrated multi-channel model.

Needless to say, these questions have become much easier to deal with, over the past few years, with the advent of Customer Relationship Management (CRM) programs. Of course, a CRM program is not a substitute for a go-to-market strategy. You must first design an integrated multi-channel model that supports your goals and aligns with your customers before a computer system can do any good or make any sense. Without a solid strategic model that assigns the right channels to the right selling tasks, an IT system can, in fact, do a great deal of harm. Once you've done the strategic work, however, and developed a sound channel integration model, a CRM system can be an invaluable tool for coordinating channel activities and, especially, managing the hand-offs between them. Channel coordination used to be a difficult, messy problem involving the tracking and frequent loss of hand-written memos, voice mails, paper lists of sales leads, and dog-eared customer history files. CRM has ushered in a new era of IT-driven channel coordination, enabling electronic transmission of leads and customer histories from one channel to another, with no loss of information or sales information falling through the cracks. Though many CRM projects fall short of the mark, well-orchestrated and thoughtful CRM initiatives can produce large top- and bottom-line gains. A good example comes to us from Hewlett-Packard, a $49 billion worldwide leader in computing and imaging solutions.

Hewlett-Packard's decision to implement enterprise-wide CRM was based on several factors. The first was a belief that an IT-enabled integrated multi-channel model would enable HP to cross-sell and 'up-sell' its products more successfully across its various markets and segments. The second was HP's recent move toward complex 'solution' sales, suggesting a need for all of the company's customer-facing employees to have a better understanding of customer needs through access to buying histories and past interactions. A third was the fact that HP had over two hundred disparate systems capturing and storing customer data, making it impossible to get a complete view of a customer without downloading and cross-referencing data from multiple channel, product, and service lines – a time-consuming and onerous task.

The fourth and perhaps most important factor was HP's strong desire to enhance the total customer experience, which the company believed it could do by coordinating the efforts of its many channels – quite a challenge, considering the complexity of its market coverage strategy. Hewlett-Packard sells directly through a field sales organization to the enterprise market; through resellers and distributor channels to the government, education and midsize business market; and through retail stores to the small office and home market. Add in its customer support channels, inside sales group, and comprehensive Web presence, and HP has an army of channels that it deploys to provide sales, service, and support to its different market segments. This multi-channel mix presents HP with many points of contact to customers, creating coordination issues and a challenge in providing a singular 'customer experience' across channels.

To deal with all of these complexities, HP's Synergy Project was launched in July of 2000. A Worldwide CRM Manager was assigned to manage a multi-faceted team of one hundred people dedicated to enterprise-wide implementation of CRM. The project's goal is to develop a unified CRM system capable of providing a 360-degree view of the customer and a seamless multi-channel experience for customers as they 'surf' across channels. Spearheaded by HP's Business Customer Organization (BCO) as the first of several business units to implement Synergy, the approach is illustrated in Figure 7.9.

To create a seamless multi-channel customer interface is, of course, a huge project for a company of HP's size. For this reason, HP is implementing the Synergy Project in phases. The first phase focused on HP's direct sales channel, which is its primary channel for enterprise customers. During this phase, HP deployed a sales force automation tool across multiple product lines and geographies. The second phase focused on integrating direct sales, inbound calls, marketing, and

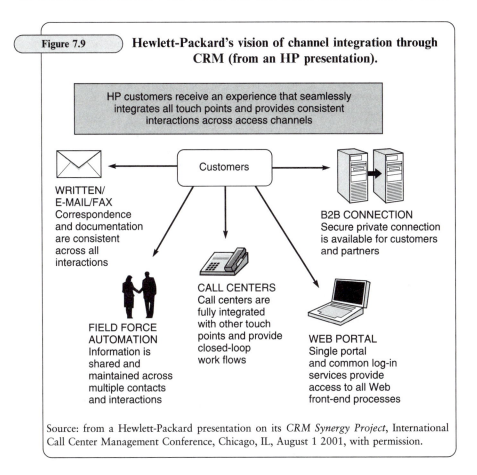

Figure 7.9 Hewlett-Packard's vision of channel integration through CRM (from an HP presentation).

HP customers receive an experience that seamlessly integrates all touch points and provides consistent interactions across access channels

Customers

WRITTEN/
E-MAIL/FAX
Correspondence
and documentation
are consistent
across all
interactions

B2B CONNECTION
Secure private connection
is available for customers
and partners

FIELD FORCE
AUTOMATION
Information is
shared and
maintained across
multiple contacts
and interactions

CALL CENTERS
Call centers are
fully integrated
with other touch
points and provide
closed-loop
work flows

WEB PORTAL
Single portal
and common log-in
services provide
access to all Web
front-end processes

Source: from a Hewlett-Packard presentation on its *CRM Synergy Project*, International Call Center Management Conference, Chicago, IL, August 1 2001, with permission.

inside sales channels. The company is now deploying a solution to bring its partners – VARs, distributors, retail stores, etc. – into the system. This phase will provide automated lead distribution to channel partners, and allow HP channel managers to keep track of partners' sales efforts in following up on those leads.

A key component of the Synergy Project is the development of a central data repository that will collect and provide an integrated source of customer data across the company. This data can be used for various purposes, such as customer segmentation and analysis of customers' demographics, needs and preferences, profitability, and potential lifetime value to HP. The central repository concept is illustrated in Figure 7.10.

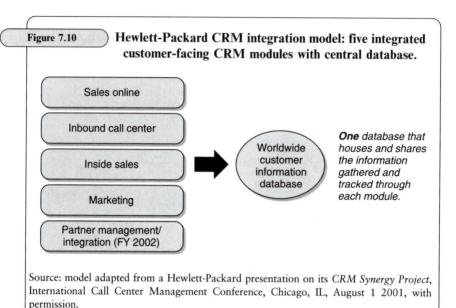

Figure 7.10   **Hewlett-Packard CRM integration model: five integrated customer-facing CRM modules with central database.**

Source: model adapted from a Hewlett-Packard presentation on its *CRM Synergy Project*, International Call Center Management Conference, Chicago, IL, August 1 2001, with permission.

To date, the benefits of Hewlett-Packard's CRM integration efforts have been impressive. During the first year, HP reduced its IT costs by $20 million, increased sales force productivity by 10 percent, boosted its marketing campaign return-on-investment by 30 percent, and reduced its cost-of-sales for transactional products by 25 percent.[150] The Synergy Project is ongoing, and HP expects to accrue further benefits as it rolls out CRM throughout its many locations and business units. Within three years following the completion of Synergy, HP expects to derive incremental revenues of $1.05 billion[151] and save $76 million in operational costs.[152]

Hewlett-Packard's experience with CRM highlights two of this technology's core strengths. First, it can enable a company to coordinate

---

[150] As quoted in Oracle Corporation's case study on Hewlett-Packard, www.oracle.com/customers/11i/hp.html)
[151] Benefit figures shown were presented by HP during the International Call Center Management conference in Chicago, August 1, 2001. They are based on the following assumptions: $300 million in increased revenues from higher conversion of leads to orders, $300 million from up-sell and cross-sell opportunities, $300 million in increased revenues from leveraging internal experiences to drive external business, and $150 million in new sales through improved account penetration and customer repurchase rates.
[152] This figure is based on an assumed $20 million in savings from reduced IT operating costs as a result of fewer people required to support a centralized system vs distributed systems, $37 million in savings from higher efficiency in sales, marketing, and operations processes, and $19 million in savings from increasing sales rep efficiency due to new processes (forecasting, call handling, knowledge management, etc.).

traditional retailers to receive no benefit for selling their customers CDs that 'channeled' those customers to Sony's online sites and away from their stores.

Being dragged into court by your distributors is a definite sign of channel conflict – specifically, the conflict that takes place not between some of a vendor's partners, but between the vendor's direct-to-customer channels and *all* of its partners.

An informative example ... but that's not the end of the story.

On November 30, 2001, NARM withdrew its lawsuit against Sony. According to NARM:[156]

In the nearly two years since the litigation initially was filed, the landscape and the facts surrounding digital distribution of music have changed dramatically. The Board believes that the interests of our retail members will be better addressed by focusing our energies and resources on educating industry executives and government officials about retail concerns relating to digital distribution, copyright law, and antitrust via other channels.

Apparently, NARM was bowing to inevitable trends. As Jupiter Medial Metrix points out, online music sales will likely grow 520 percent to $6.2 billion in 2006, making up a third of all music sales. Lawsuits or not, companies are going to sell music over the Web.[157]

The more important story here, however, is *channel power*. Sony has it. Put simply, Sony's retailers cannot boycott Sony and do business with another vendor. What would they tell their customers who want to buy a CD by Jennifer Lopez, Aerosmith, Aretha Franklin or Toad the Wet Sprocket?[158] Sony has the rights to all of these popular artists' work, and the work of hundreds of others artists too.

In fact, Sony is not slowing down its online efforts one iota. In 2000 the company rolled out Sonystyle.com, to market its notebook

---

[156] www.narm.com press release
[157] Ted Kemp, Web to account for a third of music sales by 2006. *Internet Week*, July 23, 2001.
[158] I don't know who Toad the Wet Sprocket is either, but my staff loved the name of the group.

computers, digital cameras, and other electronic products, thus expanding its direct-to-customer business and enabling it to collect invaluable consumer information which previously went to its distributors' e-commerce sites and retail stores. In July of 2001, Sony announced an agreement with Yahoo! to develop a co-branded e-commerce site to provide enterprise advisory services, content integration and promotion. According to Howard Stringer, Chairman and CEO of Sony Corporation of America:[159]

> Sony's agreement with Yahoo! will allow us to offer customers information specific to their interest in Sony. It will also give us the ability to have more direct customer relationships across all Sony companies.

Expect to see a lot more online activity from Sony – and from other eight-hundred-pound gorillas like it who can, to some degree, write the rules for sales and distribution in their markets.

The lesson from the Sony example is that if you have enough power *vis-à-vis* your partners, you can get away with a lot more than if you lack power. Many companies do not have Sony's scale, influence, or proprietary intellectual property, and deal with powerful partners that control sales in their markets and aren't beholden to any particular vendor. If that describes your situation, then you will have to take a different approach than Sony, one that accommodates the needs of resellers and attempts to resolve potential channel conflicts. There are basically four tools at your disposal to do that:

1. Market separation
2. Product configuration
3. Pricing
4. Revenue sharing.

Market separation

In the past, the most common way to minimize channel conflict was to assign different channels to cover different markets. This was the 'channel silo' approach, in which channels were kept away from each other, making it less likely that they would bump into each

---

[159] Yahoo! press release, July 31, 2001.

other or into you in the market place. For example, resellers could be assigned to distinct and separate geographical markets, such as US West Coast or the United Kingdom, or to separate vertical markets, such as manufacturing or telecommunications.

The effectiveness of this approach has been declining in recent years, mainly due to the shift toward direct-to-customer channels. These channels, and particularly Web sites, have made it virtually impossible to separate channels by geographical or vertical markets. For example, you can certainly sign up a distributor for exclusive control of the California market, but what happens when a customer from New York places an order on that distributor's Web site? Answer: the distributor is going to take the order, thus taking sales away from a distributor in New York. And what happens when a customer places an order on your Web site or with your call center? Answer: you are going to take the order, unless your Web site or call center routes the customer through to the distributor – a clumsy solution that works OK in some markets and poorly in others.

The second problem with market separation is that it applies poorly – or not at all – to integrated multi-channel selling. By definition, all channels in an integrated multi-channel model serve the same markets, since they work together on the same sales opportunities. Conflict within an integrated multi-channel model cannot be resolved by assigning sales reps, partners and other channels to different markets. Your integrated model would cease to exist. The whole point of integrated multi-channel selling is to get channels out of their silos so they can cooperate and make sales together. Market separation achieves just the opposite – it puts channels back into their silos, killing off all of the benefits of integrated multi-channel selling.

In the end, market separation is an 'old school' tactic that has lost a lot of its relevance. So let's look at some more up-to-date methods for dealing with channel conflict.

Product configuration

An approach that can sometimes really get to the root of channel conflict and wipe it out involves the development of different offerings, or at least versions of offerings, for different channels. For example, you could use sales reps to sell only higher-end, customized offerings, while using partners to sell mid-range versions at mid-level prices, and the Web to sell low-price commodity versions of those same offerings. The idea is to differentiate the products offered by different channels to prevent competition between them.

Over the last few years, this approach has proven effective in all sorts of sales, from computer systems to machine tools, and from health club exercise equipment to industrial chemicals. The advantage is that it truly minimizes channel conflict, by ensuring that each channel has something unique to sell. The disadvantage is that it may be a late-1990s strategy that's losing effectiveness.

In many markets, customers increasingly expect *all* products to be available in *all* channels. For example, they may not be willing to forego the opportunity to order expensive, high-end products over the Web, and they'll expect distributors to carry the full product range. They'll resent having to take the time to determine which channels offer which products or versions of products, and they will go over to vendors who give them simple 'buy however you want' channel flexibility.

Selling different products or configurations through different channels is still a viable approach, but it's a short-term solution. In a few years, customers will not tolerate the channel coercion that's implied in this approach.

Pricing

A much more up-to-date approach, which is particularly well suited to integrated multi-channel selling, involves price tweaking across channels. In this approach, potential conflict between channels is headed off by raising prices in some channels and reducing them in others.

This approach is particularly effective when adding new direct-to-customer channels to a channel mix that already includes business partners – as discussed, the essence of most of today's channel conflicts. Pricing differences can help resolve or even prevent this increasingly common problem.

For example, Hewlett-Packard has long sold laptop computers through its large, loyal network of resellers and distributors, but, like most other IT manufacturers, has begun offering products to customers directly over the Web. To head off conflict with its partner base, HP sells its laptops at list price over the Web, but at low enough prices to resellers so that they can 'undercut' the Web by a few percentage points. The price differential – around $100 on a $3,000 laptop – isn't enough to prevent customers who really want to use the Web from using the Web, but it's more than enough to prod the average, everyday customer over to a reseller. This approach has enabled HP to keep its resellers moderately content, while simultaneously giving HP a strong Web presence, which is in tune with the expressed channel preferences of its customers.

In sum, price tweaking across channels is an effective tool that can migrate customers into the 'right' channels and head off some potential channel conflicts.

Revenue sharing

Another way to minimize channel conflict is to develop a system that pays multiple channels for sales. For example, sales reps who refer a customer to a Web site can be paid a partial or full commission, thus reducing conflict between sales forces and newer direct-to-customer channels. Similarly, sales reps who refer leads to partners – or *vice versa* – can be given a 'cut' in order to minimize competition between direct and indirect channels. The idea is to give each channel a piece of the action, in order to reduce the incentive to cut out other channels and go it alone.

The challenge with all dual-pay compensation systems is that they lead to higher selling costs. If sales revenues go up as a result of channel cooperation, then these higher selling costs can be offset. Whether or not revenues will increase enough to offset higher selling costs, however, is difficult to predict. This is best thought of as an approach to try *after* other approaches, such as price tweaking, have been attempted.

Regardless of which approach you use, channel conflict can never fully be prevented. Channels *will* compete for sales, and they *will* come into conflict whenever they participate in the same markets and work together for the same sales. Acceptance of some channel conflict as a by-product of aggressive multi-channel selling may be wise; it is certainly wiser than wasting a lot of time, energy and money trying to eradicate something that cannot be eradicated.

In the end, the best approach may be not to try to manage channel conflict, but to address the underlying reason why channels come into conflict in the first place: competition for rewards. Ensuring that channels in an integrated multi-channel model are measured and rewarded for the right things is the easiest and most effective way to avoid channel conflict and gain their cooperation. Let's take a closer look at this.

DESIGNING PERFORMANCE METRICS FOR AN INTEGRATED MULTI-CHANNEL MODEL

In a single-channel model, the measure of success is pretty simple: *sales revenue*. A channel that makes a lot of sales and exceeds its quota is doing well. A channel that misses its sales target is doing poorly. It is that straightforward – and it's the reason why I love sales. You may not quite know whether your human resource manager is doing a good job or whether your investment in a new product or a new building is paying off, but it takes about five seconds to decide if a particular sales rep – or your entire sales force – is performing above or below expectations.

In an integrated multi-channel model, things aren't quite that simple. When different channels are assigned to different tasks in the sales cycle, sales revenue ceases to be the be-all and end-all of channel performance measurement. A more subtle approach is required.

Let's take a simple example. Suppose that you hire a telemarketing rep to generate new leads for your sales reps, and that you recruit a business partner to come in after the sale in order to configure your product and provide customer support. It's pretty clear that your sales reps should be measured by traditional sales metrics such as sales revenue, number of deals closed, etc. But how will you measure your telemarketing rep? Is it appropriate to measure this person on the basis of sales revenues – an outcome over which he or she has some influence but little control? Perhaps it would be better to measure this person on the basis of the number of leads generated or the percentage of leads that result in closed sales. Those are more appropriate and fair bases for measuring and rewarding tele-activity. And what about the business partner? On what basis will you assess performance and decide if the partner is doing a good job? Since the partner comes in after the sale, it's obvious that sales revenue would be a meaningless metric. A more likely measure of success for the partner would be something like customer satisfaction or the partner's response time in reacting to and resolving customer problems.

From this little example, it's easy to grasp the two basic design principles of performance metrics in a multi-channel environment:

1. Not every channel in an integrated multi-channel model will be measured and rewarded on sales revenue. In fact, sales revenue as a measure of success may be appropriate only for your deal-closing channel(s).
2. Each channel participating in the sales cycle will be measured on different criteria.

The essence of good performance measurement in an integrated multi-channel model is this: *you must design performance metrics that assess and monitor the performance of each channel in carrying out the specific task(s) to which they are assigned*. For example:

1. *Lead generation and qualification.* Channels responsible solely for generating leads should usually be measured on the total number of sales leads they deliver for qualification. More leads are, of course, better than fewer leads. A lead-generating channel can also be measured on the percentage of leads judged to be qualified rather than unqualified. The latter is a measure of the effectiveness of a lead-generating channel in generating not just leads, but *good* leads.

   Channels responsible for both lead generation and qualification must be measured on the basis of a more complex set of metrics. These could include the number of new leads, the percentage of those leads that are subsequently qualified, and the percentage of qualified leads that result in proposals or closed sales. Taken together, these three metrics will provide a pretty good overview of the all-around soundness and effectiveness of a lead-generation and qualification channel.

2. *Bidding and proposing*. The primary measure of the success of a bidding-and-proposing channel is the percentage of proposals that result in closed deals. Put simply, a good bidding-and-proposing channel is one that writes a high percentage of proposals that win. However, average deal size can also be a useful metric. A larger average deal size suggests that a bidding-and-proposing channel is effective at putting together winning proposals for larger, more desirable transactions.

3. *Negotiation and sale closure*. The primary measure of a negotiation and sales closure channel is, of course, sales revenue. A secondary metric might be the average deal size or average discount, both of which measure the ability of the channel to close larger, more significant deals and to 'hold its price'.

4. *Fulfillment*. Any number of metrics can be used to assess the effectiveness of a fulfillment channel, from immediate post-sale customer satisfaction to average ship-time and problem resolution response time. Obviously, fulfillment channels cannot be measured on sales revenue, because they come in *after* the sale.

5. *Customer care and support*. Channels tasked with longer-term customer care and support must be measured on how effectively they build and sustain long-term customer relationships. Metrics such as customer satisfaction are okay, but not sufficient. It's quite possible (and typical) to have customers who are satisfied but who nevertheless aren't 'sticky', and who therefore move over to a competitor as soon as they have any reason to do so. This is particularly true in the new age of impersonal direct-to-customer channels such as the phone and Web. Better measures include things such as 'likelihood to repurchase' (a question that can be asked in a post-sale survey), loss rates (i.e. percentage of customers defecting to competitors and therefore *lost* after an initial sale), and perhaps customer retention, as measured by the percentage of sales to existing customers versus new customers.

That's just a brief overview of a few of the metrics that can be used to align channel activities and performance with specific tasks in the sales cycle. The larger point is this: channels do what they are measured and rewarded for doing. The use of performance metrics to get individual channels to focus on the right activities in the sales cycle is the easiest and most effective way to get channel cooperation, avoid channel conflict, and ensure that an integrated multi-channel model runs smoothly. The development of the right channel metrics is therefore a crucial part of the overall design of a winning integrated multi-channel model.

SUMMARY

In this chapter, we looked in depth at the integrated multi-channel model: a much-discussed, much-coveted, and yet poorly understood approach for going to market through multiple, cooperating sales channels. We can thank CRM vendors and other technologists for bringing the importance of integrated multi-channel selling to the forefront of go-to-market strategy, where it belongs. However, one outcome of these companies' efforts to promote multi-channel selling has been a widespread belief that going to market through multi-channel models is fundamentally or even solely a technology issue. That is not the case. As we saw in this chapter, it is first and foremost a *strategy* issue, requiring the alignment of channels against the sales cycle with your business goals and with your customers' behaviors and needs. It is only after you have a multi-channel strategy that aligns with your customers and supports your business goals that technology becomes relevant, as a key enabler of the strategy.

This chapter focused on four key design components of integrated multi-channel modeling. The first was the assignment of channels to sales cycle tasks such as lead generation and customer support, in order to accomplish some mix of increased sales, increased profits, increased market coverage, and increased customer satisfaction and loyalty. Your choice of multi-channel models depends on the relative importance of these different business benefits. It also depends on how much time, effort, and money you are prepared to put into a new selling model. Some integrated multi-channel models, such as a simple lead-generation approach, take a lot less time and effort than other approaches, such as a maximum-growth model.

The second design component addresses the all-important issue of channel cooperation and coordination. Unless channels work well together, share customer and sales lead information, and coordinate their activities throughout the sales cycle, your integrated multi-channel model is not going to work. It will just generate customer confusion and dissatisfaction, while increasing your selling costs. The hand-offs between channels must be tightly designed and managed, and appropriate technologies such as CRM must be utilized to ensure a smooth flow of information between channels and a 'seamless' customer experience.

The third component involves the management of channel conflict – an unavoidable by-product of multi-channel selling. There are a variety of approaches for dealing with channel conflict. Some of the older approaches, such as market separation, are less effective than newer approaches, such as the tweaking of prices and product configurations across channels.

The final component of multi-channel design is the development of appropriate channel performance metrics. To make an integrated multi-channel model work, you must rethink how you measure and reward your channels. They must be measured, monitored and rewarded on the basis of how well they perform the specific tasks to which they are assigned. Design of appropriate channel performance metrics is an integral part of any winning integrated multi-channel model.

Integrated multi-channel modeling is not a simple task, and in this chapter we've covered a lot of complex areas of design and strategy. The reader can be forgiven for asking the question, 'So what am I supposed to go *do*?' Keeping in mind the old adage that a journey of a thousand miles begins with a single step, in the next chapter we'll boil all of this go-to-market strategy stuff down to a clear, concise, and very do-able ninety-day action plan for getting things underway.

8

Go-to-market strategy:

Getting started: the ninety-day go-to-market action plan

I n previous chapters, we looked at the major ingredients of a winning go-to-market strategy: targeting the right markets; aligning
with the needs and behaviors of customers; choosing the right mix
and integration of channels to serve those customers; and defining a
winning value proposition and a compelling 'channel-ready' offering
to put into those channels.

We've truly covered a lot of ground! There is definitely something to
be said for taking a broad perspective and working through the full
range of strategic issues involved in going to market. Having done
that, we're now going to shift gears and delve into perhaps the most
challenging go-to-market issue of all: *getting started*. Let's face it: in
many organizations, the most difficult part of any new initiative is to
get things underway in a practical, results-oriented, and well-organized
manner. That's exactly what we are going to focus on in this chapter.

I'll describe an approach that my own firm, The Sales Strategy
Institute, frequently uses to help clients get started with go-to-market
change. This flexible approach has been applied successfully to comprehensive go-to-market planning efforts at Fortune 500 companies as
well as to single-channel initiatives by mid-sized and small businesses.
It's based on the commonsense principle that if you collect the right
information and involve the right people early in the process, you will
acquire both the knowledge and the internal buy-in you need to make
go-to-market change and innovation succeed.

The approach is illustrated in Figure 8.1 (overleaf).

Let's take a look at each of the steps.

1. IDENTIFY AND DOCUMENT INTERNAL GO-TO-MARKET ACTIVITIES, BELIEFS AND PRIORITIES

The first order of business is to figure out what's already going on
within your own organization.

To put it plainly, many organizations don't know what they already
know. Diverse groups across multiple business units pursue markets
and customers with different coverage strategies, channels, products,

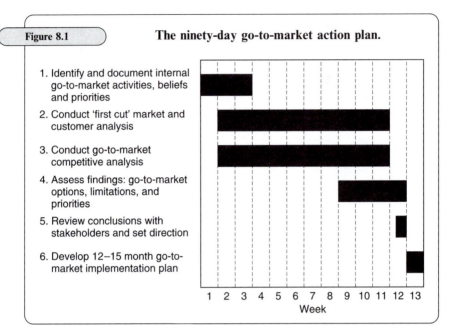

Figure 8.1   **The ninety-day go-to-market action plan.**

and messages. These groups often fail to communicate well with each other and with executive management. Headquarters executives start up new go-to-market projects, such as new channels or new vertical marketing campaigns, that have already been tried and rejected for sound reasons by groups in the field. Channel heads – the Web czar, the vice president of sales, the director of partner programs, etc. – compete for resources to move their channels forward, with little idea as to how their initiatives fit into the overall game plan, or even whether there is an overall game plan. When it comes to go-to-market strategy, internal communication and coordination is often less than stellar.

Poor communication is a significant impediment to the success of a go-to-market initiative, and it is the reason that many of them fail. Without good communication and information sharing, you will probably end up expensively reinventing wheels that have already been perfected elsewhere in the company, or developing tactics and strategies that have already been rejected by other groups for good reasons. Worst of all, you might go full-bore with a new marketing campaign or channel that lacks critical buy-in from key stakeholders – and is therefore doomed to fail.

To avoid these problems, before you even get started with a go-to-market initiative of any type, you must develop an internal fact-base: a solid understanding of what's going on in the company; what beliefs are already held about markets, customers, channels, products, and messaging; and what key stakeholders *want*.

There are two main issues to address:

1. Which people or groups do you need to include in the discussions to ensure that you're getting input and guidance from the right stakeholders?
2. What should you discuss with those people or groups, to ensure that you collect the right information and insights?

In choosing people to interview for a go-to-market initiative, the heads of sales, marketing, and finance should always be at the top of the list. Any change to a marketing or sales approach will impact all three of these functions and therefore require the input, buy-in and approval of these individuals. These people, in fact, should constitute your core go-to-market team and be included in all decisions. Other people to interview, depending on the nature and scope of the initiative, would be group heads and managers involved in the following activities:

- Evaluating and researching new markets (e.g. geographical or vertical), or developing new market penetration campaigns
- Surveying and studying customers
- Benchmarking competitors or conducting competitive intelligence
- Managing indirect channels, such as reseller and distributor networks
- Managing direct-to-customer channels, such as call centers or e-business sites
- Developing new products and solutions
- Designing marketing collateral and promotion/messaging strategies.

All of these 'go-to-market stakeholders' can be interviewed individually, although it can be far more powerful to pull the relevant people *together* for a go-to-market kick-off meeting. This will illuminate areas of consensus as well as differences of opinion – both of which will impact your decisions.

So what should you discuss with your stakeholders? It depends on the scope of your go-to-market initiative, of course. Your interviews will look different if you're evaluating the deployment of an in-house call center, evaluating a new market, or redesigning an entire global market coverage strategy. However, there are some baseline questions that can help ensure that discussions get off on the right track and include all of the relevant issues. A basic set of discussion-starter questions is provided in Table 8.1.

Once you've conducted detailed discussions on the relevant issues, a go-to-market 'state of the state' memorandum should be prepared. Divided into each of the five key go-to-market topics – markets, customers, channels, products, and message – it should document and describe current go-to-market activities, beliefs about the best courses of action, and stakeholders' top priorities, as well as any important areas of competing viewpoints on go-to-market issues. This memorandum should be distributed to *all* of the people who were involved in the discussions, in order to confirm their views. All of this may sound a little bureaucratic, but it is necessary. You must ensure that everyone is on the same page in terms of their understanding of current go-to-market activities within the organization, beliefs about go-to-market opportunities, and priorities. This will help achieve the elusive 'buy-in' and acceptance without which a go-to-market plan or new channel initiative cannot succeed.

Total elapsed time for this step: typically around three weeks.

2. CONDUCT 'FIRST CUT' MARKET AND CUSTOMER ANALYSIS

In Chapters 3 and 4 we looked in detail at tools and processes for uncovering and validating target markets, and for defining customers' needs and behaviors in those markets. Now we're going to put those tools to use. The purpose here is twofold:

1. To ensure that you are focused on the right target markets – the ones that offer the best opportunities for high growth, profitable sales, and whatever other corporate goals you are seeking to achieve.

Table 8.1   Building the internal fact-base: basic topics to explore with key stakeholders

Go-to-market topic	Questions to raise/information to collect
Markets	• What product markets are we in today? – Which markets (geographical, vertical, etc.) – With which products, services, solutions, etc. • Which *new* markets and segments are we targeting? Why? • Are there any markets we are planning to exit? Why? • How complete is the fact-base on our current and target markets and segments? Do we have all the information we need?
Customers	• Which types of customers and accounts do we most want to win? • What do we already know and believe about customers' needs? Why do they do business with us? • *How* do they do business with us or our competitors – through which channels? • What feedback or advice have we received from customers on our strategy, channels, products, etc.?
Channels	• What market coverage strategies are in use throughout the organization: – Which channels do we use? – To reach and serve which customers? – With which products? • How well are our different coverage and channel approaches working? What are the perceived strengths and weaknesses of our current approaches? • Are there any channel-building initiatives going on? What are they? • Are there any 'pet channels' that key stakeholders are anxious to build? • Are there any channels that have been ruled out?
Products	• What are our offerings (e.g. products, services, solutions)? • Which offerings are selling best 'out there'? • Which offerings aren't selling as effectively? • Are customers requesting new offerings or changes in our offerings? • Do key stakeholders have any strong views about the direction of our offerings? – What are those views?
Message	• What is our pitch? Is it the same for different customers and markets? • What media and channels do we use to promote ourselves? • How well is the pitch working in our core target markets? Is it attracting buying activity from the right customers in the right markets? • What research have we done to validate and test the pitch with target customers? • Are initiatives underway to redefine the message or the marketing collateral?

2. To ensure that you develop the in-depth knowledge of customers' needs and behaviors required to drive sales activity and to guide your channel, product, and value proposition decisions.

For best results, this step should closely follow the approaches described in Chapter 3 and 4. Those chapters can be summarized, and grossly oversimplified, as follows.

First, a Universe of Markets should be developed, in order to ensure that *all* high-potential markets have been identified – not just the ones you've already penetrated or already plan to pursue. Once you have a comprehensive picture of your potential target markets, then clear criteria for evaluating these markets must be developed, and markets under consideration should be evaluated in terms of their abilities to meet the criteria. Any markets that satisfy the criteria should be further validated with a small sample of prospects, to ensure that you haven't made inaccurate assumptions. Finally, new market opportunities should be prioritized, and a core group of markets or segments identified for immediate attention and penetration.

Second, within your highest-priority target markets, a rigorous analysis of customers must be conducted. These customers' needs, the experiences they seek from their vendors, their buying behaviors (which channels do they use today? which channels will they use in the future?), their impressions of your company, and their guidance on how to increase business with them, will all impact your go-to-market decisions, and should all be explored in depth, as discussed in Chapter 4. Until you perform this analysis, it's all just guesswork; you must get out into the target customer base and talk directly to key customers and prospects. You have lots of options for conducting the customer analysis. Tools range from written surveys to focus groups to one-on-one interviews. To get the ball rolling, telephone-based interviewing of customers in each of your high-priority markets is usually an efficient and effective approach.

The amount of market and customer analysis you perform is, of course, dependent on how much you already know. Most companies have already done some market research, and have some idea about which markets and customers they want to pursue. You might well be inclined to cut some corners, on the assumption that you already know enough about your markets and customers, combined with a desire to 'get on with it'. This can be a real mistake. Most organizations, relying too much and for far too long on generic market research reports and simplistic customer surveys, radically overestimate their knowledge of the market place. Market and customer analysis is just not the place to cut corners. The best argument for doing it right is, simply, that no one has ever suffered for investigating their market opportunities *more* thoroughly and learning *more* about their customers' needs and behaviors. On the other hand, lots of companies have lost everything by pursuing the wrong markets or failing to understand and align with their customers' needs. Regardless of your pre-existing fact-base, you could do far worse than to kick things off with a thorough analysis of your high-priority target markets and your customers.

So how long will it take to evaluate and choose markets and segments, and build the customer fact-base for those markets? There are three factors that will impact the timeline. First, the scope and ambition of your market penetration efforts will determine the amount of work required. Evaluation of one vertical market, for example, will take a lot less time than a thorough vetting of a dozen potential markets and segments. Second, the timeline will depend on the depth of your customer analysis. Are you trying to find out whether customers are receptive to e-business or some other new channel (a relatively easy thing to find out), or are you after a more complex set of insights, such as customers' interest and feedback on a variety of new vertical market solutions (a much more difficult, labor-intensive task)? Finally, the timeline depends on resources: it takes *people* to study markets and customers. The more resources you have, the faster you can get the job done. In all, depending on the complexity and scope of the effort and the resources you have at hand, it is possible to perform a rigorous market and customer analysis in approximately ten weeks.

3. CONDUCT GO-TO-MARKET COMPETITIVE BENCHMARKING

Alongside the market and customer analysis, it is important to take a close look at the go-to-market efforts – and the results – of key competitors. Competitive benchmarking is not easy to perform, and normally requires the help of consultants or researchers. However, it is a very useful and necessary tool for building your initial go-to-market fact-base, for three crucial reasons:

1. It will help you understand the go-to-market conventions and norms in your target markets, such as evolving standards for the use and integration of different types of channels, or the offering of new types of products and solutions to customers.
2. It will help you define the full range of your go-to-market options, based on the successes (and failures) of other firms who've tried them.
3. It will help you identify pockets of 'uncovered' opportunities in your target markets, as well as to identify competitively dense segments that you may choose to avoid.

While you may have many competitors, you probably don't need to research and evaluate all of them. Most companies have two to four key, direct competitors who are pursuing similar customers in similar markets with similar products and services. These are the ones you need to study.

So what topics should you include in your competitive analysis? It depends on your go-to-market objectives, of course. If your goal is to define new markets for penetration, then you'll want to analyze the market targeting, segmentation and penetration efforts of your leading competitors. If you are looking into new channels in general, then you'll want to study their overall channel mix and coverage strategies. If you are looking into e-commerce in particular, then evaluation of competitors' Web initiatives would make sense. If you want to bring new solutions to market, then benchmarking the solution development efforts of competitors – and their success or failure in promoting those solutions in particular markets and segments – will prove very useful. In short, it's situation-dependent. In defining the scope of a competitive analysis, it's helpful to begin with an overall framework of go-to-market topics, and then to choose from that framework the most relevant topics and issues to explore. A useful framework to get started with competitive analysis is shown in Table 8.2.

Now for the hard part: how do you acquire competitive information? Sources of competitive information abound, from industry analysts, corporate research reports, and business research services,[160] to competitors' Web sites and marketing collateral. You will be surprised at

---

[160] For example, Lexis-Nexis, Hoovers, etc.

Table 8.2 General framework for a go-to-market competitive analysis

Markets and customers	Channel usage	Market coverage model	Channel integration	Go-to-market results
Which markets, geographies and verticals are key, direct competitors currently targeting? In which new markets and segments are they increasing their investments and resources for future penetration? Which customers do they target/emphasize in those markets? Where are they hitting resistance or problems in their markets?	What channels are competitors using today? • Field sales force? • Business partners? • Direct-to-customer channels? Which channels are getting increased attention and investment? Which channels are getting decreased attention and investment?	How do competitors cover their markets with sales channels? • How do they cover 'premium' markets and customers? • How do they cover the middle market? • How do they reach and cover smaller accounts? Are their coverage strategies changing? Where are they increasing/decreasing channel coverage of specific segments?	How are competitors integrating multiple channels within the end-to-end sale? Which channels do what? How do they manage channel coordination and conflict? How do they measure and monitor individual channel performance and results? What have the financial results been from their channel integration efforts (top and bottom line)?	What specific benefits have been achieved as a result of competitors' go-to-market efforts? • Revenue growth? • Market share? • Margin improvement? • Customer loyalty and retention? To what specific actions, channels, or activities can these results be attributed?

how much knowledge can be gathered from a review of public sources, since many companies openly advertise and promote their expertise in their target markets, their customer reference stories, and their use of sales channels, among other things. Whether these public sources can deliver all of the insights you seek depends on what you want to find out. If you just want a basic understanding of competitors' market and channel strategies, you can probably get that through publicly available information. However, if you are after something deeper – such as competitors' emerging and newest go-to-market initiatives, the financial results they've been able to achieve, and the 'behind the scenes' issues they've encountered with new markets, channels, and products – there is no doubt that you will need to conduct primary, rather than secondary, competitive intelligence. 'Primary' competitive intelligence involves direct contacting of competitors' customers and partners, as well as competitors themselves. This is where consulting firms and researchers can usually help out, since many companies prefer not to conduct their own primary competitive intelligence.

Depending on the scope of a go-to-market competitive analysis – such as the number of competitors to include and the range of issues to explore – this effort can usually be performed in eight to twelve weeks. A ten-week effort will yield you the information shown in Table 8.2, for three to four competitors.

4. ASSESS FINDINGS: GO-TO-MARKET OPTIONS, LIMITATIONS, AND PRIORITIES

After a rigorous analysis of your company's go-to-market activities, beliefs and priorities (step 1), your markets and customers (step 2), and your competitors (step 3), you will have a solid fact-base for moving forward.

Now it's time to figure out what all that information means, so that you can do something useful with it. How do you do that without getting overwhelmed? The assessment of findings should involve four activities:

1. Identify the best go-to-market opportunities
2. Identify go-to-market limitations – the 'boundaries of the possible'

3. Develop new go-to-market scenarios
4. Develop a business case for your top go-to-market scenarios.

Identify the best go-to-market opportunities

Simply put, what are the best new opportunities to drive sales, profits, and customer loyalty? For example, from your fact-finding efforts, which markets and segments offer the best chances to achieve short-term wins and longer-term customer penetration? Which customers are ready to do business, and what are they most interested in purchasing? Which channels could most efficiently and effectively attract, reach and serve your target customers? What mix of products, services and solutions would give you the strongest competitive position and the ability to attract customer buying activity? What messages will most compel customer interest and evaluation of your offerings? These questions will all be answerable once you've thoroughly analyzed your organization, customers and competitors.

Identify go-to-market limitations – the 'boundaries of the possible'

You must also identify the *limitations* on your degrees of freedom in making go-to-market changes. For example, which markets, channels, solutions, or other go-to-market initiatives are at odds with the priorities of key stakeholders in your organization? Which markets have unacceptable entry costs or levels of competitive activity, regardless of whether they are otherwise attractive? Which channels lack 'fit' with your target customers' buying behaviors or needs? Which products, services, or solutions fail to elicit strong customer interest? All of this must be worked out. It's just as important to identify the limitations on your freedom of action as it is to identify your best new opportunities.

Develop new go-to-market scenarios

When you evaluate your best new go-to-market opportunities in light of the limitations posed by your customers, competitors and your own organization, you will be able to develop a shortlist of new go-to-market scenarios. A go-to-market scenario is a complete 'package' of market, customer, channel, product, and value proposition assumptions that hang together as a coherent go-to-market initiative. For example:

> We will target Consumer Packaged Goods (CPG) manufacturers with the new Digital Distribution 6000 solution. Since the solution is complex, we will sell it mainly through field sales reps and integrators. However, we'll also offer it over the Web in case some buyers prefer to purchase it that way, and expand the call center to make outbound telemarketing calls to generate sales leads for our top integrator partners. We'll develop a CPG-specific value proposition (message) to communicate the specific benefits these companies will accrue by purchasing the solution.

Or:

> There is a huge opportunity to sell the Digital Distribution 6000 system in many markets, so we should not limit our efforts to a particular vertical. We will target all major manufacturing segments, and expand the sales force by 40 percent to cover the opportunity. Given the broad customer base, we will also need to come out with a 'dumbed down', lower-cost version of the offering, to be called the Digital Distribution 4000 solution, in order to attract smaller customers. Larger customers will be served through field reps, while smaller customers will be served through local resellers. We will carefully position the two offerings differently in our marketing collateral, so that the lower-cost offering doesn't steal our sales of Digital Distribution 6000s to large accounts.

Of course, go-to-market scenario building is not quite as simple as these two examples suggest. It takes time and effort to put together a coherent go-to-market 'story' that accurately reflects the complexity and range of your markets, customers, channels, products, and value propositions. Yet the development of good scenarios is a crucial component of your go-to-market start-up efforts. These scenarios, based on rigorous customer, competitor, and internal analysis, will provide a realistic, market-based foundation for filling in the details and deploying a winning strategy. They will also greatly assist in getting internal buy-in for go-to-market change ... once you've developed a business case for them.

Develop a business case for your top go-to-market scenarios

The business case for a go-to-market scenario describes a 'rough cut' estimate of the benefits and costs associated with deploying the scenario in the market place. I call it a 'business case' rather than a 'business plan', because in the time it would take to create a complete business plan, your markets and customers will have already moved on. The goal is not a perfect mathematical computation of benefits and costs, but a 'sketch' of the likely outcomes of a go-to-market change.[161] In two or three pages per scenario, the business case should describe the following:

- Anticipated impact on sales – ninety days, one year, and long-term
- Anticipated impact on market share
- Anticipated impact on profits (margins) – ninety days, one year, and long-term
- Anticipated impact on customer loyalty and retention
- Costs to implement (e.g. costs to deploy and run new channels, hire and compensate sales reps, penetrate new markets with promotional campaigns, etc.)
- Time and resources required to implement.

Armed with a shortlist of top go-to-market scenarios, each of which is accompanied by a business case, you are ready to present results to your key stakeholders!

5. REVIEW CONCLUSIONS WITH STAKEHOLDERS AND SET DIRECTION

There's no great mystery in this step, which involves presentation of your findings and recommendations to key players within the organization, usually in the form of a one- or two-day meeting. What's most important is to involve the right people – the major stakeholders, such

---

[161]For a more rigorous discussion of go-to-market economic modeling, see Lawrence G. Friedman and Timothy R. Furey, *The Channel Advantage: Going to Market with Multiple Sales Channels to Reach More Customers, Sell More Products, Make More Profit*, Chapters 5 and 11. Butterworth-Heinemann, 1999.

as the heads of sales, marketing and finance, without whose acceptance a new go-to-market initiative will definitely not succeed.

The purpose of the meeting is to conduct a review and discussion of the best scenarios for go-to-market change, and to agree on priorities for moving forward. A suggested agenda for the meeting is shown in Figure 8.2.

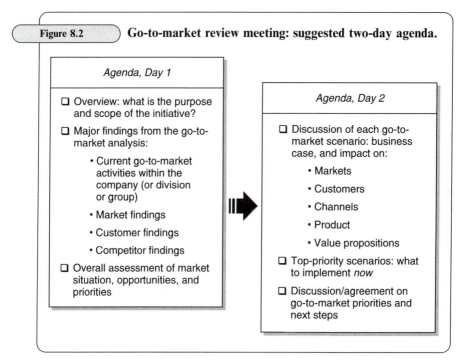

Figure 8.2   **Go-to-market review meeting: suggested two-day agenda.**

Agenda, Day 1

- ❑ Overview: what is the purpose and scope of the initiative?
- ❑ Major findings from the go-to-market analysis:
  - Current go-to-market activities within the company (or division or group)
  - Market findings
  - Customer findings
  - Competitor findings
- ❑ Overall assessment of market situation, opportunities, and priorities

Agenda, Day 2

- ❑ Discussion of each go-to-market scenario: business case, and impact on:
  - Markets
  - Customers
  - Channels
  - Product
  - Value propositions
- ❑ Top-priority scenarios: what to implement *now*
- ❑ Discussion/agreement on go-to-market priorities and next steps

6. DEVELOP TWELVE- TO FIFTEEN-MONTH GO-TO-MARKET IMPLEMENTATION PLAN

The final step in the ninety-day go-to-market action plan is to develop a plan and timeline for implementation and deployment of the top go-to-market scenario(s) approved at the review meeting in step 5.

An implementation plan and timeline can take a number of forms, but the most important issue is to set realistic expectations and timeframes for deployment. As noted earlier in Chapter 2, it can take anywhere from twelve to twenty-four months, in total, to design and deploy a new go-to-market strategy. The good news is that you have now completed the first three months of work! But that also means that you have approximately nine to twenty-one months of work in front of you. At this point, you have one or several well-developed go-to-market scenarios, complete with business cases to help you sell the approaches, along with a rough sketch of your new market, customer, channel, product and value proposition assumptions. What you *don't* have is:

■ A final selection of sales channels, and a coverage model for applying those channels against your product-markets – followed by a rigorous pilot-test of the model in your target markets
■ An updating or repackaging of your products or solutions, and your value propositions, to ensure that they fit with your new coverage model and hit on key customer needs

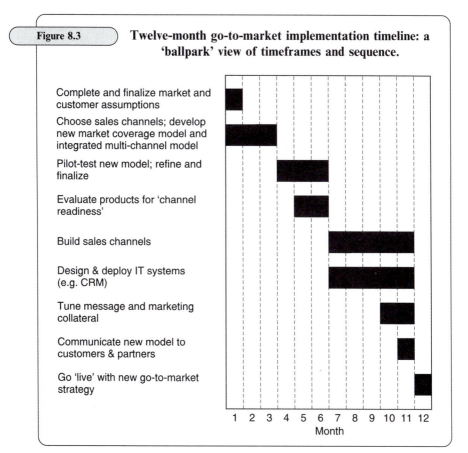

Figure 8.3 **Twelve-month go-to-market implementation timeline: a 'ballpark' view of timeframes and sequence.**

- Updated marketing collateral to support the new strategy
- The technology infrastructure needed to integrate and coordinate sales and channel activities
- etc.

In short, you have work to do, and it's going to take about a year, depending on the scope of your go-to-market initiative. The last step of the ninety-day plan is to map out the tasks and the timeline for doing this work.

A sample, generic timeline for go-to-market implementation is shown in Figure 8.3.

SUMMARY

Rethinking your go-to-market strategy is never a simple or quick-and-dirty task, and neither is implementing a new strategy. We are talking, after all, about a large undertaking: the development of a coherent, winning game plan to sell to the right customers in the right markets, through the right channels, with the right products and value propositions. That is no small endeavor, whether you're taking on the whole go-to-market enchilada or addressing just a market or channel or two. The complexity of go-to-market change leaves many organizations confused and unclear about how best to proceed. In this chapter, we looked at a straightforward process to get you organized and into the implementation of a new go-to-market approach, within a reasonable ninety-day timeframe.

That brings us to the end of the book! Let's think about how far we've truly come in the last eight chapters. In Chapter 1, I promised you, the reader, a practical approach for putting together a winning go-to-market plan – a plan that would help you align your go-to-market strategy and tactics with your customers, in order to increase sales, profits, and customer loyalty. Throughout this book we examined specific techniques and tools for doing just that – techniques that will enable you to target the right markets, align with your customers, choose the right mix of sales channels, offer the right products, and develop a winning, compelling value proposition. We have now concluded with a coherent three-month plan for getting down to business with go-to-market change and innovation.

Now, the ball is in your court! Today, go-to-market innovation is a serious and real source of competitive advantage, but to get that advantage, you have to *act*. Right now, customers expect and demand new ways of doing business, and competitors are aggressively courting those customers by rolling out new go-to-market models. Today's market leaders are all *go-to-market* leaders; they are companies that put great effort into their abilities to go to market faster, better, cheaper, and more effectively than the competition. Are you ready for this challenge? I hope this book has given you the confidence to move forward, with a clear sense of the opportunities available to go-to-market innovators – and the things you have to do to become one.

Index